EUROPEAN NATIONS

EUROPEAN NATIONS

Explaining Their Formation

Miroslav Hroch

Translated by Karolina Graham

VERSO

London • New York

Translation of this book was supported by Československá obchodní banka as a part of the project Bibliotheca Economica

This English-language edition first published by Verso 2015
Translation © Karolina Graham 2015
Previously published as *Das Europa der Nationen*
© Vandenhoeck & Ruprecht 2005

1 3 5 7 9 10 8 6 4 2

Verso
UK: 6 Meard Street, London W1F 0EG
US: 20 Jay Street, Suite 1010, Brooklyn, NY 11201
www.versobooks.com

Verso is the imprint of New Left Books

ISBN-13: 978-1-78168-834-2 (PB)
ISBN-13: 978-1-78168-833-5 (HC)
eISBN-13: 978-1-78168-835-9 (US)
eISBN-13: 978-1-78168-836-6 (UK)

British Library Cataloguing in Publication Data
A catalogue record for this book is available from the British Library

Library of Congress Cataloging-in-Publication Data
A catalog record for this book is available from the Library of Congress

Typeset in Minion by Hewer Text UK Ltd, Edinburgh, Scotland
Printed in the US by Maple Press

Contents

Preface

Anyone who has been keeping up-to-date with the world of academic publications, even from a distance, knows that 'nation' and 'nationalism' belong among the most frequently studied subject matters, and it is legitimate to question the point of adding another book on the topic. One's scepticism would be all the more justified if the aim of this book were to present yet another new 'theory of nationalism'. Any author who aspires to extend themselves beyond a mere description or narrative is, by definition, making an attempt to be original. Admittedly, such originality far too often rests either on taking one aspect of an issue out of context and blowing it out of proportion, or on presenting a new combination of already known theories and concepts. Several books, written in reaction to the sheer number and variety of publications to date, focus on a critical overview of older ideas.

This inundation of 'theories of nationalism' signals a need to take a pause and capture the present situation in research – to compile a synthesising work which focuses on those available findings that can be integrated into a coherent system. Therefore, rather than to highlight the (actual or seeming) originality of individual contributions, the aim here is to concentrate on approaches that facilitate a scholarly 'consensus'. Once we disregard the frequently presented originality of new terms, we find that the differences among individual concepts are much less marked than many of their authors may wish us to think.

The issues that this synthesis addresses must be defined at the very outset. This is not intended as a summary concerning atemporal 'nationalism', nor the present-day shape and interests of European nations. It is about their genesis, and the focal point of the historian's interest is thus the various paths that were followed in the nation-forming processes or, as some authors prefer to put it, the constructing of nations in Europe in the nineteenth century.

This type of synthesis could have been approached in two ways: by means of a narrative, or by focusing on particular factors. With the help of a narrative, one can capture the ways in which individual nations formed. Alternatively, based on one's knowledge about these nation-forming processes, an attempt can be made at discovering which elements and contexts proved decisive in these processes and, in so doing, lay foundations for a causal analysis. I have opted for the latter option: to favour generalising reflections over plain description. This is the only way in which it is possible to draw comparisons, the aim of which is to prepare material that will explain the causes of successful (or unsuccessful) modern nation-forming.

Any such approach should also contain nothing hidden – the author's points of view ought to be defined, at least in general terms, at the very outset. I do not believe that a nation is merely a cultural construct, an invention that could be brought into existence by anyone, anywhere by spreading nationalistic slogans. It is even less likely that modern nations are the result of an abstract nationalism. The vision of a nation as one form of a modern civic society proved successful only in particular social, political and cultural circumstances, which came into play independently of the wishes and ideals of the 'nationalists'. Due to the entirely divergent applications of the term 'nationalism', it is not only very difficult but actually impossible to provide a definition of the word that would achieve consensus. This is the reason why I doubt that this term can become a tool of critical analysis, and why I have made the decision not to use it in any other than its traditional sense – with a negative connotation.

All of the above has determined the basic structure of this book. Without aiming to reconcile the conflict between the 'constructivists' and the 'essentialists', I attempt to portray the historical development towards a nation 'sub specie' of both these approaches. The opening part of the book presents an overview of the development of ideas about the nation and the causes of its formation. The second part offers a summary of those objective circumstances in which nation-forming originated, and whose part in this process is generally recognised, albeit with a varying emphasis: earlier historical developments, ethnicity, political and economic modernisation. These contexts and relationships among them will be addressed as a set of prerequisites without which the forming of any nation would be unthinkable. The third part of the book is dedicated to human (patriotic) activities that aimed to facilitate nation-forming. I will summarise and interpret the available research findings concerning the role of power struggles and other nationally relevant conflicts of interest, the making of history relevant to the national framework in the construct of national history, the linguistic and cultural demands made by the leaders of national communities, and the role of myths, symbols, celebrations and so on. However, these findings will at the same time be verified against what we know about the course of development of specific nations.

No claims of any kind are made that this book will 'resolve' the issue of nation-forming. Although all chapters are units in their own right, it does not mean that I consider everything to have been answered or clarified. Indeed, it ought to be an aim of all syntheses not only to present a summary of all available findings and views, but also to open a future avenue, to become a spring-board for further research. Attentive readers will, undoubtedly, spot the blank spots, gaps in knowledge and contradictions in the interpretations of causal relationships. While some of these are a reflection of the fact that certain data are lacking and some questions have yet to be researched, others may stem from my own limited knowledge.

This book is a historical work, which endeavours to avoid projecting current conflicts and myths into the past, evaluating the past through the eyes of the present, or engaging in the selection of data according to their political 'relevance'. Such an approach would reinforce the tendency to view the matter through a false, politicised and ideologised lens. The fact that the twentieth century witnessed wars conducted in the name of the nation, ethnic cleansing, and nationalistically motivated mass murders should not prevent historians from being able to look clearly at the long historical period that preceded the outburst of these evils. We cannot simply draw single-track causal successions and look upon nineteenth-century nation-forming as a seed and a root cause of later crimes – or even as a wrong turn that European society took. Certainly, the relationship between the past and the present cannot be disregarded. However, the main aim of this book is to make a contribution by presenting findings about nineteenth-century events and relationships in order to facilitate a better understanding of events that followed later. This is another reason why the use of the term 'nationalism' has been avoided, as it conjures up the feeling of time-lessness and, indirectly, ushers in the need for a judgemental, condemning or apologetic view of events that ought to be examined *sine ira et studio*. In addition, this choice makes the task of conducting a comparative analysis easier to achieve.

Preface to the English Edition

The impetus for this book came from my German colleagues at the former Centre for Comparative European History in Berlin, who encouraged me to compile my partial studies and findings and integrate them into a system or a synthesis. I am glad I accepted this challenge, and I have made use of this opportunity to conclude and summarise my views on nation-forming processes. I decided this book should form the missing part of a 'trilogy', whose first two installments were published in English in 1985 and 2000. After asking *who*[1] the main players of the national struggles were and *what*[2] their demands were, the question I seek to answer now is *why* they succeeded.

Nevertheless, there is one important point which I would like to make clear: I regard the nation-forming process as a specifically European phenomenon. When this process had been successfully completed in most European regions, the concept of the modern nation was imported and (to varying degrees) adapted by non-European civilisations, and interpreted by diverse cultural traditions and value systems, usually far from the European roots of nation formation. Until only recently, non-European communities called 'nations' and movements called 'nationalism' had very different meanings, relating to things far removed from what those words referred to in Europe. For this reason, I do not pretend that my conclusions and models can be transferred to other continents. However, I cannot prevent other authors from doing so.

I was honoured when Verso expressed an interest in publishing an English translation, for the purposes of which I have made several amendments to my original German publication. First and foremost, I have reduced the number of references to German (and also Slavic) literature, while still leaving enough of them to enable English-speaking readers to get a sense of the fact that interesting works can be found in Central Europe. At the same time, I have deemed it unnecessary to add to the long list of authors who publish in English. I also decided not to update the literature list, despite the fact that the manuscript of this book dates back to the turn of this century. This is because it is not my aim to present a systematic 'handbook of opinions' here, not least because there are numerous such overviews of English literature.[3] My goal is to present and explain my views and how they relate to the research conducted to date. I have been on the receiving end of the positive experience of a delayed reception by the Anglophone audience. My book *Social Preconditions of National Revival*, which is still cited, and whose anniversary[4] was even remembered, was written a whole seventeen years before its English edition – during 1967–68.[5] It would be very pleasant if this delayed English edition were received, at least in part, in a similar manner to that of 1985.

The translation into English would not have been possible without financial help. It was supported by Československá obchodní banka (Czechoslovak Commercial Bank – CSOB) as a part of the project Biblitheca Economica. In preparing the English edition of my book, I was supported by the Czech Grant Agency, no. P410/12/2390 ('Myth and Reality').

Prague, August 2013

PART I

'Nation' and 'Nationalism' as Roots of Terminological Confusion

Research on nation-formation and nationalism in Europe occupies a significant place within the historical and social sciences, as is shown by the extent of public interest and the volume of scientific work on the topic. The fact that the number of published studies has grown whenever there has been an increase in nationalist tensions proves that these issues have always been connected with current policies. Indeed, the sheer quantity of partial findings and sophisticated theories appear to have turned the issues of nation and nationalism into a very chaotic terrain, within which researchers often find it hard to orientate themselves. It is not the aim of this book to present a systematic overview of existing opinions and theories.[1] However, a mutual understanding is difficult, since only a minimal consensus has been reached about the terms, hence the need to offer a clarification of the basic terms and concepts.

CHAPTER 1

Definitional Disputes

A closer examination of a number of randomly selected studies of the concepts of nation and nationalism reveals that each author interprets these terms quite differently. This is accompanied by efforts to be original, which have reached a global scale, with regard not only to definitions and interpretations but also to the creation of new terminology. The basic difficulty lies in attempting to analyse modern social and cultural processes by making use of a term that emerged in the Middle Ages and has been used continually until modern times. Although the common root of the term 'nation' was the Latin *natio*, its transfer or translations into different languages took place under a variety of circumstances, both political and social, thus giving it rather divergent meanings.

In eighteenth-century English, the term 'nation' referred to all the people who were governed by the same ruler (i.e. those living in the same state) and abided by the same laws. Whereas the first edition of the French *Grande Encyclopédie* characterised *la nation* in a similar vein, and its second edition had already added a common language to the definition. In the German linguistic tradition, *Nation* was primarily associated with culture and language, and sometimes also with a common past. An added difficulty in this case was that there was a partial overlap between this translation from Latin and the conventional German term *Volk*.[1] In the 1650s in another part of central Europe, the Czech scholar Jan Amos Komenský ('Comenius') defined a nation (*gens seu natio* in Latin) as a community of people who occupy a common territory, have a common past and a common language, and are bound by a love for their common homeland.[2] He would not have been alone in his 'premodernly modern' understanding of this term.

Another basic term within the current terminology is

'nationalism', whose genesis was very different. It was first used as a new term within political discourse, which gave it political and critical connotations. Even though the first attempts were made in the interwar period, nationalism did not become widely used as an instrument of scientific analysis until the second half of the twentieth century. The difficulty is that the term nationalism is derived from, as well as associated with, the term nation, whose historically determined connotations in various languages are very different. 'Nationalism', which was a label for a particular political or intellectual approach, was an instrument of value-orientated political controversies at the beginning of the twentieth century (and has remained such since then). It gradually came to be closely linked with the term 'nation', whose genesis is rooted in premodern times. The confusion is compounded by the fact that the way the term 'nationalism' is interpreted by members of different nationalities is largely dependent on the ways in which the term 'nation' is understood within their national linguistic traditions. In English, therefore, a connection is logically made between 'nationalism' and the state, i.e. a struggle for statehood; while in German terminology, where *die Nation* had originally been defined by culture and language, 'nationalism' has yet to find its place, and its interpretations are contradictory. In addition, in both English and German – and even more so in Russian and Czech – this term is subconsciously, if not consciously, associated with negative manifestations of national existence and struggles conducted 'in the name of the nation'. I will have the opportunity to demonstrate with a number of examples that even prominent researchers have succumbed to terminological confusion.

Perception of the Nation in the Nineteenth Century

Historians and other scientists turned their attention to the concept of 'a nation' at a time when nations had begun to form, as a result of which scientific discourse on the topic was inevitably affected by the specific circumstances of a given nation and the attitudes of the scientists in question. There was a marked difference between scientists, determined by the differing national situations in which they found themselves: those who studied the nation under the circumstances of a state nation that had existed continuously since medieval times (such as France and England) regarded the existence of a community, labelled as a 'nation', as self evident, a matter of course. Others, who approached this topic under the circumstances of a national struggle for (state or culturally defined) existence, first had to ascertain which characteristics would be appropriate in defining the new community, thereby differentiating it from the other communities.

It is no coincidence that by far the greatest number of contributions to the discussion about the definition of a nation at the end of the nineteenth and beginning of the twentieth centuries can be found in Central Europe and in German-speaking countries. As has already been mentioned, the newly forming national community was referred to using terms that were linguistically and historically anchored in the Middle Ages. All these circumstances influenced both the terminology itself and the starting points for methodologies.

A feature which most works published in the second half of the nineteenth century had in common was the axiomatic view that a nation was a perennial category, whose objective existence not only could, but also needed to be revived and renewed, as something valuable and unique to the human race. Whether we perceive this opinion as perennial or primordial, its shift from the sphere of political struggle into that of scientific research was another consequence of the fact that those who studied the nation were simultaneously members of that nation – or, more precisely, participants in the national struggle, whatever its form.

There is no need to reiterate here the views of individual historians, sociologists and political scientists about the 'nation' and its origin. It suffices to point out that works on this subject which originated in the last third of the nineteenth and the first half of the twentieth century can be roughly divided into two basic streams. The first defined a nation by *objective, empirically verifiable characteristics*, which in Central and Eastern Europe tended to comprise primarily cultural and linguistic features, in combination with various other elements ranging from political ties and ties to a territory to 'blood ties'. Anglo-Saxon authors appear to have already then had difficulty adding 'non-state' nations to the list labelled by the English term 'nation', seeking alternative terms for them, such as 'nationality', 'people' and 'national group'.[3]

However, by the turn of the twentieth century some authors had reached the conclusion that it was impossible to find a universal combination of characteristics that would apply to all communities referred to as nations at that time. Friedrich Meinecke's distinction between *Staatsnation* and *Kulturnation* proved highly influential, differentiating between whether the communities that saw themselves as national formed a state entity or were based on a common language and culture. The Austro-Marxist Otto Bauer sought another solution to the same issue by considering a common past to be the decisive factor, since it turned members of the same nation into a 'community of fate'. This in turn gave rise to the characterisation of nations as communities of a particular culture or 'character'. Over the course of centuries' worth of common history, nations progressed through a number of stages, which differed in relation to who understood themselves as a stable community – in other words, in relation to how each particular nation's social structure broadened.[4]

Only a few authors *defined a nation primarily in subjective terms* – as a community of people who were aware of their belonging to a particular nation, and desired it. This manifested itself either as an active endeavour to 'create' a nation or as a simple agreement about belonging to an already existent nation. Nowadays, this attitude is most commonly characterised by Ernest Renan's declaration about a nation being a 'daily plebiscite', but it must be remembered that it also played a major role in Germany, where it was justified by the so-called 'statistics school'.[5] Max Weber came even closer to the 'subjectivist' concept of a nation when he defined it as a group of people who feel 'a particular sense of solidarity' towards one another. He associated a nation with issues of prestige and power–prestige.[6] Such subjectivist concepts were of only marginal importance at first, and did not influence historical research significantly until the interwar era and after World War II, by which time the focal point had shifted from the nation to nationalism.

The dividing line between the two attitudes cannot be made absolute: authors who strove to define a nation by means of objective characteristics grew increasingly aware that a nation cannot exist without its members being self-aware, while, conversely, the subjectivist definition of a nation did not rule out the existence of objective ties between that nation's members.[7]

During the interwar period in Europe, studies pertaining to the concept of the nation were published primarily in Germany. Amid the nationalistic works, connected to a greater or lesser degree with or inclined towards Nazi racial concepts, some very interesting studies were published by a number of sociologists and political scientists, who built upon both Friedrich Meinecke's ideas – striving to further differentiate between his terms – and Otto Bauer's views.[8]

While European research continued to focus on the concept of the nation, a new analytical term, 'nationalism', was successfully applied in the American setting by Carlton Hayes. His definition was initially critical, in that he perceived nationalism as a 'proud, boastful way of thinking about one's own nation', accompanied by inimical attitudes towards other nations. Later, however, he defined several types of nationalism: humanist (Rousseau, Herder), Jacobite, traditionalist (Burke, the German Romantics), liberal (Welcker, Mazzini) and integral (Fascism, Nazism).[9] He also attempted to define nationalism in neutral terms – as a fusion of patriotism and an 'awareness of one's nationality'.[10]

Perception of the Nation in the Second Half of the Twentieth Century

The devastating experience of Nazism and Fascism, which World War II brought not only to Europe but the whole world, had an impact on research into the nation and nationalism. The political relevance of this type of research had grown, and with it the degree of authors' engagement. While their views continued to differ, in several respects most researchers agreed on what needed to be emphasised and what had already been resolved:

1. The vast majority of researchers distanced themselves from the perception of a nation as a 'community of blood', and decreasing interest was shown in the idea that a nation was a perennial category.
2. There was general agreement about the fact that a nation could not be defined by ethnic features (language and culture) alone.
3. A nation was now increasingly recognised as an independent community only if its members could be demonstrated to be aware of their belonging together, and to value it.
4. This gave rise to a growing emphasis on the subjectivist characterisation of a nation over the following decades, and to

'nationalism' being studied as a manifestation and even precondition for the existence of a nation.

The political context meant that the term 'nationalism' was reflected upon more frequently. Although some authors did not consider it important to define the term, they believed nationalism to be a socially dangerous, unnatural attitude that needed to be overcome.[11] The perception that nationalism was a neutral term that encompassed internal differences was initially accepted only to a very limited degree.

A polarised version of Hayes's concept, advocated by Hans Kohn, proved important.[12] Kohn defined nationalism as 'a state of mind', and in general terms related it to the nation state. In his view there were two types of nationalism. The first type was progressive – liberal and democratic – nationalism, which emerged in Western Europe, partly from English liberalism but mainly from the democratic ideals of the French Revolution. In contrast to this type, there was reactionary, 'non-Western' nationalism, dictated primarily by the German, language-based definition of the term 'nation', which Kohn saw as irrational, mythological and authoritarian. Although he later moderated this strict polarisation by acknowledging that democratic nationalism also existed in some of the smaller countries in Eastern Europe, his dichotomy directly or indirectly influenced or inspired whole generations of researchers to come.[13]

Characteristically, Kohn made no attempt to define a nation, perceiving it to be a product of nationalism. It is equally characteristic that authors who later made a critical revision of his dichotomy essentially shared his views. The Finnish historian Aira Kemiläinen, one of Kohn's first critics, convincingly demonstrated in the early 1960s that his dichotomy could not be applied along the simplified West–East axis.[14] Kohn's dichotomy was revised at the end of the century, when it was politicised rather uncritically.[15]

Of the many authors who spent the postwar decades re-examining the definition, several leaned towards the idea of a nation being determined by a loose combination of a number of types of ties. Some – Boyd Shafer, in particular – conceived of these ties as 'illusions' that led to nationalism as the main source of strength for the nation.[16] Pitirim Sorokin defined a nation as a 'multi-bounded group', comprising a group of people who were 'brought together by two or more simple ties', which may (but may not) have included language, territory, religion and physical settings. In the spirit of the older English linguistic tradition, Sorokin differentiated 'nation' from 'nationality', which he defined as an ethnic group bound by one tie alone: a language.[17]

In the decades that followed, attempts to define a nation with the help of attributes or ties were relatively infrequent, though no less important. The most significant representative of this current of thought was Anthony Smith, who characterised a nation as 'a named human population sharing an historic territory, common myths and historical memories, a mass, public culture, a common economy and common legal rights and duties for all members'.[18] I had advocated a similar notion already in 1968, when I proposed the view that the modern nation, which I distinguished from the premodern nation, was determined by relationships – i.e. ties between its members that formed gradually – and that these relationships were mutually inter-changeable. While it cannot be empirically proved that nations are characterised by a given 'binding' set of relationships, it can be proved that the community called 'nation' has always been – at least in Europe – characterised by a combination of several types of ties and relationships (linguistic, historical, economic, religious, polit-ical, and so on), and that the absence of any of these has not ruled out the existence of a given nation. However, two undeniable char-acteristics of a nation are that, firstly, its members are connected with each other by an intensity of communication and common fate that is greater than that connecting them with members of other nations, and, secondly, that they are a community of equal citizens who per-ceive themselves as members of the nation.[19] In simple terms, subjective attitudes and objective relationships form a complemen-tary structure.

Karl W. Deutsch's notions represented a significant step in the direction of resolving the debate about defining a nation by specific 'features'. In the 1950s, he defined a nation as a 'community of com-plementary social communication', and thus as a group, whose members were able to communicate with each other with ease and a greater complexity and intensity than with members of other groups. This 'community of communication' then provided the basis for a common national culture and national awareness – 'nationalism' – which needed to become sufficiently widespread for a national community to exist.[20] Members of this type of community associate their awareness of togetherness with certain values and with culture.[21]

In the first half of the twentieth century, research into the concept of the nation was conducted in German, in the second half primarily in English. Consequently, the nation was 'redefined' as a state community, in keeping with the above-mentioned English linguistic tradition, within which the term 'nation' largely overlapped with the term 'state' – i.e. it was chiefly defined by statehood. This approach can be found among authors who believed that a nation was determined by objective ties between its members, such as Stein Rokkan, Charles Tilly, John Breuilly and Louise Snyder.[22] Some researchers, such as Ernest Gellner and Eric Hobsbawm, acknowledged that a nation could in some cases be characterised not by statehood but in ethnic terms. This can be illustrated by the way in which Gellner's definition of nationalism evolved. Although he initially defined it as a 'political principle', and thus perceived nationalism as a struggle for statehood entailing efforts to make political reality match cultural or ethnic reality, he later defined a nation in terms of 'shared culture'.[23] Indeed, from the 1990s onwards, other Anglo-Saxon authors also ceased to advocate this strictly political definition of the nation. For example, Michael Keating refused to employ the term 'nation' to refer to a state, and proposed a typology that would, on one hand, take into account the presence or absence of statehood in relation to the nation and, on the other, distinguish between ethnic and civic nationalism.[24] Walker Connorts, in proposing the use of the term 'ethnonationalism', also addresses the need for a new term to label the ethnic and cultural nature of relationships that characterise one of the categories of nations.[25]

The difficulties with trying to find a binding, universally acceptable definition of a nation have left some authors resigned to the idea that it could not be achieved if specific, objectively determinable relationships were used. Instead, they have tended to define a nation in terms of subjective feelings. This group of authors comprises those who defined the nation in terms of nationalism, whether because they condemned nationalism as something deplorable (Carr, Kedourie) or because they perceived it as the main intellectual force of the present times (Hans Kohn). Even Jarosław Kilias, a contemporary Polish sociologist, appears to have given up on the definition of the term.[26] Eugen Lemberg occupies a special place in this context, as probably the first author in the whole of Europe to try to apply the Anglo-Saxon, morally neutral concept of 'nationalism', defining the nation as merely its 'object'. He defined nationalism as 'intensive loyalty' to any 'suprapersonal institution', be it a state, an ethnic group, a nation or a tribe.[27] Lemberg's work, based on extensive empirical studies, was too advanced for its times, and has remained largely unnoticed in the Anglo-Saxon world.

The search for a definition of the term 'nation' reveals that certain differences are functions of corresponding differences between scientific disciplines. Most historians and historical sociologists agree about the objective existence of the nation as a large group of people, which is characterised – in different variations – by an awareness of togetherness on the part of its members, by communication, and by cultural ties between them. Conversely, political scientists and sociologists are much more likely to define a nation chiefly in terms of subjective attitudes. This approach dates back to the 1960s, when some authors only concerned themselves with 'nationalism' in abstract terms – whatever its definition – and considered the nation to be an artificial construct, a myth or 'invention'. The roots of this concept can be found in the nineteenth century, when Lord Acton declared a nation to be 'artificial'.[28] Similarly, Elie Kedourie conceived of the nation as a European 'invention' of the turn of the nineteenth century.[29]

This interpretation has its flaws, especially when attempting to explain causal relationships. If we define a certain social group merely by reference to an awareness of belonging together among its members, we arrive at two very simple conclusions as to why a nation may only exist temporarily. Firstly, in order for a nation to come into existence, it would have sufficed if someone had spread 'nationalistic' slogans and convinced his fellow citizens of their belonging to a particular nation. Secondly, following the same logic, if the opposite, 'anti-nationalistic' ideas had been advocated vehemently enough, this awareness of national togetherness – and thus also the nation – would have ceased to exist.

Supporters of the opinion that 'nationalism' was the primary trigger and 'the nation' merely its 'invention' have not hesitated to interpret highly regarded authors in a one-sided manner. Gellner's view that the nation is a product of nationalism is frequently cited, without taking into consideration that he had studied the origins of the nation within the general context of his theory, searching for objective social roots of nationalism, which he believed to lie in the modernisation changes brought about by the era of industrialisation.[30] A similar distortion has resulted from the manner in which radical constructivist notions build upon the work by Benedict Anderson, who referred to nations as 'imagined communities'. By this he meant that a nation could exist as a group only if its members were able to imagine belonging to a community of people, most of whom they do not and will never know personally.[31] This opinion is often misinterpreted by implying that a nation could be 'invented' relatively easily as long as adequate educational and information resources were available. It tends to be overlooked that Anderson dedicated a larger part of his book to analysing the historical circumstances that were independent of the wishes of 'nationalists' and were a precondition for the creation of nations. Paul James replaced Anderson's ambiguous term 'imagined community' with the term 'abstract community', also emphasising that this type of community had formed and become integrated as a result of objective factors long before 'nationalism' emerged.[32]

The abandonment of the belief that it was possible to define a nation in terms of empirically verifiable characteristics other than national awareness on the part of its members did not necessarily rule out the acknowledgment of the fact that a nation could exist as an actual entity. Nevertheless, many authors reject this notion as unacceptable primordialism or 'essentialism'.[33] A nation is often considered to be a myth – a 'narrative' and merely an intellectual product of interest groups. Some authors have even gone so far as to propose that it was thus in the interest of the 'constructors' to conceal the fact that the nation had been constructed – i.e. that it was artificial in its essence – from the ordinary members of the nation.[34] Does this mean that the people were not only manipulated but actually deceived? Once artificially created, awareness and narrative were seen as the only things that actually existed, and any debate about the definition of a nation or search for the causes of its emergence would have been rendered superfluous. It is rather symptomatic that radical critiques that conceive of a nation as a random 'historical accident' contain parallels – although the political vocabulary may differ – with the anti-nationalistic stance of Rosa Luxemburg, as well as with the long-gone dreams of dogmatic Leninists in the Soviet Union that a nation was historically conditioned, would soon be 'naturally overcome', and then cease to exist.

Whether a nation is seen as a group that has been constructed but that, nonetheless, exists independently of individuals' wishes – as a 'substance' – or as a myth and illusion, I am of the opinion that any scientific and in particular historical study of this phenomenon cannot relinquish attempts to explain its origins. Therefore, there is a need to analyse the relationships and attitudes that led to a successful 'inventing' or forming of nations, or to the emergence of nationalism. Any quarrels over terminology become meaningful only if their aim is to arrive at a definition or a concept that allows the best possible and the most precise causal analysis. Conversely, if it is believed that the only actually existing thing is 'nationalism', the search for a definition of the nation becomes irrelevant.

Before turning our attention to the causal explanations of nation-forming, we must briefly consider a subject of dispute that was mentioned earlier: has so-called 'nationalism' been a curse or a blessing? This dispute has remained unresolved since the turn of the twentieth century, and has clearly had a political background.

It is very difficult to ascertain precisely which issues this dispute has encompassed, since the large majority of authors who have written about 'nationalism' have not defined the term. It is thus appropriate to state that the term has been used with different judgemental undertones. Three basic types of such evaluation can be differentiated: negative, positive and neutral.

1. The term 'nationalism' has been used with a negative charge on several levels. The oldest of them dates back to the rejection of 'bourgeois nationalism' by social democratic politicians, who considered it to be an instrument by which the bourgeoisie controlled the popular masses. This tradition later provided a basis for the views of authors who were closer to Marxism, such as Eric Hobsbawm. The next level of an explicitly negative connotation can be found in views contrasting national values with civic values, stressing the dangers of manipulating the masses and of abusing xenophobic tendencies.

2. The most commonly presented opinion is that 'nationalism' can have positive as well as negative effects. Tom Nairn's

contemplations of the 'Janus-faced' nature of nationalism are regarded as characteristic of this stance. He distinguished between the circumstances of colonial or other oppression, under which nationalism played a positive role, and situations in which its role was negative and repressive.[35] In fact, a great many authors have drawn attention to the dual nature of nationalism. For Étienne Balibar, for instance, the 'good' aspects of nationalism are that it facilitates state-building, the building of communities as a whole, and that it is based on the love of people and on tolerance. He lists among its 'negative' aspects its expansive nature, tendency towards hatred, and intolerance of other nationalisms.[36] According to Louis Snyder, who was in many respects inspired by Hans Kohn, nationalism could be moral as well as immoral, positive as well as negative, humane as well as inhumane.[37] It posed a danger when it combined with collectivism against the freedoms of the individual. Nationalism's positive role tends to be emphasised by authors who come from the circumstances of 'small nations', rather than those from an Anglo-American setting – for example, by the Catalan anthropologist Josep Llobera.[38] For the sake of completeness, we must remember that the official Soviet ideology also distinguished (bourgeois) nationalism from the love of the homeland, i.e. patriotism, which was compatible with (proletarian) internationalism.

Some political psychologists have attempted to apply a similar differentiation in empirical research. This has made it possible – in particular in the United States – to draw a polarisation between 'our' American patriotism and 'their' nationalism.[39]

In some cases, the ambiguity in the moral evaluation of nationalism has occurred under conditions of late industrial, liberal society, in that its humanistic, positive aspects, prevalent in older times, have been gradually replaced by aggression and animosity towards other nations. This view was already proposed by E. H. Carr in 1945.[40] Kohn's dichotomy, famous for its spatial projection of the 'dual face' of nationalism, was – as has already been stated – later adopted with various modifications by a great many authors. One example of this is the already mentioned Liah Greenfeld's seemingly independent typology of nationalism, presented in her generally rather overrated book.[41] Her dichotomy has been expanded onto a global level: the civic and individualistic American concept represents the most progressive type of nationalism, while reactionary and dangerous nationalism continues to be reserved for 'the East' – Germany, and in particular Russia.[42]

3. Nationalism has also been used as a neutral term, and an instrument of scientific analysis. Carlton Hayes was already aware that consideration needed to be given to the various attitudes the term encompassed, which could be evaluated as positive in some and negative in other cases, but that it essentially needed to be a term which helped to explain and understand social processes. Karl W. Deutsch, John Breuilly, Ernest Gellner and Benedict Anderson have adopted the same approach.

Nevertheless, the emphasis on a 'non-judgemental' use of the term 'nationalism' contains a flaw, as the following example illustrates. The vast majority of American authors employ the term 'nationalism' whenever they write about other nations and 'patriotism' in the context of the history of their own country. Any book that speaks of 'American nationalism' is generally likely to have been written by a non-American writer. Put very simply: *we* are patriots, *the others* are nationalists. The matter is even more complicated in the case of British nationalism and British patriotism.[43]

The non-judgemental, 'neutral' use of the term 'nationalism' evidently has its difficulties. Many authors are aware of the disadvantages of a term with such broad scope, which encompasses SS generals as well as the French Maquis, Johann G. Herder as well as Napoleon, Europe as well as other continents. In the same vein, the murdering of the Igbo people in Nigeria, the medieval hatred of foreigners, and Chinese foreign policy can all be explained in terms of 'nationalistic' motivations.

Which of these three concepts of 'nationalism' is a suitable instrument for an analysis of historical processes? I dare claim that not one of these is fully adequate: the first for its one-sidedness, the second for its ambiguity, and the third for its hypocrisy. Like numerous other authors, I consider it vital to adopt different terms in order to distinguish a judgemental approach from a neutral one. In this book, the term 'nationalism' is only used in the context of the former, and refers to an excessive worshipping of one's own nation, connected with overvaluing it and placing it above other nations.[44] A different term needs to be found for the positive aspect of the relationship to one's nation – i.e. for national solidarity and working for one's nation. The following terms have been employed for this purpose: national consciousness, regionalism,[45] national sentiment (Bagge), love for one's homeland and, in particular, patriotism.[46] While Gellner described nationalism as a form of patriotism, some authors propose that nationalism is one of the sources of patriotism.[47] The latter belief is an innovation that is easily discredited by the fact that 'patriotism' is an ancient term, which has different connotations in different languages. Even the term 'national consciousness' is age-old, and had been commonly used before nationalism proliferated. Its variant, 'national thought', has appeared to be most suitable in recent times.[48] In French, *patriotisme* can be understood as a synonym or even a higher form of regionalism, which in turn can be a label for a transition to nationalism.[49] *Nationalité* is another term occasionally employed in French literature, but this also has an older tradition of use.[50] The term 'belonging' (*Zugehörigkeit* in German) might hold the best prospects, as it refers merely to an awareness that an individual belongs to a larger, suprapersonal entity. An 'awareness of belonging' is an objective fact, which is non-binding and cannot be judged morally, and which can be perceived as a precondition for the existence of every group, including a nation.[51]

A number of researchers from the ranks of sociologists and anthropologists have been truly innovative with the terminology. They adopt a historical – i.e. developmental – perspective, and advocate that what is now called 'nationalism' has evolved from older attitudes and relationships, which they label 'loyalty' and, more frequently, 'identity'.

The term 'loyalty', which has so far been employed by anthropologists rather than historians, is characterised as a relationship of an individual to existing groups, events or values – i.e. to social realities – in the context of which this individual lives. This relationship implies an element of obligation or responsibility of an individual towards the suprapersonal entity or principle. It is therefore not an attitude that is a result of internalisation – based on searching for a collective 'we' or discovering 'who we are'. Instead, it is based on individuals' relationships to a particular entity (Clifford Geertz also uses the term 'primordial ties').[52] If the term 'loyalty' were applied to the process of nation-forming – i.e. to the relationship of an individual to an already-existing entity-nation – the primordial understanding of a nation would first have to be reconciled. Undoubtedly, this is one of the reasons why the term 'loyalty' is unlikely to be employed as an alternative to 'nationalism' in the context of historical research into nation-forming.

'Group identity' is an altogether different matter. Although this term is usually thought to have been pioneered by Erik H. Erikson, it is likely to have entered the world of historical and sociological research in a number of ways. The term 'identity', in the sense of 'collective identity', has most commonly been associated with 'ethnic identity'. Aware of the fact that 'nationalism' was not an appropriate term to use in the context of medieval and early modern society, John Armstrong used the term 'identity' in relation to nations in his comparative account of the journey from the medieval 'nation' to the modern one.[53] A handful of authors employed this term in the 1980s,[54] but it was not until around 1990 that greater numbers of them began to use it independently. Although Smith gained much acclaim for his systematic monograph on 'national identity', it is difficult to determine whether it was indeed his influence that proved decisive and resulted in the term being used frequently – and usually without much theoretical reflection – by researchers who study issues pertaining to nations.[55]

The advantage of using the term 'national identity' is that it is only one of many possible, mutually compatible identities, such as regional, ethnic, religious and class identity ('multiple identities'). National identity is based on ethnic elements, and encompasses the concept of a common territory (evokes the idea of a 'homeland'), common traditions and values, a common memory and myths, and common laws. It needs to be taken into consideration that national identity is not merely a variant of group identity, since is it also shaped by personal identity and social identity, both of which are an expression of how an individual presents themselves in social interaction and how, through this interaction, this individual is accepted by others. The most important function of national identity is that it is a clear manual with regard to determining an individual's place in the world by providing a definition of the individual's belonging to a 'collective self', and offering the option of identifying with it.[56]

Whereas Anthony Smith emphasises that a national identity ought to be an 'organic' extension of ethnic identity, other authors stress the importance of national identity's mobilisation potential. For William Bloom, the adoption of a national identity is the consequence of a crisis of identities, which any society undergoes from time to time. He draws attention to the fact that self-identification by large numbers of people with the nation and its symbols allows them to act as one unit, a 'psychological group', when these symbols are, or appear to be, endangered.[57] Fernand Braudel derives national identity chiefly from the national community's 'historical experience' and from the dialogue between the past and the future.[58] The Swedish historian Sven Tägil advocates differentiating 'identity', a mere awareness of belonging to a nation, from 'identification', an individual's active attitude towards the nation, the willingness to get involved on behalf of the collective self – the nation.[59]

It appears that there is justification for the use of the term 'national identity' when analysing nation-forming processes. In contrast to the term 'nationalism', it is morally neutral and not weighted down or clouded by politicised journalism. Unsurprisingly, numerous contemporary, established as well as emerging researchers have employed the term 'national identity' as one of the central terms of historical analysis, which can replace the overused and ambiguous 'nationalism'.[60] In some cases it has almost served as a synonym.

Unfortunately, 'national identity' is already beginning to suffer from the difference between the ways in which the term 'identity' is employed by the social sciences in general and by empirical studies about national identity, which regard it as a constituent part or manifestation of a group (collective) social identity.[61] Moreover, the danger is that the increased popularity of the term, together with the lack of reflection with which it is frequently used, in particular in Anglo-Saxon linguistic settings, will reduce its applicability as an instrument of scientific analysis, as has happened with the term 'nationalism'. It is thus understandable that some of the critical authors have gone so far as to propose that that the term 'identity' should be left out of the terminological repertoire and replaced by another one. Lutz Niethammer believes that this 'plastic word' ought to be abandoned altogether and replaced with more specific terms, such as 'we'. Rogers Brubaker recommends the use of 'nationness' for a sense of belonging to a national group and 'nationhood' for an objective belonging to a nationality.[62] The question is whether such an innovative approach might actually cause even greater terminological confusion.

To summarise, it can be said that the advantages of the term 'national identity' are that it is non-judgemental and can be combined with other types of identity (ethic, state or regional). Its major drawback is that it does not encompass the moment of mobilisation that is connected with nation-forming. This shortcoming is easily rectified by making use of the derivative 'identification' or – depending on the type of nation-forming in question – by using the terms 'national movement' and 'national mobilisation', which are perhaps more universally applicable. However, by no means is this meant as the final word on the topic of terminology at this point.

Whatever the objections to the term 'identity' may be, my view is that it is one of the analytical terms that can be used, albeit not the only one. Although research has so far proved both the scope and the usefulness of the term, it has also become evident that it is in danger of becoming overused in the same way as the term 'nationalism', especially if it continues to be used indiscriminately.

Presenting the Nation in a Historical Light

All attempts at defining a nation (and nationalism) implicitly contain a causal aspect: how did the object that is about to be defined come into being, and how was it shaped? Therefore, this chapter does not need to provide a list of all individual views and approaches. Instead, it will outline the general characteristic of the competing concepts, which are differentiated on the basis of their differing views with regard to the relationship between the categories 'nation' and 'nationalism'. Authors who consider the nation to be the outcome of nationalism a priori believe that nations came into existence as 'cultural constructs' and were products of intellectuals and ambitious politicians – the outcome of specific social engineering. This being said, this group contains a wide range of approaches that vary greatly, both in their radicalism – i.e. the extent to which they acknowledge that there are also 'objective' factors – and with regard to the way in which they reconcile the paradigm of cultural transfer. If nations were cultural constructs and formed across the whole of Europe, they must have been the result of the diffusion of nationalism, of 'cultural transfer'. Did this diffusion take on the form of purposeful transfers of information, or was it an autonomous force – a 'self-disseminating force', in Anthony Smith's words?[63] Was it only ideas that spread from one country to the next, or also social and political institutions? Were ideas merely imitated, or were they modified and altered? These questions are rhetorical, since there are very few unambiguous diffusionist interpretations, and most diffusionists also tend to consider other circumstances. Even Hans Kohn, who is generally regarded as the pioneer of this approach, in his dichotomy implicitly assumed the existence of objective political and social conditions and local traditions that determined the various paths of 'Western' and 'non-Western' types of nationalism.

Nevertheless, we should not let ourselves be constrained by terms. Not all explanations of modern nation-forming that claim verbal allegiance to the decisive role of 'nationalism' are constructivist, nor can all views of nations as 'images' or 'texts' be categorised as such. Let us illustrate this with Ernest Gellner who, having categorically proposed that it was nationalism that had led to the creation of nations, considered it necessary to add a causal explanation based on social transformations: If nations had been created by nationalism, where had nationalism stemmed from? Gellner explained the genesis of nationalism by such a realistic claim about the decisive role of social and economic changes, for which he uses the term 'industrialisation', that his explanation is sometimes described as historical materialism. He was conscious of the fact that national identity could not spread successfully only by chance. Similarly, many critics erroneously argue that, while Benedict Anderson's 'imagined communities' may explain how the concept of a nation spread, it says nothing about why this occurred.[64] If we read his book carefully, we cannot overlook that he also advanced a list of social and cultural preconditions that had helped create nations over the centuries since at least the Reformation, independently of the wishes of 'nationalists' who followed later. Both examples illustrate the importance of not being content with superficially adopting attractive phrases when studying the 'theories on nationalism', and the need always to examine the research techniques and findings that lie behind these phrases.

From the point of view of research methods, we can detect a certain polarity related to theories and empiricism, which to an extent corresponds with the specificity of different fields of study. At one end of the spectrum, there are empirical studies that, upon thorough examination, reveal the characteristic aspects of one particular or individual case of nation-forming. The conclusions they draw on this basis are relatively straightforward. The other end of the spectrum is occupied by sophisticated theoretical works, which are primarily concerned with the internal logic of the model. Most research projects can be found somewhere between the two extremes, and are divided into a number of categories according to how much theory or empiricism is contained in their analysis. Some authors, such as Deutsch and Gellner, work with a high level of abstraction and form generalised conclusions, which they assume will help explain individual cases. The next group of authors, including Hobsbawm and Smith, employ the 'illustrative method', form generalised observations, and prove – or rather, illustrate – their validity on more or less systematically selected examples. Other authors, such as Hechter and Nairn, analyse developments in one country and use their findings to draw generalised conclusions so as to prove or disprove various 'theories'. The present volume comes closest to the works of authors such as Breuilly, who base theirs on a comparative study of a larger number of cases – nations – and form generalised conclusions from their findings.

I do not consider it necessary to list a summary or a typology of opinions about the ways in which – and due to which factors – modern nations came into existence. However, I believe that it is worth commenting briefly on the broad and knowledgeable typology of the 'theories of nationalism' that Anthony Smith presented by categorising views on the birth of nations into five paradigms, and attributing certain partial research contributions to each of them.[65]

In my opinion, there is a fundamental flaw in singling out perennialism as a distinct 'theory' of nation-forming, in that it uses the same term for very different social forms. While we can find medieval and early modern communities whose members were aware of a long-term togetherness and common interests, the fact that they described themselves as a nation (*natio*) does not make them members of a modern nation. They differed in at least two respects, the first relating to the social base: the sense of belonging did not pertain to all the inhabitants of the country, but only to the politically privileged. Secondly, premodern societies were not communities of equal citizens, which is one of the main characteristics of modern nations. In this context, I prefer to speak about the first, premodern (or 'protonational') stage: the general preconditions for modern nation-building. We know, after all, that whenever a national movement in the nineteenth century identified itself in the spirit of perennialism with the medieval 'nation' – i.e. state – it resulted in tragic consequences. Examples include the identification of the Magyar national movement with medieval Hungary, the Polish movement with the early modern Rzeczpospolita, and the German national movement with the Holy Roman Empire.

It would have been beneficial if Smith had divided 'modernists' into further subcategories, based for instance on their relationship with the past, as many 'modernists' acknowledge the historical roots of nations, whereas others do not. The role of ethnicity ought to be another point of differentiation, since it is emphasised by some 'modernists' and seen as less important by others. It is also a reason why claims that ethnosymbolism is a distinct new theory are not entirely plausible: many modernists perceive ethnicity as one of the building blocks of modern nations. One difference perhaps lies in Smith's observation that linguistic and cultural distinctness often became a part of symbols upon which national identity rested.

Although we may have justifiable objections to Smith's characterisation of the paradigms and grouping of individual authors, his typology helps us to orientate ourselves within the superfluity of 'theories of nationalism', whose sheer number, and whose forced attempts at originality, tend to leave a chaotic impression. Smith's typology also proves how much in common different theories have – with the exception of a few marginal, extreme approaches – despite the fact that their authors pride themselves on being distinctive and original.

Perennialists inevitably work with categories determined by primordialists, as a consequence of which the two approaches overlap. Similarly, no ethnosymbolic analysis can ignore the conditions of communications or the social situation in which symbols become nationally relevant, which is usually within the framework of a modernising society. The very fact that modernists regard social, economic and cultural transformations as the key factor forces them also to take into account the changes that had occurred in premodern societies, and factors that the modern national identity was able to build upon. To put it in slightly exaggerated terms: all reputable modernists are in part perennialists and ethnosymbolists; all reputable ethnosymbolists are partially modernists and primordialists; no perennialist can deny that the nation-forming process led to modernisation – and so on. Radical constructivism, as advocated for instance by Kedouri or more recently Brubaker, has not been of much help in the historical examination of causal relationships. Indeed, the points of difference and conflict are rarely as insurmountable as they may at first appear, which is also true of the relationship between the subjective and objective aspect of the process of nation-forming. For example, the Australian political scientist Paul James noted a number of years ago that the differences between the 'essentialists' and 'constructivists' are not nearly so significant – as long as principles of scientific criticism are upheld by the authors in question.[66]

A closer examination of the concepts behind the serious attempts to explain the forming of nations in historical terms enables us to state that it is unimportant whether their authors have opted primarily to use 'nation', 'nationalism', 'nation-forming process', or any other similar term. This conclusion forms the basis of this book, which rests upon a comparative analysis of empirical materials that I have acquired by studying the nation-forming processes of most, if not all, European nations. My aim has been to detect their main similarities, differences and typological characteristics. I have limited my research to Europe alone, as I consider nations to be specifically a European phenomenon that spread to other continents by means of cultural transfer.

I do not strive to earn the label of any '-ism', since I have included primordial factors, ethnic factors, and the role of modernisation as an objective precondition, as well as the use of symbols as one of the instruments of reinforcing national identity and nationalism (in the narrower sense of the word, as mentioned above). It has been of crucial importance to me to divide the comparative analysis according to five basic aspects or perspectives, which almost all 'theories of nationalism' have taken into account.[67] These aspects can be found among objective preconditions, as well as among instruments of national mobilisation.

1. *History*: Each nation, however defined, was marked by some ties to the past, to history. All researchers query the significance of events, institutions and opinions that preceded the birth of a modern nation, how the past was perceived, and how it was made relevant to the present. While individual assessments of the role of the legacy of the past may differ, there are very few authors who reject any ties to the past.

2. *Language and ethnicity*: No one can overlook the fact that people had to communicate with each other in the process of nation-forming, and that they were aware of belonging to a group that was (or had been) ethnically or linguistically distinct. Some researchers regard this factor as decisive, others as secondary; in some cases this difference is a reflection of the fact that the role of ethnicity and culture in individual nation-forming processes varied.

3. *Modernisation*: The term 'modern nation' in itself implies a relationship to modernisation, and any historical analysis will, explicitly or implicitly, address the connection between nation-forming and the process of modernisation. No reputable author will deny the importance of school attendance, literacy, political and social emancipation, or the transformation of the social structure. The differences lie only in the place they occupy within their explanation.

4. *Conflict of interest*: Only a few researchers perceive the nation-building process as an entirely harmonious transformation of identities. Most take into account at least some conflicts, whether these stem from revolutionary and other struggles for power, from economic position or prestige, from the differences between regions and the interests of their elites, or from the relationship between the centre and the provinces, and between social groups and classes.

5. *Emotions and identity*: Nations are no longer considered natural communities whose members are unaware of their belonging together ('a nation by itself'). Once we accept the view that the existence of a nation depends on national identity being adopted by the masses, we must give regard to the ways and means by which this identity spread and gained ground. Naturally, individual authors differ on whether an awareness of belonging to a nation forms the central theme of their research, or whether they

confine themselves to stating that it was an integral part of the nation-building process, the causes of which could be found in each of the four aforementioned spheres and processes.

Differences among authors and paradigms are thus not a result of a one-sided orientation towards a single circumstance or relationship. Instead, they are determined by the varying degrees of emphasis on each one of these circumstances, and the range of opinions about its importance for particular national movements or the whole European continent.

Consideration must also be given to the fact that the need to make one's mark in the professional world and among all the scientific findings is facilitated by being original and inventive. This leads some, in particular young, authors to draw attention to themselves with the help of one-sided perspectives and novel expressions, neologisms and controversial statements. In so doing, some of these authors develop and expand older concepts and, by applying new techniques and methods, make new findings. Only time will reveal which concepts will gain general acceptance and which will prove to be marginal deviations and, as such, forgotten.

It is not the objective of this book to be original for originality's sake. It aims to explore the possibilities of a general consensus, a 'compatibility' of opinions, and to verify whether the above-mentioned five 'fields' address all of the important contexts of the nation-forming processes, regardless of whether these processes have been approached from a constructivist point of view or not. The preliminary working hypothesis that will need to be confirmed is that there is much more consensus about the outcomes of the research to date than we may be led to believe by numerous verbal proclamations and artificially created conceptual differences. It is vital to distinguish genuinely different approaches (and theoretical starting points) from more or less sophisticated and original terminological innovations and plays with words, which are often a source of misunderstanding.

Last but not least, we must note two marked flaws, which – despite all the differences – are common to all the research conducted to date. The first flaw is that analyses of manifestations and sources of what is labelled 'nationalism' (and in some cases also 'nation-forming') somehow automatically assume that all parts of Europe (and perhaps even other parts of the world) were affected by the same 'nationalism'. As a mere product of this nationalism, the phenomenon of the 'nation' was also one and the same. It is rarely taken into account that the modern nation is part of the process of nation-building, and that it is thus essential to respect that different regions and continents developed at different stages. This in turn determined the civilisational differences and, consequently, differences in what have been described as 'nations' in different places at different times. Researchers tend to underestimate variations in time and the causal diachronic interpretation. 'Nationalism' is too often studied as an atemporal category, and little regard is given to the differences between the social and cultural situations in which 'classic' modern nation-formation occurred and those characterising the current situation. Consequently, findings about current national identity and the factors that have shaped it are used to advance ahistorical – and thus inevitably distorted – interpretations of past developments.

The second flaw, commonly seen particularly in Anglo-Saxon literature, is that researchers disregard the important fact that modern nation-forming followed two markedly different types of path in Europe. With very few exceptions, it is completely overlooked that the use of the vague, undifferentiating term 'nationalism' obscures the fundamental difference between modern nation-forming in the context of state-nations and of national movements.[68] As a result, findings about the nationalism of a particular state-nation, such as the French, are generalised without restraint to explain all nation-forming processes.

In practice, this means that the vast majority of works conducted within the territories of state-nations have ignored or completely marginalised the forming of small nations, as though they were exceptions to the rule or historical mistakes.[69] It is as if an old geo-political concept of the nineteenth century lived on in this approach, according to which it is a natural part of the life of state-nations to continue to expand their territories and integrate or control small nations. However, if we choose not to view historical developments from the perspective of great-power politics, for which the interesting and important parties are only those who rule the world, we must also alter the way in which we look upon the importance of the history of individual nations. From the point of view of studying the process of nation-forming, it is not important how large different communities were or whether or not they formed within their own nation-state.[70] Just as social historians are equally interested in the poor and the rich, in large landowners as well as in small peasants, for historians who study 'nationalism' the development of each nation is equally interesting and relevant, regardless of how many members this nation had. This makes it all the more essential to pay attention to the typology of modern nation-forming addressed in the following chapter.

CHAPTER 2

Typological Characterisation

As the previous chapter revealed, one of the fundamental shortcomings of the modern study of the historical contexts of nationalism is that important typological variations in the process of nation-building are often disregarded. The term 'nationalism' is used irrespective of historical and social context, and regardless of its initial objective. Even if we accept the view that a nation is merely a product of nationalism, we should not overlook the fact that the journey from nationalism to a nation cannot be described using one model, as if it were a mono-dimensional process. It had two radically different starting points – 'state-nation',[1] on one hand, and ethnic group, on the other – and this difference will invariably have affected the outcome of the journey.

Basic Types of European Nation-Building

Theodor Schieder differentiated three types of nation-building in Europe.[2] The first consisted of state-nations of the 'Western European type', such as France and England, i.e. modern nations formed by means of internal revolutions or reforms. The second type constituted 'nation-states', created by the coming together of state entities whose peoples were close both culturally and linguistically, such as the Germans and the Italians. John Breuilly used the term 'unification nationalism', and justifiably also added the Polish to this group.[3] The third type comprised nation-states, which had been formed by splitting away from their supranational, multi-ethnic state entities.

Schieder's typology proved most influential within German historiography, and while an analogous approach can be found in the Anglo-Saxon context, it tends to be the domain of historical sociologists. For instance, during his studies of the history of state power, Michael Mann concluded (in a striking correspondence with Schieder, whom he is unlikely to have known) that when modern

nations started to emerge after 1840, they did so on three levels: as
communities that strengthened the state (France and England), as
communities that created the state (Germany), or as communities
that dismantled the state – i.e. seceded from it.[4] Charles Tilly simplified the differentiation of nation-building processes by grouping
them into two types: those driven by state-led nationalism and those
driven by state-seeking efforts. In the former, the ruling classes
demanded, in the name of the nation, that all citizens self-identify
with the state, and subordinate their personal interests to the higher
interests of that state. In the latter, the representatives of the part of
the population that had no collective control over the state demanded
that they be granted autonomy.[5]

No major objections can be raised to this typology as long as we
share the view that it is the state that lies at the centre of historical
events. However, if we believe that statehood is not a necessary prerequisite for the existence of a nation, then this typology is not
appropriate, because it fails to encompass the crucial difference
between the two possible paths to a modern nation (and nationalism)
in Europe. The first one took place within a state-nation, i.e. a state
that had developed its own distinctive culture in the medieval or early
modern periods. Nation-building in these 'states-thus-nations' took
on the shape of intra-state transformation. The second path arose
from the circumstances of non-ruling ethnic groups, and assumed the
form of national movements – purposeful efforts to attain all the
attributes of distinct national existence. However, statehood – i.e. full
independence – was not one of these attributes; nor was it a historical
necessity, since the existence of a nation is not determined by whether
or not it has achieved statehood. Both the German and the Italian
paths to becoming nations lie on the dividing line between the two
basic types. In keeping with a state-nation, they exhibit complete social
structures with their own 'national' elites, as well as continuity of
developed culture and literature in their national languages. What they
have in common with the second type of nation-building is the absence
of statehood, and thus, among other things, also the fact that their
members did not regard their national existence as inevitable but as
something they needed to strive for. Conscious of exaggeration, we
can therefore accept the notion that, typologically, Germany and Italy
belong alongside the states that sprang from the national movements
within the Austro-Hungarian Empire.[6]

What purpose does such typological differentiation serve in the study of nation-building processes? When comparing the political map of Europe around the year 1800 with the situation in 2000, we will see there are marked differences. At the outset of the nineteenth century there were only a handful of state-nations in Europe with ethnically homogenous populations, full social structure and only one national culture: France, the Netherlands, Sweden, Portugal and, with some reservation, possibly Spain. Beside these, there were five multi-ethnic empires: Great Britain and Denmark, both dominated by one developed national culture, and Austria, the Ottoman Empire and Russia, which exhibited clear multicultural characteristics – i.e. other cultures existed alongside the state culture with which most of the ruling classes identified. More than twenty non-ruling ethnic groups lived within these five multi-ethnic empires. Several of them were still, in Anthony Smith's terms, in the stage of 'ethnic category', while others were already 'ethnic communities'.[7] It should be emphasised, however, that such differentiation simplifies matters greatly, since an 'ethnic category' will usually already contain small segments that could qualify as 'ethnic communities', and vice versa. As their national movements achieved success, a majority of these non-ruling ethnic groups adopted national identities and developed distinct national cultures. Over the next two hundred years, these 'communities' gradually gained a degree of autonomy, and eventually also independence, reaching a stage here labelled 'small nation'.

In typologically simplified terms, these ethnic communities differed from modern nations in that they lacked complete social structures, cultures in their national language (or these cultures had been weakened), and, of course, political autonomy. As was stated earlier, nation-building within these ethnic groups assumed the form of national movements seeking to attain all the essential attributes of a distinct nation – i.e. to develop a complete social structure with its own business and academic elites, create a national culture in its national language, and gain a political voice, although not necessarily as a state. 'A nation' was initially a programme, a vision for the future, and the ensuing of national movements was neither a matter of course nor a necessity. Neither was their success seen as assured, as they would invariably come into conflict with the elites of the ruling nation (or of the multi-ethnic empire) and with the old regime as a whole. In this sense, all the national movements were closely linked to the struggle for political modernisation and the disposal of old sources of legitimacy. This was reflected in the national programmes and auto-stereotypes of the nations fighting for justice and democracy.

The roots of state-nations can be seen in the centralisation of the late medieval and early modern 'national monarchies'. Again, centralised monarchies and state-nations were neither the inevitable nor the only possible outcome of the medieval developments. The aforementioned multi-ethnic empires, the evolution towards a political 'federation' such as that of the Holy Roman Empire of the German Nation, and the tendency towards the establishment of municipal and theocratic church-states are all good examples of alternatives. The early modern states tended further to centralise their administration in order to increase its reliability, and to introduce effective tax systems in order to secure funding for the administration and royal court, as well as the army and any military pursuits. These states had their own ruling classes, and gradually developed their own educated elites and their own police apparatuses so as to ensure that the law was abided by. In cooperation with the church, they also monitored their subjects' way of thinking. The legitimacy of the monarch's power rested on religion, and political rights were reserved for a privileged few (either the aristocracy alone or also the urban middle classes). In 'Latin Europe', they adopted the term *natio* and its equivalents in individual languages (for example, *národ* in Czech) as a way of labelling their togetherness. They tended to see themselves as representative of the interests of the entire country.

In the era of absolutism, any building of a modern state as a community of equal citizens could only become effective if it was a response to the crisis of the old legitimacies of the monarch and the religion – i.e. when the ruler's political sovereignty had passed to the nation (or was expected to have done so). State policy – domestic or foreign – would no longer be conducted in the name of 'a monarch by divine right', but in the name of 'a nation'. A community of citizens – members of a modern nation – would leave no room for any feudal political privileges or hierarchical non-economic dependence. Specific historical circumstances determined whether or not the building of a modern civic nation was accompanied by the replacement of a large proportion of the old elites, as was the case of France, or by reaching a compromise with them, such as in England or Germany.

The state and its power apparatus had been created before the transformation into civic society began. Consequently, mass mobilization was not a prerequisite for the existence of this type of modern nation. In fact, the new elites leading these modern civic nations were seldom eager to share power with the lower social strata, or promote the adoption of a national identity in the form of democratisation, thereby opening doors to mass participation. In contrast to state-nations, the success of national movements, which were essentially movements from the ground up, was completely dependent on the active participation of the masses, and on their engagement in political decision-making. It thus comes as no surprise that, as long as national agitation proved successful, the degree of mass participation within national movements was substantially higher than the extent to which masses were mobilised under the conditions of internal transformation of state-nations.

The building of the German and Italian nations transformed them into national movements, which focused on their one fundamental shortcoming with regard to their full national existence – the need to create a nation-state. It holds true even for these nations that full national existence, which in their case included a nation-state, was not something automatic, but rather a value that needed to be fought for. This fight was greatly facilitated by the fact that a large majority of the old regime's educated elites, and even a proportion of those in power, adopted the idea of a nation as their own. It was perhaps precisely because the striving for a nation-state was headed by the power elites that, in both cases, it achieved full statehood in a historically short time – certainly before the masses were fully mobilised. This is what led to the post-1860 efforts to 'create the Italians' for the already-existing Italy. It also explains why there was such a drive within the newly formed German Empire to establish an integral, truly national, German (Prussian-Protestant) identity as against the 'foreign' (Catholic and socialist) elements.

Periodisation of the Path to the Modern Nation

Injudicious use of the term 'nationalism' has caused much difficulty in attempts both to typologise and to periodise nation-building processes. When and where is the label 'nationalism' justified? Is it when it is used to refer to the eighteenth-century philologists who sought and created the grammar rules of modern languages? Or when describing patriots as national agitators? Or perhaps when it is employed to represent the attitude of landowners arriving at harvest celebrations that were decorated with state or national flags? The answer in each of these cases can be both positive and negative, but neither will aid our understanding or insight. We can attempt to periodise these heterogeneous processes, which are (often injudiciously) listed under the term 'nationalism', by 'playing around with adjectives'. Even this, however, would shed no more light on the causal relationships, and is thus of no value.

Rather than engage in terminological speculations, it will be more useful to identify chronological differences – i.e. whether and how individual phases of nation-building differed. At the very outset, it is crucial to address the question of whether it is at all possible to periodise two such dissimilar paths to a nation as were discussed in the previous chapter. It is also essential to decide how we define 'a nation', and this will, in turn, determine our selection of the starting periodisation criterion. In my approach to the definition of the term 'nation', I have opted for a compromise, and worked with the one characteristic that almost all authors agree on: a modern nation becomes fully existent only when everyone, or almost everyone, who qualifies as its potential member, identifies with it. This understanding of the term helps select a functional periodisation criterion, and I will be examining how national identity spread and was received, and in what time-frame ethnic communities (within any state or empire) gradually transformed into conscious communities of citizens – members of nations.

The first prerequisite for identification with 'a nation' was the existence of some pointers by which 'national identity' could navigate. There was thus a need to define 'national territory', gain knowledge of the past events that had helped develop an awareness of national belonging, codify the language, characterise the national cultural tradition, and identify the members of the nation – i.e. the ethnic groups, their customs and ways of life. This was achieved in state-nations by erudite scholars. They had been scrutinising facts about their own countries and nations since at least the seventeenth century, partly on their own initiative but increasingly by reason of having been commissioned by the state or monarch. They perceived the existence of 'a nation' as given and inevitable.

While this type of scholar can also be found among the non-ruling ethnic groups, they tended to be private individuals and did not appear until the era of enlightened patriotism. It should be remembered that this scholarly 'phase A' only ever had a faint presence in some cases – for example, in the Serbian, Belarusian and Basque national movements – and that at times the epicentre of scholarly interest lay partly outside the ethic group's territory (for example, in Lithuania and Greece). Moreover, it holds true for national movements – but not only for them – that erudite patriots did not necessarily come from the ethnic group to which they devoted their scholarly efforts. A closer examination will reveal that their scholarly interest was usually accompanied by an emotional interest in the subject, as was typical of all Enlightenment scholars. Although their studies were an important prerequisite to the formation of a concept of the modern nation, it would be an ahistorical update if we asserted that it was each of these scholars' subjective intention to pave the way for or initiate a national movement. The determination to learn about the distinctive features of an ethnic group only occasionally went hand-in-hand with the vision of its further development towards a nation.

In the narrower sense of the word, 'national' movements came into being as soon as several members of an ethnic group – usually those who had had access to higher education – decided to spread national awareness and offer a new national identity, presenting it as something of a specific value and a commitment for all members of the group. In most cases the focus was on cultural, linguistic and social goals, but at times political demands were added too (for example, by the Norwegians, the Irish and the Greeks). 'Phase B' rarely progressed as a linear correlation between agitation and mass mobilisation. Being limited to a small circle of patriots, it initially acted in something of a social vacuum. In time, however, there was a shift in attitudes, and calls for patriotism gained wider appeal.

The question is whether or not state-nations underwent a parallel phase to the 'phase B' of national movements, during which, as has been mentioned, the success of nation-building usually took on the form of an intra-state struggle for political and civic rights.

Whether it occurred as a revolution or as gradual reforms, it was always a struggle of active minorities, who provided political and cultural coordinates for the forming nation. Once these coordinates were established as more or less consistent and indisputable, efforts to mobilise the masses took place. The intensity of these efforts corresponded with the degree to which the new power elites felt they needed to reinforce their power within 'their' state and/or with their growing interest in defensive, expansive or even war politics. In state-nations, the power struggle was an intrinsic part of national mobilisation from the very beginning. However, the success of the nation-building processes in these nations was clearly not dependent on mass mobilisation.

National movements were a different case. Their path to a modern nation became irreversible only when the national agitation of phase B succeeded, and gained the support of the decisive part of the non-ruling ethnic group. Once national identity was embraced by the masses, it turned into a 'material force'. National political programmes were usually not formed or made distinctive anywhere until phase C – when a mass national movement occurred. We can talk of ultimate success, and thus of the national movement coming to an end, only once a national community had developed a complete social structure and the movement attained political autonomy or independence. In the case of state-nations, the equivalent of phase C was full national mass mobilisation, sometimes referred to as 'integral nationalism'.

It is evident that any analysis or characterisation of the terms 'nation' and 'nationalism' should be based on typological classification. At the same time, it also ought to take into account which development phase of modern nation-building is being discussed. However, all the considerations mentioned above illustrate that using the terms 'national identity', 'national consciousness' and 'national mobilisation' proves much more beneficial and useful than the nebulous term 'nationalism'. Another advantage could be used, when typological specification of nation-building processes and their periodisation are concerned.

PART II

The Sources and Elements of Nation-Building Processes

As was stated at the outset, the premise of this book is that the process of modern state-building was not purely an intellectual construct 'without any foundations', but rather a process, driven by human intent in the shape of subjective 'nationalistic' dreams and hopes. There were, of course, circumstances and developments at play that were independent of these wishes, but may have become their building blocks, or even an impulse for their conceptualisation. Whether or not we regard the subjective and objective components of the modern nation-building process as equally essential and mutually determining, developments that had emerged from the social, political and cultural circumstances of the earlier times had provided a natural basis for them. Therefore, the first part of the book will focus on the objective factors and processes that the bearers and protagonists of modern nation-building efforts drew on, or relied on in any way. They have been grouped under the following three themes: the legacy of the past, linguistic and cultural links, and the major 'modernising' changes within the economic, social, political, cultural and educational spheres.

CHAPTER 3

The Legacy of the Past

Present-day research often mistakenly reduces the importance of history in nation-building merely to the results of historical investigation, whose selection and evaluation is frequently manipulated to suit the current needs and interests of a given nation. Such an approach is one-sided and, more importantly, fallacious. It ignores the fact that the members of any forming nation perceived history not only through information about the past – at the level of cultural construction or collective memory – but also through institutional and objectively existing relics of the past, i.e. those relics which existed independently of their hopes and visions. It was not possible to completely 'invent' national histories, disregarding what had happened in the past; they could not contradict the way people perceived the past through architecture, historical sites, state and political institutions, the local rule of law, preserved documents, religious paintings and texts, and so on. Moreover, not all constructions of the past and 'invented traditions' proved truly effective and produced the desired results. For all these reasons, when we examine the role history played in the process of nation-building, it is crucial to distinguish the 'objectively surviving past', which interests us in this part of the analysis, from 'historical consciousness', which encompassed a wide range of representations of the past, ranging from scientific interpretations of national history to myths and family traditions.

History Perceived Directly

Statehood and its institutions were the most significant forms and manifestations of the past, which most members of the developing nations were, to a greater or lesser degree, in direct contact with. It may be valuable to remind ourselves here of a number of commonly known facts from the history of European states.

Most references are usually made to the evolution of France from an absolutist state to a modern nation – a nation that had been developing continuously since the Middle Ages and which a revolution had transformed into a state-nation – i.e. a state inhabited and governed by a community of equal citizens. The claims that the first mention of 'France' had not appeared until the thirteenth century and that the ensuing *francisation de le France* lasted centuries are fully justified. By the eighteenth century, in spite of all the tribulations of the Hundred Years' War and the religious wars of the sixteenth century, the French state was a consolidated entity with a homogenous culture and a rich, developed literary language. Thanks to its centralised administration and its organisation of the tax system, practically all members of the population knew which state they lived in and who their ruler was. Paris, the age-old metropolis and royal residence, had become a tangible demonstration of the monarchy's existence, and also, therefore, of the state-nation. The church administration had been made to suit the interests of the French kingdom, and served it. Undoubtedly, only a small part of the population would have identified themselves with this type of state – mainly the privileged elites and the wealthy inhabitants the administration cities and centres. Nonetheless, this was a sufficient psychological prerequisite and, to a certain degree, also a social base for the forming of the new elites of the state-nation.

The French king was presented as an embodiment of the state and its interests, which included expansion as well as the protection of internal order. Not even in times of greatest decline was there any real chance of the whole of France becoming part of another state – i.e. another state-nation. Its borders had been set by the eighteenth century, and although the majority of the population did not have a command of standard French, they spoke in dialects close to it. Beyond the borders of France, French was the mother tongue of a large group of people only in the Habsburg southern Netherlands. The civic national identity, which was asserting itself in revolutionary terms, knew no other national allegiance. Any generalisation to the effect that the evolution of France represents a standard nation-building process is an exaggeration. It would be equally justified to propose that France's evolution towards a modern nation was more of an exception than a rule in the European context.

A parallel development took place in England, where absolutism did not prevail but where aristocratic and municipal participation played a very effective integrating role, resulting by the eighteenth century in a stable, albeit far from democratic, parliamentary system. A factor that strengthened a sense of belonging among a relatively large part of the population had been the creation of the 'specifically national', Anglican Church, whose integrating role was only slightly disrupted by Puritanism and Nonconformism. The stability of the English borders, predetermined by the island location, had been further reinforced by the occupation and integration of Wales and the creation of a union with Scotland. Once the Norman conquerors had been anglicised, there had therefore been no alternative to English identity until the eighteenth century. The union with Scotland marked the beginning of the development of British identity, and contributed to the specific blurring of English identity. British identity gradually became accepted by the Scots and the Welsh (or, more accurately, by the elites of these groups) and predominated over their Scottish or Welsh identity, mainly because it offered the opportunity to participate in colonial expansion. In England, by contrast, British and English identities overlapped (as they still do), with no clear dividing line between them. A long tradition of statehood was an indisputable legacy in all parts of Great Britain, and also a framework for national identification.

Spanish national identity, too, was able to lean on the existence of an absolutist centralised state, although its statehood was markedly younger. All the small kingdoms had gradually united during the Reconquista, the crowns of Castile and Aragon being the last two entities to merge. Their autonomy remained more or less intact, despite Castilian dominance. Individual regions continued to have their own *cortes*, their own legal systems, and the organisation of the church had also been partially preserved. Their autonomy was continually curtailed, but was not taken away completely until the Bourbons assumed the Spanish throne at the turn of the eighteenth century. After that, Spanish state identity became an expression of and synonym for Castilian identity, even more so than the degree of overlap between English and British identities. The institution of royal power proved to be an integrating historical relic here, as well. Its geographic location had provided the kingdom with relatively fixed borders, although this did not rule out border disputes with France, and the 1580–1640 attempts to integrate Portugal within the realm of Spanish kings were unsuccessful. The civic notion of the

Spanish nation struggled to gain ground over the course of the five revolutions of the nineteenth century and, although the old regime was eventually defeated in the 1870s, it soon became clear that at least two ethnic communities – the Basques and the Catalans – would have some difficulty in adopting the Spanish 'state-national' identity. The two regions' historical distinctness, coupled with their ethnic dissimilarity, had created alternatives to this state identity.

The other state entity that had survived in the Iberian Peninsula since the Middle Ages was Portugal. It had also risen from the Reconquista, and was also subsequently united as a result of colonial pursuits. In the middle of the seventeenth century, the Portuguese aristocracy successfully averted Spanish attempts to take over the country permanently, and Portuguese statehood, defined in opposition to Spain and still on the basis of failing colonial dominion, became an obvious foundation for development towards a modern nation. However, the state institutions of the authoritarian regime and remnants of feudalism hindered the civic component of this development until the twentieth century.

The Netherlands was the only European state-nation to be created in the second half of the sixteenth century, by a revolution that brought together entities that had until then been almost entirely independent, but which then preserved their autonomous status and self-government. The integrating force within the new state was Calvinism. Although the autonomy enjoyed by individual lands that had emerged from the revolution slowly degenerated into oligarchy, the fact remains that, in the second half of the eighteenth century, the Netherlands – a confederation of autonomous provinces with traditional town centres and political institutions – was a stable state. There were growing groups of intellectuals among its elites who were, in the name of patriotism, willing and able to adopt a civic national identity. That said, the sixteenth-century revolution was only successful in the northern, Dutch-speaking provinces, and the ethnically diverse southern part remained under Habsburg rule. The Congress of Vienna decided to create the Kingdom of the Netherlands – a conservative, monarchic 'union' of the northern and southern provinces; but this was to be short-lived. A mere fifteen years later, the Belgium revolution of 1830 gave rise to a new state, whose population consisted of two ethnic communities of approximately the same size.

Sweden had set out to become a multi-ethnic empire at the beginning of the seventeenth century, and remained so until the beginning of the nineteenth century. As a result of Finland's annexation by Russia, it then became a mono-ethnic state, in which there was no alternative to the ethnically and politically defined Swedish state-national identity. Since free landowners were also part of the Estates in Sweden, a large part of the population had been aware of the kingdom's political history.

All these cases were situations in which a modern nation developed as a direct consequence of a civic society forming within an established state whose right to exist was not disputed by anyone. Its educated elites had very quickly – by the early modern period – created a distinct national culture that a majority of the population found easy to understand and accept. The state's territory easily became the national territory, and the state culture was easily turned into the national culture; identification with the state could organically, although not always nonviolently, come to mean identification with the nation. While the administrative apparatus of these states was not defined explicitly as 'national', it either already possessed or was developing features and relationships that, in certain circumstances, could prove nationally integrating. What became decisive for the actual shift towards 'nationalism' was the struggle for political participation and for civic rights in general, which, at the same time, sought to transform the state into a modern national community. Chronologically speaking, England was perhaps where this occurred first.

The situation in many of the other European states at the end of the early modern period was very different. Most of these were multi-ethnic empires, which had been created by the coming-together of several once-independent entities. The members of the ruling classes and the educated elites in these empires usually spoke the same language; but whether their *lingua franca* was German, Russian or Latin, it tended to be unintelligible to the rest of the population. The way in which the past and its relics were perceived by the people of these empires depended on their status. The difference between the attitudes 'from above' and those 'from below' can be observed on two corresponding and interrelated levels. Firstly, in geopolitical terms, the legacy of the past was seen differently by the members of the 'ruling nation' and by the non-dominant ethnic communities.

Secondly, from the point of view of social differentiation, there was a difference between the perception of history of the ruling elites and that of the underprivileged, from whose ranks educated individuals were already beginning to rise. Historical consciousness and the interpretation of relics for the purposes of the present varied correspondingly.

The types of empire that continued to exist beyond the early modern period were conglomerates of essentially autonomous entities with varying administrative and legal traditions, cultures, and, in some cases, even social composition. Some of these entities had once been politically independent. The political and intellectual elites had not created a distinct 'state-national' culture that would be embraced by the people of all the countries that became part of the given empire. They also had difficulties in developing a unified system of administration and government. To the ruling elites, 'the past' referred to the past of the political entity, the empire, while the histories of its constituent parts were only relevant in specific escalated situations. This is why the metropolis and the monarch (more precisely, the ruling dynasty) were the bearers of continuity with the past. Tsarist Russia is one of the empires in this category. Its ruling class was closely knit by the system of tsarist autocracy and the increasingly centralised administration, and had gradually developed a strongly religious culture. Several factors thus favoured the formation of the Russian state-nation, albeit on a territory containing numerous ethnic minorities. Another member of this group, the Habsburg monarchy, possessed much less potential to evolve towards an all-encompassing state-national entity, mainly because only a small part of the population shared a vernacular with the German-speaking elites. An important factor was the existence of the obviously distinct legacies of the medieval Hungarian, Croatian and Bohemian kingdoms. Moreover, neither the dynasty nor the aristocratic elites had made any effort to create a unitary state before the second half of the eighteenth century. In fact, the conglomerate of states ruled by the Habsburgs had borne no official name until the Austrian Empire was founded. In Poland, attempts to transform the multi-ethnic confederation into a modernised state through reforms in the second half of the eighteenth century relied on political and national unification, but failed as a result of the second and the third partitions. Within the Ottoman Empire, history was commandeered by the Ottomans, for whom it was a reminder of glorious expansion and forcible conquest, while the only factor that reminded the members of the Christian ethnic groups of their past was their different religion.

Non-dominant ethnic groups perceived history from a very different angle, and its legacy for them was also markedly different. For now, let us put aside situations in which neither institutional nor cultural remnants of political links with the past had survived – usually since they had never existed (as in the case of the Slovenians, Slovaks, Estonians and Latvians), and occasionally because they had been completely destroyed and forgotten (as in the Bulgarian case). It is not an accident that these peoples were, to use Anthony Smith's words, still in the stage of an ethnic category. In contrast, most European peoples had by the turn of the nineteenth century become ethnic communities, had a name, and lived on the territories of once-independent states, which may have lost their autonomy through dynastic contracts or as victims of external aggression. It would be a mistake to assume that these populations were not directly affected by the history of their lost autonomy and only encountered it in the form of a myth. Many aspects of their long-lost statehood had survived: stable political borders, administrative centres, royal palaces, courts, political institutions (rules of the court), religious and administrative organisations, and, above all, the name of their land and its symbols.

Most remnants of statehood were preserved in Hungary. Its provincial and regional assemblies were the living, institutionalised legacy of the past – not only a reminder of lost statehood, but also of the noblemen's revolt against the Habsburgs. There were also the autonomous Hungarian Catholic Church, the cult of St Stephen, the crown jewels, and, ultimately, the name of the kingdom itself and the term for its ruling class, 'Natio Hungarica'. The late-medieval myth of Hungary as the stronghold of European Christianity in the defensive fight against unbelievers also retained its salience.

It was much harder for relics of statehood to survive in the Triune of Croatia, Slavonia and Dalmatia within the Hungarian Empire. The kingdom had undergone a complex territorial evolution and, at the turn of the nineteenth century, was not homogenous. Its historical territory had lost Dalmatia at the outset of the fifteenth century, and the military frontier in the early modern period, which then remained under the direct rule of Vienna until the 1880s. The provincial assembly of the so-called Banska Croatia, and its capital Zagreb, were both reminders of history, but their borders and structure of administration differed markedly from their previous forms.

The provincial assembly also remained intact in the Czech lands (Bohemia, Moravia and Silesia), together with provincial autonomy, of which Prague had been the centre since medieval times. While the Catholic Church was organised provincially, it was independent in Bohemia and Moravia, heavily promoting the cult of St Wenceslas in Bohemia, the cult of Saints Cyril and Methodius in Moravia, and the cult of the 'modern' St Jan Nepomucký in both. The stable provincial borders, the plight of the kingdom and its monarchs, the architectural heritage, especially in Prague, and the remnants of royal town privileges were all reminiscent of the past. However, the national relevance of a common historical legacy was complicated by the fact that each of the Czech lands (Bohemia, Moravia and a small part of Silesia) represented an autonomous entity with its own assembly, court system and distinct geopolitical location. Their populations thus perceived history differently.

In Norway, the only surviving aspect of the medieval kingdom was its name. The country was not an administrative entity, had been completely bound to Denmark since 1535, and did not have its own capital city, while the Danish language was used by the Norwegian Church. Despite this, the memory of King Olav the Holy, associated with the coronation cathedral in Trondheim and the long-lost independence of Norway, had retained its continuity. Otherwise, however, the distinctness of Norway rested in its geographic location and economy, and the specific social structure of the countryside (free landowners), rather than its relics from the past.

Similarly, there was little left of the once-independent medieval Grand Duchy of Lithuania. It had lost some of its autonomy through the Union of Lublin, but retained its traditional provincial offices and a degree of judicial autonomy until the Partition of the Polish-Lithuanian Commonwealth. However, none of these remnants of its distinctness were incorporated in the 1791 constitution, which counted on a unitary Poland. The importance of Vilnius, the capital of medieval Lithuania, was now only symbolic.

Although the absolutist rule of Philip V had destroyed all that was left of the institutions of Catalan's self-government, culture and judicial system, its capital, Barcelona, and many of its historical buildings in the countryside continued to act as reminders of past glories. Scotland and Wales followed a very similar path, the difference being that their statehood was not destroyed by absolutist centralism but by their incorporation into Great Britain, within which England played a dominant role. In Provence, in southern France, it was particularly the relics of the rich medieval architecture that constituted 'adaptable history'.

There were many other non-dominant ethnic groups, living in the territories of their former medieval states, which had left no 'tangible' relics, only vague mythology and church buildings. Of these ethnic groups, the Irish were reminded of their common past most strongly. Their history was based on the continuity of their religious tradition (and its persecution), symbolised by St Patrick – who was not, in contrast to Saints Wenceslas, Stephen and Olav, a medieval ruler. For the Irish, as for the Icelanders, their territory was determined by their island location. For the Serbs and Bulgarians, just as for the Irish, any awareness of history derived from a vague oral tradition. The important relic for these two peoples was their cultural distinctness from the ruling Ottomans. This lay in their religious allegiance, whose historical symbolism was mainly expressed by old Orthodox monasteries. Unlike the Bulgarians, the Serbs managed to keep their church administration autonomous for a time. The Greeks would have identified with their history to a greater degree. Although no state institutions had survived from the times of the Greek state, Macedonia or the Byzantine Empire, the Greek Orthodox Church had retained full continuity, including numerous Byzantine architectural works. In addition, works of antiquity and of Greek and Hellenistic art were easily adapted to suit the Greek national heritage.

The institutional legacy of medieval times was rather more complicated in the Flemish case, where Flanders as a historical entity had become something of a substitute for the common past of all the Flemings. The Ukrainian relics of the Zaporozhian Cossacks are an even stronger example of how a constituent region had come to be perceived and adopted as a *pars pro toto* for the history of the whole nation.

Several autonomous medieval states had ceased to exist, and never again became objects of national identification, even though a great many of their relics remained, as was the case of the architectural relics of the Caliphate of Cordoba, the County of Toulouse, the Teutonic Knights, and of Aragon, Lorraine and Dubrovnik.

History would have played quite a different role within national movements that were trying to appeal to members of ethnic categories, but could not present them with any relics of a political past with which to identify themselves. They were usually also unable to appropriate architectural remnants as a 'national legacy'. The Finns, Estonians, Latvians and Belarusians, among others, rarely encountered anything that would be reminiscent of their belonging together or having a common past – and which could become the main driving force behind their striving for a modern national identity – other than their natural surroundings, the architecture in their countryside, and their myths.

When we study the importance of historical relics, special attention must be given to the German and Italian nation-forming processes. In both cases, various small states, their administration, and political institutions had survived and retained continuity with the past; but, not being state-nations, they complicated and hindered the formation of national relations. This was especially true of Italy, which never became a political entity again after the Western Roman Empire had disintegrated and – if we ignore the nostalgic dreams of Humanistic scholars for now – it only lived on as a name and a distinct geographic unit. Rather than the state or administrative institutions, it was the rich legacy of fine art which gave very clear proof of a common past, and provided arguments in favour of the nation's future.

To the inhabitants of the German states, the Holy Roman Empire of the German Nation, which still technically survived, conveyed the image of a 'national' supra-state community, but it ceased to exist completely at the point when the national movement emerged. Although the institutional connections within the empire were very weak, the fact that a large majority of the constituent states were, in contrast to most Italian states, ruled by native 'national' dynasties with centuries-old histories, must have played an important role. Imperial institutions – imperial towns included – were a living reminder of the past that could easily be 'translated' into a modern language, and that, in the nineteenth century, enabled a smooth transition in turning the history of the empire into German national history.

Historical legacy must be understood to encompass more than only institutional and architectural relics. What had also survived was the legacy of thought and traditions – which will be addressed in the following chapter, on 'national' medieval myths. Political theories and concepts (together with terminology) also form part of the political legacy of the past, since they helped create the foundations for modern national consciousness. It must not be overlooked that the state-political definition of the term 'nation' in English and French was not an invention of the nineteenth-century 'nationalists' but an aspect of cultural heritage stemming from Humanism. The term entered common usage in the period of modern state-building, which was long before the appearance of the term 'nationalism'. This explains the closeness of the terms 'state' and 'nation' in both English and French; they were easily interchangeable, and thus *raison d'état* – 'state interests' – came to be easily interpreted as 'national interests'.

Surviving notions of a chosen nation, a mission, the Promised Land, nations as God's creation and such like were forms of a historical relic of pan-European significance and, primarily, a Biblical heritage that had been adapted by the Reformation. The very term 'nation' was thus an objectively existing 'mould' – a template for certain value connotations, however vague. As a term, it was sufficiently general, yet attractive, and could therefore act as a simplified, intelligible and functional means of describing a positively defined community, which was emerging (or should have been emerging) from the process of modernisation.

The idea of the homeland was an even more important pre-existing concept, and a model adopted from the past; Enlightenment patriotism can be seen as the prototype of national identity. Love of the homeland had been fostered and celebrated for hundreds of years. It was often a poetic celebration of one's motherland, and can be found in the landowners' relationship to their native soil and its defence as early as the late Middle Ages. The political concept *communis patria* is even more significant. It is a term for the motherland associated with *publica utilitas*, which became part of the terminological repertoire of chroniclers and theorists in the second half of the thirteenth century. The term *patria* became the normative category in the political sense of the word when the state ceased to be seen as the property of the ruler – i.e. when it was demanded that there should be a strong bond between the bearers of political power (usually the aristocracy) and the state.

Enlightenment patriotism was an obvious historical legacy of which the processes of nation-building could make use. It obliged scholars to work towards the common good delimited by a relationship to a particular territory. Enlightenment theory saw patriots as cosmopolitans, but their service to mankind was expected to manifest itself through specific acts on behalf of those closest to them; they were to feel responsible for the flourishing of their homeland and for its inhabitants' good fortune. 'Homeland' could mean the state, but equally only its constituent part (land or region), and it was not defined – patriots were free to choose and even change it later in life. An active relationship to their homeland, including work towards its welfare, was decisive. The importance of patriotism as a historical foundation of national consciousness did not lie only in this notion that an individual had a commitment and responsibility towards mankind through working for the homeland. It also expressed the idea of the freedom of an individual, and thus offered a possible (but not inevitable) alternative to absolutism.

It would be an oversimplification to say that the 'love of homeland' and 'love of the nation' defined and postulated in the nineteenth century were the same. Enlightenment patriotism may have been cosmopolitan, but it was also elitist; patriots wished to work for mankind but did not see themselves as part of it – nor did they necessarily identify with it. Frederick II, who presented himself as the homeland's 'first servant', was an archetype of such a patriot. The idea of a nation was more inclusive – it promoted the civic equality of all members of the nation while demanding that 'patriots' identify with this nation, and thus also with its members.

'National' History as Part of the Premodern Historical Tradition

A brief overview of the relics of 'historical reality' was necessary in order to substantiate the fundamental claim that history could not be freely created to suit the needs of the forming nations, as is asserted in some radical interpretations of the thesis of 'invented tradition'. It was equally impossible first to 'invent' and then to succeed in building an independent national community and provide it with an arbitrary 'nationalistic' content. The search for a national past had its limitations – in the era of scientific criticism, national histories could only be constructed or interpreted if they were based on existing and critically verified sources of information. It was unfeasible, for instance, to devise a history of Finnish kings, of an Italian medieval state, or of a victory of the Serbs over the Ottomans at the Battle of Kosovo. That said, there was still the possibility of contradictory interpretations of national histories, and the existence of different criteria according to which information about the past was selected or, as the case may be, manipulated.

The construction of national histories and the revival and crea- tion of national myths constituted key activities of national mobilisation, and will be the focus of the second part of this book. For now, it suffices to point out that the images of the national his- tories forming in the nineteenth century had not been shaped only by the above-mentioned historical relics, which had a direct impact on the people. They were also influenced by the premodern 'histori- ographic tradition' – i.e. the transfer of facts (and myths) about national or state histories in the same form in which they had been recorded in historical works since the Middle Ages. These medieval and early modern images of the past, especially chronicles and his- torical epics preserved mainly in written but also oral form, became an important component of the living legacy of the old times. They were expressions of the past that scholars, and to a lesser degree also the wider public, had identified with even before the emergence of national movements.

It is of little relevance in this context whether or not we accept the older terminology by the medievalist František Graus, who dif- ferentiated between chroniclers' 'historiographic' and 'mythological' data. The former were a manifestation of attempts to depict historical facts, while the latter were created and passed on in efforts to learn about these facts.[1] Alternatively, there is the later view of Jan Assmann, who perceived chronicle accounts as belonging to the same genre as myths and the oral tradition.[2] This difference may be important when investigating the genesis of the 'collective memory' and examining the circumstances under which historical data were presented, and with what aim this was done. For our purposes, how- ever, it is much more important to study the manner in which information, which had been communicated through the medieval and early modern sources, influenced national argumentation in the nineteenth century, and how this was received. From the point of view of reception and instrumentalisation, it is irrelevant whether a source of information was in essence a chronicle or a record of group traditions and myths. It is similarly inconsequential to ask how chronicle accounts and myths were received at the time of their origin – during the Middle Ages or the early modern period. The decisive factor in the context of modern nation-building was how much scope and credibility information, and possibly also stereotypes and judgements, had during the construction of the modern nations' new histories.

The modern scientific construction of national histories (and creation of national myths) built upon an earlier, usually written tradition, whose terminology, value judgements and selection of facts could not be entirely ignored. The nineteenth-century arguments invoking the national past tended to build on information, and partly also terminology, that had communicated the older adaptations of history. The subject matter of these adaptations had been regions and ethnic communities which, at the time of their existence, may have been – but were not necessarily – 'national' entities. Something seemingly obvious must always be borne in mind: that any given image of the past presented by chronicles and myths was shaped in relation to the times of their origin, and was therefore independent of the historical consciousness or national aspirations of the nineteenth-century scholars.[3]

Historical tradition acted as a 'natural basis' for the construction of national histories, especially in situations where nation-forming built on an older tradition of statehood. This is because, in the European context, interest in the past had been an organic part of the existence of a state since the Middle Ages. Comparing the historical consciousness of medieval chroniclers with that of early modern Humanistic (Baroque) historiographers would require a separate comparative investigation. Here, however, we have to restrict ourselves to the fundamental and necessarily simplified outlines and a few characteristic examples.

Every medieval state or political entity had its own medieval chronicles, which gradually moved away from narrating the heroic deeds of their rulers and noblemen to narrating the history of the state and its politically privileged classes. Although the term 'nation' appeared explicitly for the first time in Humanistic historiography, medieval chronicles had already contained definite evidence of identification with politically – and often also ethnically – defined communities. They also documented xenophobia, exclusivity and group stereotypes, which some authors classify as 'proto-nationalism'. By the late Middle Ages, linguistic differentiation had come to be commonly seen as a criterion for political belonging and an argument in favour of group solidarity.[4]

The question 'Where do we come from?' had already been posed by medieval chroniclers, and they had gathered enough materials to create national myths over the centuries that followed. One of them was the Trojan myth of descent as a 'dynastic mythomoteur' of the Franks, which dates as far back as the sixth century. It was later overshadowed by the Arthurian myth, and later still by identification with the old Gauls. The Dutch based their myth of origin on the heroisation of the Batavi tribe, which had risen against Roman domination in the middle of the first century. The Spanish aristocracy derived its origin from the Visigoths, but also shared a belief that its roots lay in antiquity. The Swedish Baroque poet and scientist Olof Rudbeckius revived the myth of the Goths as heroic conquerors and ancestors of the Swedes.

By the first half of the twelfth century, Geoffrey of Monmouth had created in his chronicle, the *History of the Kings of Britain*, not only the story of the Arthurian wizard Merlin but also the influential myth of Brutus, the great-grandson of Aeneas, who had landed in Albion, founded a kingdom and split it between his three sons. The oldest son received England, the middle one was given Wales, while Scotland was allocated to the youngest. This legend survived until the early modern period, and served as the basis for claims during the rule of the Plantagenets and the Tudors that England was entitled to rule over Wales and Scotland.

Searching for and retelling a story of origin was not purely a game of prestige. It was also a source of auto-stereotypes, which were not only able to help achieve cohesiveness among the citizens of the early modern states, but also shaped the national auto-stereotypes of the nineteenth century. Were 'our forefathers' peace-loving farmers or hostile warriors? Did they conquer foreign lands, like the Germanic peoples and the Vikings, or did they defend their countries from invaders, like the Batavi?

The diametrically opposed Czech and Hungarian myths of origin demonstrate a symptomatic dichotomy, which survived the Middle Ages and continued to influence auto-stereotypes until the nineteenth century. Cosmas of Prague, the oldest Czech chronicler, depicted the common origin of the Czech peoples at the turn of the twelfth century. In his account, the first Czechs arrived at Říp Mountain in the central Bohemian plain, discovered that the region was fertile and hospitable, and so settled in the land that lay before them as if it was uninhabited. Medieval mythology later added the story of the two brothers, Čech and Lech. The common origin of the Hungarians was presented very differently – in accordance with reality. According to one of the first chroniclers, Gallus Anonymus, the first Hungarians, arriving in Pannonia, found it to their liking, and settled there permanently – once they had killed or conquered the native population. In the fourteenth century, this image of origin fused with the Hunnic legend – which consisted of the claim that the Huns were the Hungarians' ancestors and teachers, even their actual blood brothers. Humanism later also incorporated the idea that the Hungarians had an innate sense of freedom, as demonstrated by the Golden Bull of 1222, which had established the rights of the Hungarian nobility, and of Hungary being the stronghold of Christianity against the Turks.[5]

All the medieval myths of origin were based on the view that having been long settled in one's own land was a virtue and somehow conferred a right to that land. By and large, state-nations tended not to have any difficulty in uncovering their ancient roots, since they could relatively easily lay claim to being autochthonous to 'their own' state territory. The French and Spanish myths of origin, too, were based on the story of the arrival of existing ruling medieval 'nations', whose right to dominance had never been called into question. The English situation was rather more complicated, and the original Celtic peoples were omitted from the myth of origin there. The Hungarians were, relatively speaking, the last to arrive in Europe. They satisfied their need to demonstrate that they had inhabited it for long enough by creating the so-called 'Hunnic myth', laying claim to Attila – who had owned Pannonia long before the first Slavs arrived – as their forefather. It is noteworthy that, in a large majority of the cases, the medieval or early modern notion of the roots of existence – i.e. of a common origin – reached back to pre-Christian times.

Besides the myth of origin, the concept of a 'Golden Age' was often another important component of historical mythology. It was looked back on nostalgically, as a time of glory and a source of consolation and encouragement. Examples of Golden Ages include the English-Celtic myth of King Arthur, the celebration of Charles the Great, the memory of Ireland during the time of St Patrick, and later also the myths of Imperial or Republican Rome as the golden era of the Italian past, and of free, pre-Norman society as a source of inspiration for the English revolutionary ideals of 1640–60. However, during the medieval and early modern periods the Christian myth was generally binding. This greatly limited the role that legends of a Golden Age could play, as they could not be projected back to pre-Christian – i.e. pagan – times.[6]

Old myths proved no less troublesome. The dispute over Charles the Great, for instance, dates back to the Middle Ages, since he was appropriated by the French as well as the Germans. In the late medieval period, the French and Italian Humanists began to compete over whose culture was more advanced. The English–French rivalry, which culminated during the Hundred Years' War, contained enough substance to produce contrasting interpretations of the two countries' pasts, starting with the Norman occupation of England after the Battle of Hastings in 1066.

Humanistic historiography helped to strengthen the sense of belonging within the heterogeneous Swiss Confederation. The depiction of successful battles in defensive wars against the Habsburgs, portrayed as ancient tyrants, significantly aided the creation of the Swiss image of the past, centred on the myth of William Tell. Swedish early modern historiography supplemented the myth of the Gothic origin of the Swedes with the legend of King Gustavus Adolphus and, given that he had saved European Protestantism, presented him as the rightful descendant of the heroic Goths. The historical concept of the Dutch nation was also based on an old myth of origin – in this case the Batavi origin. The successful revolution against the Spanish led to the revival of the noble Batavi virtues and, at the same time, to the creation of the Calvinist notion of the 'New Israel'.

Italian Humanistic historians were less politically successful in their attempts to create an image of an all-Italian history that would connect seamlessly to the Roman Empire and point to national togetherness. As a result, they turned to the histories of individual political entities, using the term *nazione* much less frequently than the term 'nation', for instance, was deployed within the German framework. Similarly, a failed sixteenth-century revolution caused Flemish patriotic chronicling to lose its national relevance, as this had been based on the Flemish townsmen's victorious resistance against the French king, culminating at the Battle of Courtrai.

The Humanists also propagated and justified the view that the Germanic tribes were the earliest ancestors of the German nation. Tacitus's *Germania* naturally became an important source of information not only within the German setting. The German concept of a nation, as defined by ethnicity and blood lineage, thus already has its roots in Humanism. The English term 'nation' followed a similar path, in that Humanistic dictionaries of the second half of the sixteenth century define it primarily as 'country', which was the equivalent of the Latin *patria*. Therefore, it already referred to an area then defined as a state. In the first half of the seventeenth century, the Czech Humanist Pavel Stránský defined the Czech nation as based on its territory and language. Clearly, the primary aim of all these definitions was not to define the abstract term 'nation', but rather the nation itself (English, Czech or other) in a way that corresponded to the situation at the time.

Although the list of examples given here is necessarily limited, it allows us to conclude that premodern historiographic tradition provided the emerging, modern national consciousness with a rich body of information. Firstly, it defined national existence in terms of time – i.e. it determined the 'origins of nations'. Secondly, it delineated national territories, including any potential claims over regions that overlapped with another national territory. Thirdly, it conceptualised the term 'nation', which had been crystallising since the sixteenth century. Fourthly, national existence came to be characterised by key events, which provided fertile ground for feelings of both pride and injustice. Last but not least, it became a source of national auto- and hetero-stereotypes and, consequently, of national prejudices. National mythology, however, also encompasses the cult of 'national' saints.

Historiographic tradition was not all-pervasive. It only played its part in regions that were home to the premodern tradition of statehood, regardless of whether this evolved into a state-nation (as in France, Sweden and Spain) or became weakened during the early modern period (as in Catalonia, or the Czech and Norwegian king-doms). It was much less influential in regions where statehood had been completely discontinued (such as the Balkans under Ottoman occupation), and it was altogether absent in settings where 'ethnies' remained 'ethnic categories' until the early modern period. Whatever the causes, it is clear that the ancient, medieval and early modern historiographic traditions, and the role that the scholarly phase of modern nation-building played from the mid eighteenth century, are closely interrelated and linked – especially as regards the pre-paratory work on the construction of national histories.

CHAPTER 4

Ethnic Roots

The opening overview of how the terms 'nation' and 'nationalism' were perceived revealed how much the opinions of individual scholars differed on the role of ethnicity, culture and language in modern nation-building. That said, however important they considered ethnic differences to be, it is indisputable that any study of the nation-building processes in Europe must not disregard the linguistic, ethnic and cultural diversity that had characterised European society since the Middle Ages. The different peoples had obviously been aware of this diversity since that time, and thus it cannot be seen as pertaining merely to the different categories of 'printed' languages.

Ethnic Diversity in Premodern Europe

The ethnic diversity of the European population is a historical legacy, and thus also a 'historical burden' upon modernity. There were lots of mutually unintelligible vernaculars at the time when medieval states were developing, albeit bridged temporarily by the use of a universally comprehensible, 'supranational' language of scholars – Latin in the West and Greek in the East. When the Frankish Empire was being divided, consideration was already given to the fact that the Germanic and Roman fighters did not understand each other, and so the Verdun vows were drawn up in two different languages. The Slavs referred to the speakers of Germanic dialects as 'Nemci' – the 'mute people', with whom one cannot communicate.

It is not an easy task to reconstruct the ethnic map of Europe in such a way as to explain the nation-building processes that followed, or make them easier to understand. Again, the problem starts with the terminology itself. Literary languages have been relatively clearly identified for some time, and those adopted as the languages of state administration can be labelled proto-national. While this was the case in most early modern European state-nations, the state language and the newly dominant literary language were not always one and the same. Latin, for instance, remained the language of state administration in the Polish-Lithuanian Commonwealth, the Hungarian Empire and Croatia until the eighteenth century, despite the fact that Polish literature, for example, had become very rich. It also holds true that a large majority of citizens in any of the medieval or early modern states will clearly have spoken in dialect, and used neither the official state language nor the 'national' literary one, as they usually did not even understand them. Despite this fact, it can be said that it is easier to reconstruct the linguistic map of premodern Europe in regions where a literary language had developed, kept evolving more or less continuously and, as the case may be, had possibly also become the language of state administration.

Reconstructing the ethnic composition of regions where the literary or state language differed fundamentally from the dialects spoken by most of the population is much more complicated. Backward-projection is usually employed in these cases, and it is based on the assumption that, for instance, a region where Estonian dialects were prevalent in the nineteenth century would have been ethnically mostly Estonian in medieval times. Assimilation processes must be taken into account, and so it is impossible to apply this projection in reverse – the fact that only a few hundred people speak Livonian or north Frisian dialects today, or that the number of Sorbs (Lusatian Serbs) have declined to a few tens of thousands, does not imply that these ethnic groups were equally small in medieval times. The same applies to the Provençal and Irish dialects.

Since this part of the book is mainly interested in the ethnic roots of modern nations, attention is mostly being paid to the evolution and changes in those vernaculars and literary languages that were affected by the nation-building processes of the nineteenth century. This approach is in no way based on the teleological notion that modern nations had existed, or that their existence had been predetermined, since medieval times. This is why consideration will also be given to alternative developments of the vernaculars that never evolved into printed languages – i.e. to ethnies that never developed their own literary language, and were assimilated.

Latin and Greek retained their dominant role in culture and state administration until approximately the thirteenth or fourteenth centuries, when 'national' languages came to the fore and began to take over this function. Paradoxically, the peripheral regions of Europe were an exception to this rule, as the local languages there had already assumed the form of written languages in the early Middle Ages – for example, Irish Gaelic in the western-most part of Europe and Old Norse in the north (as a language of chronicles and legal codes, as well as epics). In the course of the twelfth century, distinct literary languages began to form in Western and Southern Europe, although they initially remained overshadowed by Latin: Provençal, French, Catalan, Galician, Welsh, Upper German, Low German (*Plattdeutsch*) and Tuscan. One to three centuries later, they were joined by the literary forms of English, Castilian, Czech, Polish and Danish. In Eastern Europe it was Old Church Slavic (with modifications according to local vernaculars) that played the role of a universal literary language throughout medieval times.

As the Reformation spread and modern centralised states and multi-ethnic empires began to develop, the number of literary languages that had survived the Middle Ages started to decline. At the same time, in countries that embraced the Reformation, vernaculars started to become the new printed languages, and were used for religious purposes. English, French, Portuguese, Castilian, Danish, Swedish and, for the time being, also Czech and Catalan, maintained their dominant position as the languages of state administration. They were newly joined by Russian, Dutch and Polish. Luther's German and Tuscan Italian played specific roles in the forming of national cultures in politically fragmented circumstances. Conversely, several medieval languages were pushed out, albeit not always necessarily in direct relation to the Reformation: the Provençal language almost completely disappeared, as did Old Norse and Galician, while Welsh, Irish, Low German, Catalan and Czech began to fade dramatically at the very point when everywhere else in Europe printed languages started to emerge, during the sixteenth to eighteenth centuries.

All printed languages were, above all, the languages of the educated elites, and their 'reception' by the common people was mostly (but not exclusively) limited to religious contexts. Their vernaculars were either dialects of one of the literary or state languages, or, just as often, dialects that were unrelated to the state language, and thus mutually incomprehensible. Scotland, England, Brittany, the Basque country, Lusatia, Hungary, Poland, Russia, the Ottoman Empire and Sweden were all inhabited by ethnic groups of varying sizes whose dialects did not attain their literary form until the nineteenth century. Nor was it necessarily a sign of successful nation-building. Some of these languages played only a limited role as secular literary languages, in that they had – thanks to the Reformation – become the language of church services and religious texts. This is, for instance, how Finnish, Estonian, Latvian, Hungarian, Slovenian and Lower Sorbian came into being.

States and their rulers had seldom cared for 'national languages' until the sixteenth century, when the more or less conscious efforts to achieve linguistic homogenisation emerged in most European states. This was undoubtedly a consequence of the rising power of the monarch, centralisation and bureaucracy – a manifestation of absolutist efforts to unify all the components of the life of a state: the legal system, religion and language. It is significant that the Académie Française, the first institution to oversee the unification and purity of the state language, was established in a country that was to become the model absolutist state.

Linguistic Homogenisation in the Early Modern State

It would be a great oversimplification if the ethnic foundations of modern states were evaluated by pointing to the greater or lesser degrees to which the medieval 'national' languages had 'survived'. It is true, for instance, that Czech, and until the eighteenth century also Catalan, had retained a certain degree of continuity with the respective literary languages of the late medieval and early modern periods. But this continuity was lost in Ireland, Norway and Wales, where the medieval literary languages had almost disappeared. Most European national movements were unable to build on a literary tradition, and yet they succeeded in creating a developed culture in their national language as well as in applying their new literary language in other spheres of life. Therefore, the level of development that a medieval national language had reached does not appear to have been crucial for the modern nations.[1]

It is indisputable that a long linguistic tradition was important for the evolution of modern national cultures and languages, but it was the early modern era that played a decisive role in the formation of the ethnic prerequisites for nation-building. This period was char-acterised by the establishment of absolutist regimes in most European states, and the spread of absolutism constitutes a decisive starting point in the creation of a relationship with the language. This can be studied from two perspectives: 'from above', at the level of the state apparatus, and 'from below', at the level of the controlled regions (or provinces) and their populations.

Sooner or later, the absolutist principle of unifying all aspects of society affected the language as well.[2] The interest in language homo-geneity on the part of the state apparatus focused on implementing and reinforcing a single official language, and it was irrelevant whether the regions, which the central power considered to be the peripheries, spoke in dialects of the same (state) language or a com-pletely different literary language. As the peculiarities of historical entities were gradually overcome, consideration lessened for lands whose literary language differed from the state language.

The objection can be raised that the dividing line between a 'lit-erary language' and a 'dialect' of premodern times is not very clear, but this is a matter to be dealt with by linguists. In order to differen-tiate between a 'language' and a 'dialect' for the purposes of historical analysis, it will suffice to make use of Benedict Anderson's criterion of a 'print-language'.[3] The very existence of print-languages as an accepted means of communication proves that they were compre-hensible, and thus easily used, with certain groups of readers, regardless of whether or not they were identical to their 'mother' vernaculars. The role attributed to the print-language by the abso-lutist state determined further developments and the building of modern nations that followed. While in some situations the printed language became the language of state power permanently, in other situations it lost this function as a result of absolutist centralism, as in the previously discussed cases of Czech, Catalan and Norwegian. Religious literature enjoyed the distinct, non-state status of a printed language, and grew in size and importance especially in the countries that had embraced the Reformation. Modern standard languages were not necessarily developed from printed languages.

Educated aristocratic circles often tended to regard the difference between a spoken language (a dialect) and the language of state power as a manifestation of a 'degeneration' of the popular language, rather than a consequence of the creation of a developed literary language. Dialects are documented to have been used in the eighteenth century to entertain educated aristocrats and demonstrate their superiority over the popular strata[4] – the exact opposite of the way the popular language was treated by the Romantics and the patriots in numerous national movements a few decades later.

The revolutionary rise of civic society did not lead to any dramatic changes in the attitudes of the state, the new ruling classes or intellectuals towards the language. The French Revolution continued with the homogenisation efforts of absolutist centralism, and even accentuated them. Paris supported and initiated campaigns for the eradication of *patios* as a relic of feudalism, while regarding the remnants of the 'hostile' German language of the Rhine provinces as the most dangerous.[5] It was only half a century later that the German and Magyar Liberals employed similar arguments in their language assimilation policies to those which the French Liberals and Democrats had used in theirs, as was manifest in the Czech and Slovenian national struggles in the 1848 revolutions, the Slovak, Romanian and Serbian national struggles within the Hungarian kingdom, and the Polish struggle within Prussia.

At the same time, the language policies of the rising civic revolutions were not identical with the policies of feudal absolutism, and at least two fundamental differences need to be stressed:

1. While the attitude of absolutism was based on the idea of a homogeneous state comprising subjects, the language policy of revolutions was based on the idea of a nation as a stable organism, which had its own personality and perceived itself as a state-nation. Inevitably, such a personality-nation would have to use a single language, since the term 'dialect' continued to be understood in its Enlightenment sense – i.e. referring to a degenerate language, whose survival would weaken the national organism. Besides its communication value, a language was also becoming a means for the state's population to self-identify as members of a national community, whether this self-identification assumed the form of their internal integration within the state-nation or a contrasting self-identification, anchored in the realisation that their non-ruling ethnic group was linguistically different from the other groups.[6] This in turn enhanced the symbolic value of the language. Significantly, this permanent shift in the function

of a language occurred even in countries where a revolution did not take place.

2.   The absolutist state considered a single language to be an instrument of effective communication and a means of homogenising its subjects in the spirit of traditional relations, whereas in a civic society a single language became a value in itself. Herder (and the Romantics) regarded it as the soul of the nation manifesting itself; for the revolutions, the implementation and use of a single language was a way to 'create a new man' – to transform ('re-form') the structures of his thinking.[7]

Having addressed the perspective 'from above', I will now examine the perspective 'from below', looking into how language policies were received by individual provinces and the wider population. It needs to be emphasised that the policy of linguistic unification was only one of the components of centralisation and homogenisation pursued by feudal absolutism, and rarely the most important one. It was not the language policies but those of centralisation that were met with the greatest opposition and dissatisfaction within the provinces. The strength and success of this resistance varied greatly, as did the arguments the provinces used against absolutist centralism. There is not enough room to go into detail here, and it thus remains a task for the future to conduct a comparative study and develop a typology of manifestations of attitudes towards centralism among the nobility and the commoners in individual parts of Europe (the Habsburg monarchy as well as France and Spain).[8] The same applies to research into what role efforts either to preserve or eliminate local vernaculars played in the opposition to centralism.

It is a well-known fact that some of those opposed to absolutism argued that the provinces, whose rights absolutism had reduced or eliminated, differed not only in terms of language and literary culture, but also by having a distinct history. It is worth recalling the attitudes of the Czech and Hungarian provincial patriots toward Joseph II's policies, or the Finnish nobility's opposition to the Gustav III's absolutism at the end of the eighteenth century. Similar arguments, albeit less frequent, can be found in the displays of the rising Scottish and Irish resistance to London centralism, and by the end of the nineteenth century these arguments were even more noticeable in the federalist attitudes in Catalonia and the Basque provinces against Castilian centralism, and in the Baltic provinces against Russification.

The issue of uneven assimilation becomes relevant in this context, and the question arises as to why assimilation in the early modern period proved more successful in some parts of (particularly Western) Europe, where most ethnic groups were integrated, whereas elsewhere ethnic variety prevailed and became the basis of national movements. In other words, why were the assimilation capabilities of France and Great Britain greater than those of the Habsburg monarchy, Russia or the Ottoman Empire? Answers commonly point to two factors: firstly, the ruling classes in the eastern empires never aimed for linguistic assimilation among their subjects and, secondly, state-nations with a homogenised approach to language appeared earlier in Western Europe than in Eastern Europe.

While both these answers are correct, they are far from sufficient, and need to be clarified by further, deeper connections:

1.   The level of economic growth and the corresponding levels of social mobility and economic integration of the provinces were much higher in France and Great Britain than in other parts of Europe. It was economic growth that allowed people from the provinces (members of the marginal ethnic groups) to benefit from migrating to the centres of development, and from becoming assimilated.

2.   The unevenness of economic growth corresponded with a varying intensity of social communication. The more developed Western states enjoyed higher levels of communication, and the state language became the dominant language of communication within state administration as well as day-to-day economic life. This made the journey from *la langue du pain* (language of employment) to the mother tongue shorter and easier.

3.   The effectiveness of public administration and its influence on daily life were more pronounced in early modern western monarchies than in eastern and south-eastern Europe.

4.   Natural assimilation of ethnic groups did not take place in regions where the ruling classes used their linguistic difference as a social barrier, aiming to hinder upward social mobility among the members of the popular strata – for example, in the Ottoman Empire and the Baltic provinces of Tsarist Russia.

Conversely, conditions were much more favourable for natural assimilation when large parts of the provincial population contributed to the centre's prosperity, as was the case in the British and Danish states, as well as perhaps the Spanish.

5. We must not overlook the importance of timing in combination with social development. In France and Great Britain, the process of assimilation began while the feudal system was still in place – i.e. in premodern society. In contrast, the multi-ethnic eastern monarchies did not pursue their assimilation policies until the onset of the modern period – under the Habsburg monarchy at the end of the eighteenth century, and in Tsarist Russia a whole century later. Even if we disregarded the fact that these places had reached a very different level of overall social development, their assimilation policies simply had too little time to succeed before they came up against the rise of national movements.

As a result of these factors, the non-dominant ethnic groups within central and eastern European countries (particularly the three multi-ethnic empires) inhabited compact territories and, if any assimilation took place at all, it happened only in peripheral regions and was rarely accompanied by upward social mobility. By and large, members of these groups – even those who had become urbanised – remained out of reach of the state language and the secular segments of the ruling culture. Nevertheless, the opportunity to communicate with them in their dialects remained open.[9]

Whether the transition to civic societies occurred through revolution or reform, it is significant that diglossia – a situation in which two or more languages or dialects were used in one area concurrently, but only one of them had the role of the official, state language – had survived from premodern times in certain parts of the state territories. But these linguistic differences did not appear to cause any difficulties owing to the low density of communication ties,[10] and neither bilingualism nor assimilation became a common occurrence in this type of situation. Following the model of the socio-linguist Joshua Fishman, we can distinguish a number of cases of diglossia in the period prior to the emergence of national movements.[11] The most prevalent was a situation in which the ruling elites used a literary 'H-language' and the popular masses spoke an 'L-language'

– a dialect related to the ruling 'H-language'. Nevertheless, two further cases, which Fishman's model does not take into account, are crucial for a better understanding and interpretation of the aims pursued by national movements:

1.   While the elites used an 'H-language', a proportion of the masses used an 'L-language' that was markedly different from the state language. It either belonged to a different language family (as for the Slovenians in Carniola, Styria and Carinthia, the Masurians in East Prussia and the Finns in Sweden), or it was a different 'H-language', used by a different state (as for the pockets of German-speakers within the Hungarian Empire, the Croatians in Venetian Dalmatia and the Romanians in Transylvania).
2.   In addition to the 'H-language', the language of state power, another 'H*-language' was used in some provinces of the multi-ethnic empires, which naturally also had a corresponding 'L*-language'. This was true of Polish in the annexed areas, Czech in Bohemia and Moravia, Finnish and German in east-central Europe, Catalan in Spain, and finally Dutch in the south Netherlands (Belgium).

It holds true for all the cases where diglossia was to be found that one of the languages always occupied a hegemonic position, and that this was regarded as a matter of course. But differences existed in the degree to which the non-ruling ethnic groups' specific cultures and languages were tolerated by the ruling elites and, as has been mentioned, this tolerance diminished with the arrival of modernisation.[12] In this context, the variations in the language policies of individual states need to be kept in mind, since they were the primary issue that needed to be confronted by protagonists of the national movements.

Languages in the Era of Nation-Building

The basic typology of the nation-building processes demonstrated that, at the turn of the nineteenth century, there were only a few state-nations in Europe with a long tradition of culture in a codified national language, but many ethnic groups without such a tradition that gradually gave rise to national movements. It has been reiterated that, within the two fundamental types of nation-building processes there were numerous transitional cases. We will follow the developments that European languages underwent in the process of modern nation-building by comparing the situation at two points in time: around the year 1800 and at the end of the nineteenth century. The question that will have to be addressed is to what extent the ethnic groups' sense of belonging reflected their linguistic distinctness.

Let us first examine the situation in Europe at the turn of the nineteenth century. Among the national languages that had developed during the Middle Ages and then continued to evolve, only French, English, Castilian (Spanish), Portuguese and German had reached the level of a codified state language. Of the languages that developed later, Swedish, Danish, Russian, Dutch and, until the state ceased to exist, also Polish served the function of state-nation languages. Italian was, in its different varieties, the language of Italian states, but the search for a consensus about its codified form (modified Tuscan) was to take a few more centuries.

The territories of state-nations were not ethnically homogeneous, despite the successes of earlier assimilation policies. The countries that came closest to mono-ethnic states were Portugal and, once it had lost Finland, also Sweden. France was inhabited by large Breton, Occitan (Provençal) and German minorities, and by smaller groups that spoke Catalan, Basque and Flemish dialects. In Spain, Catalan dialects had remained in existence in historical Catalonia, in the province of Valencia and on the Balearic Islands, and there were also the Basque and Galician ethnies. The Netherlands was not mono-ethnic, owing to the presence of the Frisian ethnie and, during the short-lived Kingdom of the Netherlands, also a large minority of French-speaking Walloons.

Denmark was essentially a multi-ethnic empire. Even after it lost Norway in 1814, its territory was inhabited by a sizable German minority in Holstein and southern Schleswig, and by distinct ethnic communities of Icelanders, Faroe Islanders and Greenlanders. Similarly, while England itself was mono-ethnic in its make-up, Celtic minorities had survived elsewhere in Great Britain, of which the Welsh was the largest. Gaelic prevailed only in the remote parts of the Highlands in Scotland, and the specifics of the Irish situation will be addressed at a later stage.

As regards the language situation, the non-ruling ethnic

communities can be divided into two groups. There were those who were able to build on an older tradition of a standard language, which had been weakened to a greater or lesser degree – for example, the Greeks, Czechs, Hungarians, Croatians, Finns, Catalans and Welsh. Then there were those who could not build on such a tradition directly, either because it had been completely discontinued or because it had never existed. The latter group comprised the Estonians, Latvians, Lithuanians, Ukrainians, Belarusians, Slovaks, Slovenians, Basques, Galicians, Bulgarians, Serbians and Romanians, as well as the Irish and Norwegians. Their much later efforts to codify their standard languages centred on the spoken vernaculars and, in the Protestant countries, also on the printed tradition of religious texts that dated back to the Reformation. However, there were three cases where an established 'foreign' language, with an old tradition of a 'printed language', had been embraced by the educated future leaders of national movements: Dutch by the Flemish, Danish by most of the Norwegians, and English by the Irish and the Scots.

The characterisation of ethnic groups cannot be restricted by focusing on the developmental stage of their languages alone. Since these communities were defined not only in linguistic but also in cultural and social terms, the extent to which cultural or linguistic distinctness was reflected in self-awareness among their members also has to be considered.[13] Smith's typology of ethnies is also appropriate in this context, but with one fundamental modification – without his tendency to label individual ethnies as definite 'communities' or 'categories'. Taking into account empirical data, we can assert that, at the turn of the nineteenth century, every territory defined as belonging to an 'ethnic community' contained compact areas (groups of dialects) that qualified as 'ethnic categories'. Conversely, among 'ethnic categories' there were groups of varying sizes whose self-identification was already at the level of 'ethnic communities'. It is with this reservation in mind that the two terms shall be used here.[14]

What set an ethnic category apart from its neighbouring groups was an objectively different language (dialect) and popular culture. However, this distinctness did not translate into a clear sense of belonging among its members, despite their inhabiting the same area. At the beginning of the nineteenth century, this was true of most Estonians, Latvians and Lithuanians, and later also of the

Belarusians, Ukrainians, Slovenians, Bosnian Muslims, Macedonians and Galicians.

In contrast, an ethnic community was characterised by having a name that most of its members were familiar with, by the fact that its members (or a proportion of them) were conscious of their common origin or collective destiny (a form of 'collective memory'), and by elemental manifestations of mutual solidarity.[15] This applied fully to the Hungarians, Norwegians, Icelanders, Finns, Czechs, Irish, Serbs and Greeks, but only to some parts of the territories inhabited by ethnic Croatians, Romanians, Bulgarians, Basques, Catalans, Slovaks and the Flemish.

In order to differentiate the various levels of self-awareness, the subject of social stratification needs to be addressed. As we have seen, non-ruling ethnic groups differed from members of state-nations by the lack of a complete social structure. According to Anthony Smith, an ethnic community consisted of three social groups: peasants and rural artisans; small townsmen, who were exposed to the pressures from town elites and bureaucracies; and monks and clergyman, who represented their ethnic community and determined its common faith.[16] Smith's emphasis on the importance of an ethnic group's social structure is undoubtedly meaningful, but requires further specification and application in differentiating between ethnic communities and categories. A closer examination of the social structure of ethnic categories reveals that, in most cases, they only comprised peasants and rural artisans. As regards ethnic communities, two corrections are needed, one relating to the clergy and the other to the wealthy elites. Firstly, while educated individuals could be found in all communities, they were not necessarily clergymen. Secondly, by the turn of the nineteenth century some of the non-ruling ethnic groups that qualified as ethnic communities had wealthy elites among their members, such as the aristocracy among the Hungarians and Croatians or the business bourgeoisie and high clerks among the Norwegians. Indeed, the social structure of the Greek, Irish, Flemish and Catalan ethnic communities also comprised not only peasants, urban artisans and the low clergy.

If we superimpose the ethnic groups' linguistic characteristic onto their varied social structures, we will discover notable parallels. Unsurprisingly, ethnic categories either had never had a literary or 'printed' language, or this tradition had been completely discontinued. In contrast, the language situation among ethnic communities was characterised by variety: some of them – including the Czechs and the Greeks – maintained their weakened, but not discontinued, language tradition; some – including the Irish and the Norwegians – chose to make use of a 'foreign' state language; and many – including the Slovenes – had to create their own literary language first, and did so by basing it partly on the reformation tradition of religious literature.

Let us now turn to the ethno-linguistic situation in Europe at the close of the nineteenth century. Over the hundred years from 1800, the asynchronous national movements had ushered in some important changes – not only in relation to the level of mobilisation of ethnic groups, but also to the mutual relations and internal structures of the multi-ethnic monarchies and state-nations. It will be useful, therefore, to examine the language situation in Europe at the end of the century – i.e. at a time when the majority of the nation-building processes here had reached the decisive stage.

By 1900, west and central European state-nations had undergone a certain degree of differentiation. While the French and English languages had reinforced their position in France and Great Britain respectively, leading to an almost complete assimilation of ethnic minorities, the dominant role of Castilian had begun to be questioned in Catalonia and the Basque provinces. Two new large states had emerged: the practically mono-ethnic Italy, with its recently codified literary language, and Germany with its large Polish and small Danish minorities. There was also a new small state, Belgium, with a strong Flemish ethnic community. Having lost Holstein and Schleswig, Denmark itself had become a mono-ethnic state, but the 'island' ethnic communities on Iceland, Greenland and the Faroe Islands remained part of the kingdom.

Non-ruling ethnic groups, which I have categorised as ethnic communities, had undergone a marked transformation. Some of them had succeeded in gaining statehood: the Serbian, Greek, Romanian and Bulgarian nation-states were created, each with its own codified state language, although in Greece the elitist Katharevousa tradition continued to rival Dimotiki, the colloquial language form. Some national movements had achieved so much that we can refer to their nation-building processes as having reached completion: in linguistic terms, the Magyar national movement paved the way for Magyar to become the dominant language within the Hungarian Empire, while the Norwegian national movement divided the public into supporters of the Danish-based Riksmål and those supporting Landsmål, which was based on dialects of rural Norway. In several other cases, the completion of the nation-building process was not accompanied by the national language reaching full equality within the multi-ethnic empire: Czech continued to struggle against German, which dominated within the Habsburg monarchy; Finnish became only partially successful against the dominant Swedish; Estonian against German; and Ukrainian in Galicia against Polish. For various reasons, the Catalan, Basque, Welsh, Lithuanian, Ukrainian (in Russia), Slovak and Flemish national movements had yet to reach phase C of their mass movement.

I should also mention those ethnies that were unlikely to achieve significant success due to their small size. In some of these, leaders had voiced certain national ambitions during the nineteenth century, but limited them mostly to linguistic and cultural goals, while in others agitation efforts had yet to 'awaken' the ethnic category. Some ethnies remained regionally restricted 'folk communities', and it is noteworthy that these were largely groups with far fewer than 500,000 members, whereas the smallest ethnies that developed into successful national movements had around 1,000,000 members (for example, the Estonians and Slovenes). The Icelanders were the exception to this rule, with their geographic location probably making up for the small size of their ethnic group.

These ethnies were, by and large, remnants of a long-gone ethnic diversity that had at some stage stopped short of undergoing complete assimilation. The best-known examples of these were perhaps the inhabitants of some of the valleys on both the Italian and Swiss sides of the Alps: the Romansh people, and the inhabitants of the Aosta Valley. There were also the Bretons and the Corsicans within the French territory, the (West) Frisians in the Netherlands, the North Frisians and the Faroe Islanders in Denmark, the Sami people in the very north of Europe, the Upper and Lower Sorbs and the Kashubians in central Europe, and the Karelians, Ingrians, Livonians, Gagauzians, Lemkos and Hungarian (Carpathian) Ruthenians in eastern Europe. If we can speak of any national movement at all in all of these cases, it never attained any significant results.

Consequently, they will not be addressed in the following analyses of nation-building processes.

There are two ethnies that occupy a specific place in all ethnic maps of Europe, since they differed greatly from the other peoples around them but did not inhabit a compact, enclosed territory – the Jewish and the Roma. The Jewish people were ethnically different primarily on the basis of their religious distinctness, which was maintained by their exclusion from the Christian community and, in some parts of Europe, was combined with their speaking a different language – especially Yiddish in eastern-central Europe. The ethnic difference of the Roma people rested mainly in their nomadic way of life and the language they spoke. Of the two, it was the Jewish community that directed its attention to a national movement, whether in the form of the successful Zionist movement or the unsuccessful Bundist movements. But these movements were so specific that, in the context of the other movements, we will only concern ourselves with them tangentially.

Since medieval times, linguistic differences had played an important role in communication, in fostering a sense of belonging and being alike, and in cultivating an awareness of being different. As seen 'from below', people who spoke the same dialect (or vernacular) would have been closer to each other, and would not only have communicated with ease but also showed solidarity with each other. Seen 'from above', members of the elites could form special interest and power groups more easily if they spoke the same language. An essential prerequisite in either case was the existence of a literary language or, at the very least, the ability of those concerned to see beyond the differences in the dialects of the same language family, focusing instead on the similarities among them. Neither could have taken place without a degree of congruence between the linguistic and political entities, since language has always been a means of communicating as well as identifying with a whole.

To summarise, the ethnic diversity in Europe had deep historical roots, and it was irrelevant what wishes the nineteenth-century intellectuals had for the future shape of Europe – it was the relevant ethnic situation that determined both their hopes and dreams and the actual outcome. In spite of all the prognoses of the rationalists of the time, modernisation did not lead to the merging of 'nations', but rather its opposite. Over the course of the nineteenth century, most large ethnic groups assumed a definite form, delineating themselves and adopting a new identity by identifying with a civic community that had embraced 'the nation', whether this had attained statehood or not. The factors that activated the struggle for language will be addressed in the context of the activities that were conducted in the name of a nation.

It should be emphasised that one cannot prove that there was a direct causal relation between linguistic differences (i.e. various vernaculars) and the emergence of modern nations. In other words, linguistic distinctness did not necessarily lead to the creation of a nation, even though linguistic requirements would usually have ranked high among the priorities laid out by the protagonists of the national movements. Linguistic differences alone do not explain why language-based ethnic distinctness very quickly became one of the factors in nation-building in some cases but not in others – and other relevant circumstances will therefore have to be considered.

CHAPTER 5

Modernisation

The term 'modernisation' is not used here with the intention of entering the contentious field of the theory of modernisation, or as a means of promoting the 'modernist interpretation' of modern nation-building and nationalism. It serves merely as an all-encompassing label for one of the fundamental processes that most authors associate with modern nation-building. Regardless of whether we agree with them fully or only in part, we need to determine how individual modernisation processes may have been linked and related to national mobilisation. Was this relationship causal, conditional, or a result of random coincidence?

It is undeniable that major transformation processes took place in European economics, politics and culture in the early modern period. Consequently, nineteenth-century society was quite unlike that of the seventeenth century – in terms of lifestyle, ways of thinking, and ways in which wealth was accumulated and redistributed, and in terms of living standards. Moreover, the social structures and political systems had been profoundly transformed as well. In the context of this book, it is unimportant whether all these changes are labelled 'modernisation', as a transformation from a traditional into a modern society, or as a shift from a feudal to a capitalist formation.[1] What is extremely significant, however, is that among the many new phenomena and types of relationship that arose from these transformations was a large social group – the modern nation. The working hypothesis here is that the time correlation between the transformation of the whole of society and the new type of national community was neither an accident nor a pure and simple coincidence.

The aim of this chapter is to establish the possible relationships between the different modernisation processes, on one hand, and national mobilisation – i.e. the spreading of national identity – on the other. As with ethnic factors, the idea that national mobilisation was somehow dependent on modernisation is rejected, while keeping in mind that modernisation processes took place objectively – i.e. independently of the wishes and interests of the 'nationalists', or national mobilisation activists. The possibility that these activists might have been making use of the processes is not ruled out.

While it is unquestionable that modernisation processes were mutually interconnected, for the purposes of exploring their significance for nation-building it is helpful to make some distinctions between them. Therefore, for entirely pragmatic reasons rather than out of an ambition to engage in theoretical discussion, the processes have been divided into four categories, each of which will be examined for its role as an objective prerequisite of nineteenth-century nation-building. The first category contains changes related to the modernisation of the state, of which bureaucracy and militarisation were the most important for nation-building. The second category encompasses social and political emancipation – i.e. the ways in which civic societies were built and the forms they assumed – and includes the emancipation of peasants, constitutionality, political participation, and the promotion of civic equality. The third group relates to modernisation in the economic sphere. The fourth, labelled 'social communication', comprises specific transformations – primarily changes to social mobility and the educational systems and the emergence of public opinion.

The fact that modernisation processes did not occur evenly across Europe complicates matters; they were all interconnected, but affected the various European macro-regions at different times and in a different sequence. Therefore, their role in modern nation-building has to be assessed with caution, with respect both to the modernisation categories and, above all, to the territorial variations in their implementation. This is achieved by drawing comparisons, while taking into account analogous historical developments elsewhere in Europe.

Modernisation of the State

In most cases, early modern state-building rested on centralisation and reinforcement of state power, and thus required a growing workforce – bureaucrats. The bureaucratic post ceased to be a profitable sinecure for the noblemen or the wealthy; the bureaucrat was no longer a servant of the ruler, personally dependent on him, but rather a link within an apparatus whose purpose was to serve the state. Reforms of the state administration called for the expansion of the state apparatus and a shift in the bureaucratic mentality and, holding this office under such circumstances therefore required qualifications rather than rank, which retained its privileged position only in diplomatic service. The perception of bureaucratic loyalty began to change as bureaucrats no longer served the ruler alone but increasingly the state as well, a fact which later combined with the expectation that they should work for the common good. This gave rise to a class of well-paid officials who were (at least in relative terms) reliably loyal to the state which they served. That being said, the bureaucrats' loyalty to the state did not predetermine their positive or negative attitudes towards national identity. These were dependent on what form the modernising state assumed and, above all, on whether it came closer to a mono-ethnic state-nation or a multi-ethnic monarchy.

The situation was straightforward in mono-ethnic state-nations where the bureaucracy's self-identification with the modernising state-nation more or less coincided with what was seen as 'national identification'. In contrast, the settings of multi-ethnic monarchies proved rather more complicated: officials were expected to self-iden-tify with the state, but since this did not allow for a clear identification with a nation, their loyalty to the state showed strong characteristics of loyalty to the ruling dynasty. When members of non-dominant ethnies joined the ranks of state administration, they could identify with the state and the dynasty, but this, with the exception of the Ottoman Empire, did not prevent them from continuing to identify with the ethnic community (and later with the forming nation) from which they originated. The Hungarian and the Polish-Galician offi-cials in the service of the Habsburgs and the Baltic-German officials in the service of the Tsar are good examples of this.

The modernisation of administration was in essence about cen-tralisation, and affected people's lives by reviving the old issues regarding the relationship between the provinces and the centre. It raised the questions of how regions should be territorially delineated and relate to the centre. In Austria, centralisation was accompanied by language unification and disputes over what degree of autonomy individual lands should retain. The national movements in the Russian and Habsburg monarchies entered their phase B in the context of major administrative reforms – those imposed by Joseph II at the end of the eighteenth century in Austria and by Alexander II in the 1860s in Russia. Similarly, the Enlightenment reforms in Denmark at the end of the eighteenth century preceded the rise of the Norwegian national movement, and Catalan and Basque movements emerged after the victory of centralism following the Spanish revolution of 1873.

If those members of non-dominant ethnic groups who had succeeded in rising to the ranks of state bureaucracy had previously been almost automatically assimilated into the empire's official culture and language, the emergence of national movements changed this dramatically. Those who had become educated increasingly retained their ethnic (national) identity, and became the potential supporters and proponents of national efforts. As national movements grew more successful, patriots made increasingly conscious efforts to join the state apparatus, not only for existential reasons but also so that they could help the national cause. It is in this sense that we can modify Stein Rokkan's thesis that the provincial elites' penetration of the state apparatus strengthened the position of the given provinces within the state.[2]

Although patriots could theoretically become part of the state apparatus everywhere, in practice there were significant limitations. Joining the ranks of state bureaucracy was difficult for members of non-dominant ethnic groups (who usually belonged to the lower classes), and in the Ottoman Empire it was also conditional on religious conversion. In addition, active participation in any national activities, especially those that included political demands, could easily come into conflict with the requirement that a state official should be loyal to the empire.

Bureaucratisation affected the intensity and nature of social communication as well. The state permeated the day-to-day lives of the wider population on a growing scale, making its presence felt through the increasingly effective system of tax collection, the forced unification of municipal administration – which it subjected to frequent checks – and even occasional interference in the civic role of the church. Once the constitutional regime was established, the state involved its people (at least the wealthy ones) in electoral political decision-making, at times by bringing them into contact with elected representatives.

Bureaucratisation of the state administration created only a small proportion of new vacancies for those with higher education seeking employment in the administrative sphere. Growing numbers of individuals with secondary education found employment as officials or clerks at new institutions – the land registries, the post offices, railway stations, and so on. New posts were also created within local and municipal services and in the private sphere – legal firms offered employment to those with legal education, while factories and businesses (including large estates) required workers qualified in technical subjects. The demand for people with academic or secondary education was thus on the increase, which naturally led to higher numbers of students at secondary schools and universities and, consequently, greater numbers of highly qualified teaching staff.

All countries witnessed a rise of the educated strata of the population – people who earned their living outside the state services and were thus largely independent of state supervision. While this was likely to have increased the numbers of people who could be easily mobilised to take part in national movements, our ability to verify this theoretical supposition empirically is limited. For example, we know that in the Hungarian Empire, where modernisation was not particularly marked, the number of officials and independent professionals almost doubled between 1787 and 1843, growing from 27,000 to 50,000. But these data do not reveal anything about what proportions of these figures apply to Slovak, German or other non-Hungarian ethnic groups.

The implementation of compulsory military service was another act of the modernising states, and had a specific effect on nation-building in that it integrated the majority of the population, men directly and women indirectly. Military service had a certain 'educational' effect, in that it extended people's perspectives beyond the local horizon and allowed them to discover distant lands, while also strengthening their loyalty to the state. Once 'wars in the name of the king' turned into 'wars in the name of state interests' (and subsequently into 'wars in the name of the nation'), soldiers were expected to demonstrate a certain type of patriotism, and this may have reinforced their loyalty either to the dynasty or to the nation.

From this perspective, we can differentiate between two fundamentally distinct effects of military service, based on whether this service took place within state-nations or multi-ethnic empires:

1. Service in the army of the French state-nation, and later also in the armies of German, Serbian, Greek and other nation-states, prepared the soldiers 'to fight for their homeland', which became increasingly referred to as 'their nation'. The language of the army and most soldiers' mother tongue were usually one and the same, and this type of military service fostered national awareness, and at times even provided elements of national mobilisation. The fact that in critical periods of nation-building the professed 'fight for the homeland' often entailed military pursuits or colonial expansion is irrelevant in this context.

2. Service in the army of a multi-ethnic empire posed a confusing dilemma for soldiers from non-dominant ethnic groups, stemming from being expected to serve their 'homeland' – i.e. a state that was defined not in national but in dynastic terms. Unconditional loyalty to the ruler was often demanded of them, while the army language usually differed from their vernacular, the impact of which tended to be ambiguous. On one hand, it was putting them in a situation where they were made clearly aware of being different from the members of other ethnies and, as the case may have been, of their resulting inferiority, which made it easier for them to adopt a national identity. On the other hand, military service reinforced the dynastic identity of the empire, and thus could not act as an instrument for awakening national awareness among members of an ethnic group. In theory, this may have changed once the national movement had reached its mass mobilisation phase and the soldiers, whose national self-awareness had already been clearly formed, had begun to regard military service in the interests of the multi-ethnic empire as more of a service to a foreign power and foreign interests. However, studies into the fighting morale of the soldiers on the fronts during World War I reveal that the reality was not necessarily clear-cut.

The journey from a premodern to a modern state was characterised by the establishment of continual and effective bureaucratic and military control over one's own, precisely demarcated territory.[3] The government of the state-national elites from the centre had been primed for this, unlike the provincial elites and the non-dominant ethnic groups. Wherever the leaders of the non-dominant ethnic communities had yet to formulate their national demands, ethnies continued to be seen in the context of provinces – which defined themselves in contrast to the centre but were, nonetheless, compatible with the modernisation of the state. This was certainly the case of the German-speaking lands within the Austrian monarchy but, for a time, also of Scotland and Catalonia. Conversely, the leaders of emerging national movements no longer fitted this framework, since they aimed to create their own autonomous power centres and thus emancipate the provinces as national territories.

Political and Social Equality

The presence of political revolutions, the exercising of civic rights, and industrialisation are among the characteristics most commonly accepted as those distinguishing modern society from its 'older' counterpart. Freeing people from the shackles of the traditional, hierarchically organised feudal society and making them equal entails political and social components. If all members of society were to be politically and socially equal and become fully accepted members of a national community defined in civic terms, they could not be bound by feudal obligations to the old ruling classes. Two fundamental changes, which occurred on the brink of the French Revolution – and the way one immediately followed the other – offer a truly symbolical representation of this: the parliament announced the 'Declaration of the Rights of Man and of the Citizen' at the same time as it abolished the feudal privileges of the aristocracy, all in the name of the newly forming, one and indivisible nation. Although such a concurrence of these three civic emancipations – social, political, national – can also be found in central Europe during the revolutionary year 1848, it was more of an exception. More commonly, the legal or social emancipation of the masses took place before political participation was achieved, as was the case in semi-feudal Prussia and Russia, and in capitalist England. How did the two changes relate to the process of modern nation-building?

Social emancipation

Social emancipation is most commonly associated with the idea of subjects gaining equality. Nevertheless, the nature of the state and the transformation of society were most significantly affected by the social emancipation of the Third Estate – i.e. the emergence of confident, economically independent entrepreneurs in spheres of production, commerce and services. A modern, secularised national state could hardly exist without the presence of an enterprising bourgeoisie and wealthy middle classes.[4] While such emancipation, symbolised by the revolutionary self-identification of the Third Estate with a nation, corresponded in content and timing with the nation-building processes in state-nations, it also occurred within the German and Italian struggles for national unification. The comparison between the German and French paths to a modern society tends to be used to illustrate that the Third Estate's emancipation often led to different outcomes, but this difference is overplayed. It is true that differences in outcomes and the nature of nation-building should be considered in relation to whether the changes took place mainly through revolution or through compromise-based reform. Nonetheless, the common denominator in both of these cases was a shift away from a system based on privileges, economic regulations and religious legitimisation. The secularisation of the value system and principles of civic society consequently opened the doors to a new community, a new type of togetherness and solidarity, that best corresponded to the model of 'nationalism'.[5] It was only in situations where the state-nation's Third Estate had become emancipated that intellectuals could create and propagate 'patriotic codes' and search for ways to reach a new collective identity.[6]

Among the changes aimed at overcoming social inequality, freeing peasants from their dependence on the former feudal landlords had the widest impact. The form this emancipation assumed in different parts of Europe varied according to the local peasantry's status. While in several countries, such as England and the Netherlands, peasants had gained their independence earlier, most of Europe only began to address the peasant question shortly prior to the onset of modern state-nation building, or phase B of their national movements. In France, the 'classic' state-nation, emancipation of peasants from their feudal obligations and dependence was declared in the context of the emerging revolution, but this by no means meant that all peasants would continue to support the revolution. The freeing of the peasantry in Denmark was made possible by the reforms at the end of the eighteenth century, and Norwegian peasants, who had always enjoyed personal freedom, were freed of other aspects of dependence in the same century. In the south of Europe – for example, in Castile and some parts of Italy – modernisation initially brought about only small changes to the lives of tenant peasants, while the social situation of peasants in Ireland and the Balkans only significantly improved during their respective national movements.

Social modernisation had the most profound effect in areas where the forms of servitude that had survived since medieval times were the most oppressive, and where peasants had often become serfs bound to the land. The transformation of unfree peasants into equal citizens was most striking in the region of the so-called 'second serfdom' – the eastern part of Central Europe and most of Eastern Europe. This phenomenon deserves closer attention because it occurred in two out of three large multi-ethnic empires, and thus on the territory of 'classic' national movements. The fact that social emancipation and national movements were interrelated, or at least coincided, is clearly evident in these cases.

The emancipation of serfs took place on two levels. Firstly, their personal dependence and compulsory attachment to the land were eliminated (usually without any payment involved), and, secondly, they were freed of their financial and other duties, and also from corvée (usually for a redemption payment). The abolition of serfdom in the Habsburg Monarchy is associated with Joseph II, and occurred in the Czech and Austrian lands in 1781 and in Hungary four years later. While in the eastern Baltic provinces of Russia and in so-called 'Congress Poland' serfdom was abolished in the second decade of the nineteenth century, Tsarist Russia itself did not follow suit until 1861. That said, beside the Russians, most members of the Lithuanian, Belarusian and Ukrainian ethnic groups were also freed during the 1860s, as were those small proportions of the Polish and Latvian populations that had not previously gained freedom.

It is noteworthy that, in all territories inhabited by non-dominant ethnic groups, national movements (or, more precisely, their 'agitation phase B') started approximately one generation after serfdom had been abolished. There was thus no immediate causal relation between the two phenomena. Neither the abolition of serfdom nor manifestations of resistance to oppression by landlords resulted directly in the national mobilisation of peasants. For instance, the demands raised by the rebelling Czech peasants in 1775 or the Estonian peasants in the 1850s contained no explicit national elements. It can be assumed, however, that the two phenomena were indirectly related. Being no longer bound to the land may have enabled at least some of the sons among the peasantry to obtain a higher education (in the Habsburg lands earlier, and in Russia much later). Certain material and psychological conditions will also have been created, which would later aid national agitation. Peasants ceased to be seen as a 'backward mass', or as an object of ethnographic interest, and instead grew to be seen as an organic part of society – and later even as the core of the forming nation.

The eastern Baltic was the one area where feudal landowners and the elites of the ruling nation began to thematise the 'national' aspects of the abolition of serfdom immediately after the peasants had become free. Representatives of the German intellectuals (members of the so-called 'Literaten') gathered there in 1819 in order to discuss whether the newly freed 'non-Germans' (i.e. peasants speaking the local vernaculars) in the provinces of Estland, Livonia and Courland should be assimilated and integrated into German-speaking society, or whether the language and cultural barriers, which maintained a distance between them and the German-speaking higher orders of society, ought to be preserved. The conservative majority regarded their ethnic distinctness as something valuable, and wished for it to be retained, together with the differences as regards their Estate and education. The ruling German-speaking elites thus became aware of the potential difficulties with nationality issues much earlier than the multitudes of Estonian and Latvian subjects, whose national mobilisation did not begin for almost another fifty years.[7]

The second phase of peasant emancipation – the elimination of servitude and the relics of feudal obligation – tended to occur once national movements had emerged, and was therefore often thematised in national discourse as a part of the national programme. The elimination of both servitude and its remnants was, for example, demanded by the Czech, Magyar, Slovenian and Estonian national movements. It can be assumed that such demands will have won the peasants over to these movements, similarly to the effect of the adoption of Home Rule in Ireland. Symptomatically, the late incorporation of peasant emancipation in the Polish national programme corresponded with the late mass mobilisation of peasants in favour of the Polish national movement.

When examining the significance of peasant emancipation for modern nation-building, a number of factors need to be considered. Most importantly, we cannot automatically correlate the degree of feudal dependence (oppression) with the quality of the peasants' living conditions. In the eighteenth century, serfs living in the fertile parts of the Czech lands would have been substantially wealthier than free tenant peasants in Castile, free peasants in Finland, or peasants living in the less fertile parts of France. Similarly, a Ukrainian peasant in Galicia at the beginning of the nineteenth century was economically and culturally worse off than serfs in some Lithuanian regions. The peasants in the Balkans and the poverty-stricken tenant peasants in Ireland were, in fact, also free. In other words, peasants' wealth was not directly proportional to the degree of non-economic oppression they endured. Therefore, their participation in national movements must be studied in the broader context of modernisation changes.

One should also avoid automatically assuming that a change in peasants' legal or economic status would necessarily lead to a change in their mentality, social mobility, or position within society. It has been established that in the Czech regions the number of countrymen moving to the towns had started to increase even before serfdom was abolished. It seems that, more significant than the formal act of making peasants free was the process by which they became free, and the degree to which they became aware that their status, rights and obligations were in the interest of the whole state and the 'better' society. This was, of course, dependent on how wealthy, educated and informed they were, and only one general conclusion can be drawn for all regions.

A comparison of the points in time when peasant emancipation occurred in different countries with the timing of phase B of their respective national movements reveals a clear correlation. The earlier the peasantry was freed, the sooner the leaders of national movements began to strive for the mobilisation of the masses in the countryside – albeit always one generation after the emancipation itself. In simple terms, national agitation began approximately thirty to sixty years earlier in the Habsburg Monarchy than in Tsarist Russia. In the latter case, national movements first took place within the Baltic provinces (Latvia and Estonia) where serfdom had been abolished earlier, and only later in the territory that was integrated to Russia itself (Lithuania, the Ukraine and Belarus). This is the context that perhaps also provides an explanation for the faster and earlier success of national agitation in the countryside of south-western and central Germany than in the northern and eastern parts of the country.

This generalisation is, nonetheless, only partially valid, as it does not apply to regions where classic serfdom did not exist, such as the Balkans or western and northern Europe. Attending to the varying levels of economic development among the regions also offers only incomplete answers, as it would suggest that the Catalans and the Flemish, for example, should have been among the first peoples to start their national movements, whereas the Irish movement should have followed much later. Other factors must therefore have influenced peasant mobilisation in western and northern Europe.

An examination of the chances among members of non-dominant ethnic communities to rise socially offers another explanation. One of the main effects of serf dependence was that the children of the serfs were extremely unlikely to gain access to anything other than basic levels of education (in Tsarist Russia and the Baltic provinces they were forbidden to access higher levels of education by law). When the non-dominant ethnic groups largely comprised peasant serfs, the rise of an intelligentsia from within these groups was only possible once they were no longer tied to the land, with the attendant limitations.

At this stage we need to remind ourselves of the difficulty in accounting for the marked differences in the levels of education among rural populations, and of the fact that there was no direct relationship between the education of peasants and their legal and social standing. In the Habsburg Monarchy, for instance, school education was made free and compulsory before the abolition of serfdom, and more than a hundred years earlier than in a number of economically more advanced west European countries. This will inevitably have affected the peasants' willingness to respond to national agitation in the wake of their emancipation, which is one of the reasons why the relationship between school education and national mobilisation needs to be examined in the context of modernisation processes.

The path to civic society

Political modernisation entailed a whole range of crucial changes that happened neither simultaneously nor concurrently, and which replaced the late-feudal system based on privileges and religious legitimisation. Primarily, a constitutional regime was established guaranteeing basic civic rights, and stipulating the principles of equality and the political participation of all citizens, including those belonging to non-dominant ethnic communities. In addition, life within society became politicised, public opinion emerged, economies were liberalised, and there was a drive for a gradual democratisation of the political system. All these processes took place within politically defined territories – i.e. states. We thus need to differentiate between the two ways in which political modernisation and nation-building related, according to whether they occurred within state-nations or multi-ethnic empires.

In state-nations, the struggle against the old regime and for constitutionalism was a struggle between two classes of the same nation, while also taking the shape of a battle over that nation's new form. The conclusion of the process saw the defeated representatives and supporters of the old regime (French monarchists, for example) being gradually integrated into the new civic national community.

There is a tendency to distinguish between two basic paths to civic society, depending on the nature of the national struggle: the revolutionary path, represented by France (and, outside Europe, the United States), and the evolutionary path, of which the English case is often seen as the archetype. However, it would be more appropriate to acknowledge that political modernisation came about as a result of revolutionary transformations combining with gradual reforms. The 'evolutionary' English journey to civic society, which dominated the nineteenth century, had been ushered in by two revolutions – that of 1640–60, and that of 1688–89. Several political revolutions over the course of the nineteenth century led to the permanent establishment of civic societies in France, Italy and Spain. In contrast, in certain regions of the German Confederation, for example, the political revolution of 1848 did not take place until after a period of partial reforms. Denmark and Sweden were perhaps the only countries where political modernisation and the establishment of a constitutional regime took place exclusively through reforms 'from above'.

Incorporating the old regimes' educated elites and ruling classes in the national communities was inevitably more difficult in places where transformation was achieved mainly by revolutionary means. Despite this, the integration of modern national societies was completed by the end of the nineteenth century, once 'integral nationalism' – or, more precisely, a general adoption of national identity – had brought together members of state-national communities that had risen from political revolutions and, equally, members of communities that were modernised through reforms and compromise.

The principle of political equality was associated with the relationships between citizens, and it also affected the ways in which relations between nations were evaluated. A view that was becoming commonplace was that, if equality and mutual respect applied to citizens, they should also apply to nations. While Liberals were happy to embrace the idea of all nations being equal, there was disagreement about what should determine which communities deserved to be recognised as nations, and thus entitled to belong among 'the equals'. Consequently, the struggle for equal civic rights coincided with the notion that the battle was also being fought over the equality of the civic nations, but this could only be achieved free of misunderstandings within and between state-nations.

Potential nations – ethnic communities which lacked their own statehood but whose leaders (and increasingly also whose members) believed that they had the right to exist as equal nations – occupied a different position in the context of struggle for equality, and it should be noted that national movements played a different role in the process of political modernisation. Both the members and the leaders of ethnic communities rarely shared the political power enjoyed by the privileged orders, or dictated what should be encompassed in the struggle for civic rights. Consequently, specialist literature tends to present the view that political modernisation somehow bypassed national movements, and some authors even go as far as to claim that national movements had no interest in political emancipation at all. The validity of these beliefs can be verified by analysing the political demands made by national movements. The very logic of the struggle for modernisation calls into question the commonly held construct of 'ethos versus demos' – i.e. the idea that national movements were a priori 'anti-modernist', and that struggles for national rights and civic emancipation somehow 'missed each other'. Quite the contrary is true: they were mutually interdependent.

National movements were in their essence movements that sought support from the public, and were thereby a political phenomenon. National agitation was bound to be more effective in circumstances of political freedom rather than those of oppressive censorship and political control. Similarly, the range of national demands would have been limited by the ways in which they could be spread – or, rather, by the principles and rules of the political system governing all parts of the multi-ethnic empires.

In the situation of political oppression as we know it from Tsarist Russia prior to 1905, the Austrian Empire prior to 1848, and the Ottoman Empire, only cultural (and to a very limited degree also social) demands could be expressed publicly, while any public agitation in favour of liberalisation, political participation or civic rights were precluded. Not a single province managed to accomplish changes within the centre, in the sense of its national movement succeeding in bringing about political changes in the whole of the multi-ethnic empire. Such vision, however, perhaps lay beyond the imagination of the leaders of the national movements. Only the leaders of the Hungarian revolution of 1848 almost managed to achieve changes in the whole of the Austrian Empire – but even they did so unwittingly, as their aim was secession.

Political circumstances dictated whether or not national movements were successful, and these proved most favourable in countries without censorship and political oppression, such as Great Britain, Belgium and the Swedish-Norwegian kingdom. In Austria, the first wave of civic emancipation made itself temporarily felt during the 1848–49 revolution, and permanently so when the constitutional regime was established in 1861. The implementation of Austro-Hungarian dualism meant a relative freedom for national movements within Cisleithania, but led to the introduction of restrictive measures against non-Hungarian national movements in Transleithania (Hungary), despite its otherwise liberal regime. In Spain, the situation did not begin to ease permanently until the 1870s, while the first wave of liberalisation connected to national movements in Tsarist

Russia occurred even later – during the 1905 revolution. The Ottoman Empire retained its authoritarian and despotic system for a long time, and only began its hesitant liberalisation efforts through the reforms of the 1830s – i.e. after the Serbian and Greek national movements had achieved their decisive successes.

Sooner or later, nation-building reached a stage where national movements became a political factor – i.e. the subject of political activities. We should take into account the varying natures of political determinants that resulted from the very genesis of individual multi-ethnic empires. Within the Habsburg Monarchy, the Czech, Hungarian and Croatian national movements were able to claim the 'old rights' of the political entities they associated themselves with. In contrast, in the Russian Empire, only Baltic Germans and Finns could use this line of argument before 1905, while the national movements within the Ottoman Empire could claim hardly any 'rights' at all. Characteristically, these national movements found themselves in situations of conflict by the time their 'agitation phase' had begun, culminating in wars for national liberation. It is these wars that bring into question the notion that national movements could not pursue political goals in circumstances of political oppression. The Polish uprisings against Russian and Prussian dominance provide a similar illustration, and pose the open question of why some national movements responded to political oppression by aggressive means while others did not.

It would be a gross oversimplification if we adopted the extreme view that the conditions were only favourable to national movements when political liberalisation encompassed the entire country. The Flemish and Welsh movements, for instance, both occurred in states regarded as bastions of political liberalism, but both had great difficulty in achieving mass national mobilisation. In other words, neither the level of success nor the methods employed by the national movements could have stemmed solely from the way political modernisation evolved in the given multi-ethnic empire.

Similarly, no generalisations can be made when the aims of national movements are placed in the context of civic demands, since this relationship, as will be shown, varied greatly. Some national movements swiftly embraced a programme of democratic transformation of the political system, while others claimed allegiance to the 'traditional' values of the old society. But even such conservative declarations did not automatically lead to a rejection of the basic principles of civic equality.

As has already been pointed out, the requirement that all nations should be equal, irrespective of how large, powerful or wealthy they may be, corresponded with the demand that all citizens should be equal, regardless of their origin or wealth. However, the term 'equality of nations' was understood very differently by the nineteenth-century politicians within state-nations, on one hand, and leaders of national movements, on the other. The very notion of the 'sovereignty' of a state, which was replacing its religiously justified, dynastic, divine legitimisation, was in fact a legacy of the Enlightenment, and was formulated according to the principle of all nations being equal.[8] Once national movements achieved mass acceptance, opinions about the equality of nations, which had provided a common ground in the struggle against the old regime, became a source of divisions and conflicts. The political elites of the long-established state-nations began to question whether they should grant the same recognition to all nations that declared themselves to be independent and equal, and demanded to be seen as such, no matter how small they or their 'historical grounds' might be. This gave rise to the term 'unhistorical nation', and the argument that small nations were 'not viable enough'. Parallels can be drawn between the various approaches to these issues and the differing attitudes of liberalism and democratism to the notion of equal civic rights to political participation.

In a similar manner, we can examine how national movements related to political revolutions – and this investigation, too, reveals a striking compatibility between the two processes, irrespective of whether political and national demands were clearly expressed. Both national and revolutionary movements shared the common feature that they had turned against the existing order as represented by the old regime, and intended to fundamentally change it. Both strove to introduce a new, secularised legitimacy, based on government by the 'people' and their sovereignty, and to implement a new value system based on natural rights and the principles of civic equality. The French Revolution represents a model of unity between political and national emancipation – but the same can also be said of the 1848 revolution in Central Europe and also of the 1905 revolution in Russia.

A model does not rule out the presence of deviations or inner conflicts in cases that may follow it. For example, a clash between national and civic principles manifested itself during the 1848–49 revolution in relations between the Hungarian and non-Hungarian nationalities in Hungary, and between the Germans and the Czechs in the Austrian Empire. This clash must not be interpreted as proof that the two principles were somehow a priori incompatible. It was an outcome of the fact that the participants in the conflict failed to understand or perceive the shift in the timing of individual phases within the process of modern nation-building. As a result, the compatibility of national with civic emancipation was questioned at the time for two reasons: firstly, national movements were entering their 'agitation phase B' later than state-nations; and, secondly, they embraced a definition of the term 'nation' that did not place the state above the nation. But this type of controversy was not confined to central Europe alone. The specific aspects of the Irish–English, Catalan–Spanish and many other conflicts were a result of the fact that their national movements emerged only after the political revolutions and reforms, which aimed to modernise the state-nation on a countrywide scale, had achieved their goals.

Economic Development and Social Communication

There was, naturally, an important economic component to modernisation but here again the utmost care has to be taken so as not to make any presumptions. Therefore, the construct of a direct link between industrialisation and nation-building will be regarded as a hypothesis which needs to be verified and completed by the secondary consequences of this process. In addition, the chapter on economic modernisation also contains a section which addresses the most important accompanying effect and a by-product of modernisation – social communication.

From proto-industrialisation to industrialisation

It is easy to prove empirically that modern nation-building coincided with the gradual establishment of the various capitalist economies, but the question remains whether or not this indicates a causal relationship and, if so, in what sense. Can we verify the thesis that modern nation-building was a by-product or a consequence of the emergence of capitalist enterprise? According to orthodox Marxism, the answer is definitely positive – capitalism gave rise to national markets, and as the established bourgeoisie began to fight over them, bourgeois nationalism came about. The role of economic changes has also been emphasised by other authors. Ernest Gellner, who explicitly distanced himself from Marxism, regarded industrialisation – i.e. a distinctly economic process – as the key factor on the path to nationalism. Two decades before him, Karl W. Deutsch (and Otto Bauer even earlier than him) pointed out how important the new ways of doing business were with regard to people's need to form groups that would be better equipped to face new challenges.[9] This opinion was even shared by some of the nineteenth-century Liberal theorists, such as Friedrich List, who believed that the battle over markets played a crucial role in nation-building. Conversely, it can be argued that dividing markets along national borders is inefficient and goes against the spirit of capitalist enterprise and the true interests of transnational capital.[10]

It is relatively easy to prove that the correlation between economic modernisation and nationalism cannot be reduced to industrialisation alone. Admittedly, the rise of so-called patriotism in England dates back to the second half of the eighteenth century, when the industrial revolution also took place, but the concept of a modern nation began to form long before France embarked on industrialisation. For Belgium (the Southern Netherlands under Austrian rule), which underwent industrialisation, annexation by the First French Republic proved advantageous, as its industry gained access to the substantial French market. Although political development in Belgium culminated in the 1830 revolution, which brought the country independence, it also brought about serious economic problems. In Belgium, the logic of political power outweighed the logic of economic interests, but this is by no means an isolated example in Europe.[11]

The differences between industrial and agrarian countries were becoming more marked during the nineteenth century, but this had no effect on the speed or nature of nation-forming. While certainly Russia, the Ottoman Empire and the Hungarian part of the Habsburg Monarchy can all be justifiably seen as agrarian countries, not every state-nation can automatically be labelled industrial. If there was any universal correspondence between industrialisation and nation-building processes at all, it was the fact that industrial regions developed in all states except for the Balkans, and profited from advantageous trade in agrarian regions within the same state. This was true of the agrarian parts of the Czech lands within Cisleithania, agrarian parts of Catalonia, and the Basque country in Spain, and of Italy, France, and even Russia.

The fact remains (and can be empirically verified) that almost everywhere in Europe the phase B of national movements had been achieved before the onset of industrialisation, and could not therefore have stemmed from it. In some cases, such as in the Czech and Slovenian Lands, Finland and the Baltic states, industry had started emerging before the rise of mass movements, but even this does not make industrialisation decidedly 'nation-forming'. In the Czech lands the epicentre of industrialisation lay in the German-speaking regions, ruling out almost entirely any direct influence on the Czech national movement; few industrial workers, and no entrepreneurs, in the early phase of industrialisation were ethnically Czech. Similarly, the industrial revolution in the Ukraine originated in the Odessa region in the south, which had been almost entirely Russified. The centre of industrialisation in Belgium was in the southern, French-speaking areas. In contrast, the rising wood and paper industries in Finland were mostly located in the Finnish-speaking areas and, similarly, a number of Slovenian-speaking regions were involved in industrial production. In the Balkans, where the national movement was the most radical in its nature, industrial production continued to be negligible even at the time when mass movements occurred. For instance, the index of the volume of industrial production in the whole of the Balkans in the second half of the nineteenth century was less than 1 per cent of the volume of industrial production in Great Britain.[12]

The issue becomes clearer if we adopt a broader interpretation of 'industrialisation'. Let us assume that Gellner used the term to label the changes and shifts in way of life and in interpersonal relationships that manifested themselves with the development of domestic and factory production, and included an intensification of market relations between the towns and countryside. In the past, the term that referred to these transformations was 'commercial capitalism',[13] while the historiography of the last few decades tends to use the term 'proto-industrialisation', emphasising changes to the manner of production and life-style, rather than technology.[14] In this sense of the word, 'industrialisation' is no longer understood to stand for the volume of production and fundamental changes to business structures through the creation of industrial centres. Rather, it has to do with the broadening of horizons and changes to the life-styles of the majority of the population in the countryside, and thus represents a disruption of the premodern economic, cultural and mental fragmentation of agrarian society. This 'preindustrial industrialisation' led to truly substantial increases in social mobility and communication, which is the subject of the following chapter.

In connection with economic transformations, we need to ask whether or not the level of economic development and the chances of evolving into a modern nation correlated in any way. Was the speed with which nations were being built, or the success of national agitation, a reflection of the differences in economic development?

When considering the issue of unevenness of industrialisation, criteria according to which this unevenness is assessed should first be selected. Undoubtedly, volume of production is one of them, as are living standards or 'quality of life'. However, if we limited ourselves to only economic criteria we would be justifiably criticised for a simplified, materialistic belief that the 'cultural superstructure' is automatically dependent on the existence of 'economic foundations', as if it were true that faster economic development brought about faster changes to the cultural sphere, and thus also to national agitation and the spreading of national identity.

The criteria of uneven development are manifold, as is unevenness itself – underdevelopment in the handicraft and industrial sphere of production was not necessarily matched by underdevelopment of the state administration. The presence of grand church or secular buildings in the Baroque era, for instance, did not necessarily reflect economic prosperity or high levels of education.

Can the tempo at which political participation and political systems evolve be a criterion of development? Any answers to this question are limited by the need to take into account whether political participation involved all citizens or only the privileged classes. Poland, for instance, enjoyed a far greater degree of political freedom and participation prior to its partition than France, for example, but this freedom and participation were exclusive to the aristocracy. It is equally difficult to make the criteria of the level of the political system's development objective: Should centralism and absolutism be regarded as 'better' than a system based on privileges of the Estates? Perhaps it is only the attainment of modern constitutionalism or parliamentarism that provides a more acceptable criterion of a higher stage of development.

State administrations and political systems were closely interconnected with state-nation building. How was an uneven bureaucratisation of state administration – i.e. political modernisation – related to the level of economic development and to nation-building processes? While it cannot be said that there is a direct correspondence between the speed of political modernisation and that of economic growth, a stable state administration is inconceivable without a certain degree of economic development. It was income from their developing economies that enabled modern states to create strong bureaucratic apparatuses and armies, as well as more refined forms of internal surveillance and public discipline. This may equally have resulted in more oppressive forms of the authoritarian regimes just as in democratisation of the states.[15]

Only in situations where higher levels of economic development coincided with a tradition of an internally consolidated state unity, in which the ruling state-nation had a clear dominance over other ethnic groups, did conditions evolve favouring fast development towards a modern mono-ethnic nation-state. This was the case of France, Sweden and the Netherlands; in England matters were complicated by the dichotomy between English and British identities. Evidently, such a situation of coincidence between strengthening economy and consolidated state-nation applied to a small minority of nation-building processes in Europe and could be regarded as a specific sub-type of these processes.

The previous chapter, which addressed the ethnic roots of nations, revealed that the medieval linguistic assimilation of non-dominant ethnies proved more marked in states understood to be more economically advanced and administratively consolidated than those in central and eastern Europe. We must be careful not to assume automatically that assimilation was a consequence of economic prosperity, which is the causal interpretation that offers itself here, as the opposite may have been true: assimilation may have created the conditions for economic development. However, if we recall the conclusions of the analysis of the assimilation processes from the previous chapter, we will realise that neither argument is presented correctly, as both are limited to the economic sector alone. Assimilation within medieval and early modern societies was largely dependent on the level of development and centralisation of state administration, and on the intensity of market relations and social mobility – circumstances that were not necessarily linked to economic advancement.

To return to the phenomenon of unevenness, it is not only its criteria that are manifold but also its territorialisation (its projection into space). The question that needs to be answered here is what constitutes the basic territorial unit of unevenness. Until this point, unevenness and underdevelopment had only been considered in terms of entire states, without acknowledging two important circumstances of nation-building: the size of state territories and the internal economic heterogeneity of multi-ethnic empires. The former makes it complicated to draw comparisons between, for instance, Tuscany and France, the Netherlands and the Habsburg Monarchy, or Ireland and the Ukraine. The latter takes account of the fact that every state territory contained historically more developed, less developed, and even fundamentally underdeveloped regions.

Making connections between the various sizes of the state territories and the fact that great economic differences existed within the larger ones helps us to reveal some crucial aspects of national development. The size of the state territories corresponded directly with their internal heterogeneity. We also know that in early modern Denmark, Austria and the Ottoman Empire, economic (and cultural–political) fragmentation combined with ethnic diversity. Consequently, the unevenness discerned in examining large states may not prove to be the same when the basic unit of comparison is a region. The Habsburg Monarchy as a whole was certainly less developed than Great Britain, but the level of economic development in northern Bohemia was definitely higher than that of southern Ireland or northern Wales. While Catalonia was more advanced than Hungary, the situation looks very different if we compare the more developed regions of the 'east European' Hungary with some of the Castilian regions of 'west European' Spain. The levels of production in southern Italy and in Finland were probably very comparable, but 'east European' Finland had much higher levels of education. A majority of national movements occurred at this level – the level of unevenly developing sub-regions of large empires – and they were based on specific aspects of the life of local ethnic communities.[16]

We need to abandon assessment of the degree of 'industrialisation' only from the macro-analytical, 'state-wide' perspective of economic history, and look into the internal structures of the state territories – i.e. regional unevenness. Only by doing this will we obtain meaningful data that will allow us to discuss the role of uneven economic and social modernisation in nation-building processes. In this context we must also remember the aforementioned issue of the economic effects of nation-building processes, which cannot be dealt with by superficially contrasting 'effective' state-nation forming with the 'ineffectiveness' of the so-called secessionist national movements. Admittedly, the centuries-old ties among the people of France, for example, easily explain the transformation from an absolutist state community into a modern national society as decidedly effective, but can the same claim be made of the Austrian and Russian empires?

The strengthening of social communication

Whether early modern transformations are classified as 'commercial capitalism' or 'proto-industrialisation', their impact on the speed and volume of transferred information was immense. To prove that this increase in the intensity of social communication played a significant role in modern nation-building, as had been pointed out by Karl W. Deutsch, we need to focus on aspects other than the improvement of roads, construction of canals, the increase in scope, speed and regularity of postal connections, the possibility of subscribing to newspapers or journals, the increasing speed of boats, and the building of railways. All these changes were, undoubtedly, crucial for both macro-economic development and the emerging fascination with economic progress, but, from the point of view of national movements and of national mobilisation within state-nations, their importance lay primarily in speeding up the flow of information from the 'big wide world' into the existing network of local communications.

Ordinary people (in both state-nations and multi-ethnic empires) gained no immediate benefit from the fact that the postal connection between Vienna and Berlin, for instance, became twice as fast. Nor did they benefit from the newly built long-haul railways. Much more relevantly, the improvements to long-distance connections meant that – through subscription periodicals, in state documents or by other means – information now reached smaller regions and then spread within them through the traditional routes.

We can distinguish between the importance that growing social communication had for the elites and for the wider masses of members of ethnic communities. Leaders of national movements, politicians of state-nations, entrepreneurs, and also members of the educated elites, will have profited from being able to exchange letters quickly and receive printed materials, and, later, from the invention of the telegraph and telephone. This way they could gain access to information, exchange opinions, arrange and coordinate joint events, critically assess outcomes, and pass among themselves organisational instructions for political and national activities. All this will have strengthened the sense of togetherness and search for common interests on the part of both actual and potential elites.[17]

There is not enough room in this chapter to give consideration to the various processes of social communication or the spread of education, even if we disregard the contents they managed to communicate. Therefore, reflections on 'objective' factors will address certain aspects of national activities, and focus – especially in the context of examining the contents of social communication – on the nationally relevant elements.

The success of national mobilisation depended on communication with the ordinary people. Characteristically, leaders of national movements initially tried more consciously than the political elites in state-nations to integrate the masses into the national community. This was also the case in France, which is traditionally designated as a 'model' nation. The peasant masses were integrated into Czech, Estonian and Slovenian national communities faster than their counterparts in France or Spain.[18]

When examining what role social communication played in the spreading of national identity, and thus in modern nation-building, a fact that is commonly disregarded is that the acceptance of national awareness among the broad masses was of utmost importance. We need to remember that, even in the nineteenth century, information was mostly still transferred by traditional means, which had been firmly in place since at least early modern times. It was mainly spread through the pulpit, and through regular contact between the clergy and believers – but also through people coming to town markets, which usually entailed a visit to the public house, coming into contact with the local nobility and municipal authorities. Later on, people also became part of the communication system by means of attending school or serving in the army. These traditional forms of communication retained their function even after the majority of populations learned how to read and write, partly because most of those who could now read lacked the means to take out regular subscriptions to journals.

It was not only the volume of information that was important, but also the way in which its content was altered. The more people discovered what was happening and changing in their wider surroundings, the greater their 'imagination which transcended the system' (Jürgen Habermas), which then enabled them to understand change – or, rather, the idea of change – regardless of whether it concerned them directly. Newspapers and magazines increasingly wrote about 'the others', i.e. 'foreign' (not 'our') people and communities, and states ruled by 'foreign' rulers. It was crucially important whether these 'foreign states' were characterised or defined as 'belonging to foreign rulers' or 'inhabited by a foreign people or nation'.

Let us illustrate this claim with an example. In the 1790s, the media in central Europe began to present news about the wars against revolutionary France by referring to the enemy not by the name of the ruler or the state, but by using the ethnonym – the war was fought 'against the French'. This tendency continued throughout the nineteenth century, and applied not only to war reporting. Group labelling started to be used mainly in connection with religious conflicts and, depending on the situation, the enemies were the Catholics, Lutherans, Calvinists or Orthodox Jews. Unintentionally, perhaps, this type of information about the hostile 'others' easily became the new national terminology, and thus the training ground for national awareness.

As national integration progressed, the role of periodicals became increasingly educational – or, more precisely, nationally educational. Facts that have been established about large nations have their parallels in national movements, and so the publication of patriotic periodicals, for instance, tended to signal an onset of national agitation. Examples of such publications were the Czech journal *Hlasatel český* ('Czech Herald') from 1806, the Finnish weekly newspaper *Saima* from 1844, the Latvian *Petersburg Newspaper* (Peterburgas Avizes) from 1862, the Estonian *Sakala* from 1878, and the Lithuanian journal *Aušra* from 1883. Most of these were short-lived projects, but were a sign of a fundamental shift that was soon to follow. The more successful national agitation grew, the more magazines were published, and the larger their print-runs. In a sense, the growth or stagnation in numbers of patriotic periodicals indicated whether national agitation was progressively more or less successful. It reflected the number of readers as well as authors.

Communication provided by the press had the specific task of organising public collections in support of national interests, of which the so-called *matice* were the most famous in the Slavic context. They were associations whose aim was to secure the financial means for costly national projects – such as scientific writings, cultural magazines and highbrow fiction – and which had their counterparts in other parts of Europe. There were also collections for the construction of schools, such as those that took place during the Estonian national movement. Since the press published the names of contributors as well as subscribers, each contributor could easily discover where else there were people who he might not have known but who held similar views. This form of indirect contact proved to be one of the tools for 'imagining the nation'.

The printed word could never achieve as much as either personal contact, whose reach went beyond the local village and marketplace, or the secular public – neither of which would have been possible without a certain degree of political relaxation and liberalisation in state surveillance, i.e. without the implementation of civic rights. It was freedom of assembly, together with freedom of expression and the media, that gave rise to public opinion, one of the first signs of which was the emergence of private associations. People had gathered in politically neutral religious and reading groups, choirs and professional associations even before the constitutional era commenced. Once civic rights were established, they also started joining political parties and interest associations. The importance of group activities as a prerequisite to strengthening communication within the forming national communities should by no means be reduced solely to modes of association whose goals were explicitly national.

People's mobility played a crucial role in the context of intensifying social communication and vertical mobility – the possibility of rising socially. Of prime importance when discussing communication, however, is the increase in horizontal mobility – the number of people leaving their homes either temporarily or permanently in order to seek employment or education. This type of mobility was no longer limited to spending time as a wandering journeyman; it also included migration to industrial centres and areas where there were colleges and universities. In both cases, such migration reached beyond ethnic borders and may have influenced the assimilation of members of non-dominant ethnic groups. Whatever its other potential consequences, migration always led to new personal experiences and an exchange of information with the migrant's neighbours in both lands – that of his origin as well as that of his destination.

As in the case of industrialisation, the intensity of social communication was not the same across all parts of individual states. If we looked into how the varying speed of economic growth affected the spread of national identity, we could make the hypothetical claim that social communication acted as a transmission mechanism between economic – or, rather, civilisational – development and national activation. Can the fact that social communication was more intensive in towns than in the countryside account for why national agitation in distinctly rural areas followed much later?[19]

The almost textbook example of a comparison between Wales and Belarusian Polesia reveals much about the nature and limitations of the influence social communication had on nation-forming. When asked about their nationality in the 1919 census in Polesia (then a part of Poland), the majority of the rural population who spoke in Belarusian dialects responded by describing themselves as *tutejsi* (meaning 'from here' or 'local'). This lack of national identification is often explained by low population density of the region, by the network of roads being very thin, and by the exceptionally low levels of literacy in the countryside. Rather than taking their goods to the fairs, the peasants tended to trade the most essential items with (usually Jewish) middlemen who came to them. In contrast, south Wales was an industrialised area, with highly developed market relations and social mobility and a dense network of roads and railways.

Despite this, the Welsh movement was never mobilised, and instead the Celtic population was assimilated. Conversely, the Celts prevailed in the northern parts of the country, where social communication was markedly less developed. This comparison supports the thesis that the success of national movements was not determined by the level of social communication alone.[20]

Schools and national education

From the point of view of forming national identity, there are two reasons why schools occupied a crucial place among the new aspects of social communication. Firstly, they provided room for the transfer of nationally formative information to the wider population; and, secondly, they paved the way for a strong communication network by being an essential tool for attaining literacy. In addition, they played an important role in moral education and public discipline within the state. The question arises of how these functions interrelated. This section analyses schooling and literacy as objective prerequisites for nation-building processes, and as a platform for fostering national identity. For the time being, the issues of national activists' ability and willingness to make use of this platform is disregarded.

Literacy tends to be seen as one of the prerequisites for successful national agitation, but such generalisation is questionable, given how fast national mobilisation was achieved among the mostly illiterate Christian population in the Ottoman Empire. This poses an interesting question, which has so far not been explored in greater depth: did national identity or nationalism (and do they still) differ in relation to the levels of literacy of the populations concerned?

The implementation of compulsory schooling in Europe between the middle of the eighteenth and the beginning of the twentieth centuries was far from even. Although the Habsburg Monarchy, Prussia and some other German states were the first to prescribe it by law – by the third quarter of the eighteenth century – it was not accomplished in practice for a number of decades in the western part of the monarchy, and for almost a whole century in its eastern parts. Similarly, little progress was achieved by the introduction of compulsory schooling in France, whereas the northern countries proved much more successful in implementing it (Denmark since 1814,

Sweden since 1842, and Finland since 1866). Throughout the nineteenth century, people were entitled but not obliged to attend elementary schools in developed western Europe (Great Britain, Belgium and the Netherlands). The rich and developed Netherlands, for example, did not make schooling legally obligatory until 1900.

Data about populations' literacy is much more revealing than the state of the law. Almost 90 per cent of the populations in the Czech and Austrian lands were able to read and write by the 1860s – i.e. at the onset of the constitutional era – and the figures were similar in most German lands. In contrast, 45 per cent of the population in Croatia was still illiterate at the end of the nineteenth century, and, in spite of education being compulsory by law, only about 60 per cent of children attended schools in the second half of the nineteenth century, due to a lack of both schools and teachers. In 1871, a whole two-thirds of the adult population in Tuscany, Veneto and Lazio were illiterate, compared to only 40 per cent in Lombardy. Only 25 per cent of children attended schools in Spain in 1830, and one-third of the conscripts in Belgium were unable to read or write in 1860. In the Russian Ukraine, illiteracy remained at 80 per cent at the end of the nineteenth century, while the Latvian, Estonian and Lithuanian countryside reached much higher levels of literacy than the rest of Russia.

The teaching of reading and writing was not the only function schools served. Their principle role was to provide moral education and teach children social and political discipline, which is why religious education occupied a central position in elementary schools in most European countries, and especially at schools that were directly controlled by the church, as in the Orthodox areas during and after the Ottoman rule. Besides moral education, schools also fostered 'civic' virtues, and those that were controlled directly by the state, which applied in most European countries, were the most influential in this respect. Civic education encompassed specific 'national' dimensions, intended to teach pupils to love their homeland and those who governed it.

Again, we should differentiate between the impact of civic education within state-nations and within multi-ethnic empires. In the former, love towards the French, Portuguese or Swedish homelands, for instance, more or less correlated with state loyalty, as well as national identification. In the latter, elementary schools placed emphasis on the state's 'imperial' identity and pupils, like soldiers, were expected to regard the whole of the empire – all the countries reigned over by the ruler by divine right – as their homeland, regardless of their ethnic background.[21]

The language in which schooling took place was not always employed as a disciplinary tool, or as part of the inculcation of state loyalty. It is true that French schools gained a reputation for harsh enforcement of French as the only permissible language in class, and that Anglicisation of schools in the Celtic areas of Wales, which started taking place in the mid nineteenth century, followed a similar path. Catalan was also banned from all schools by Spain's King Carlos III in 1768. Russian was naturally the language used in elementary schools in Orthodox Russia, but began to be employed in elementary schools in the annexed parts of Poland after 1864, and in all other parts of Russia (with the exception of Finland) after 1885. This gave rise to secret private schools – or, more precisely, educational systems – in Lithuania, Russian-occupied Poland, and the Baltic region, based on teachers travelling from village to village and teaching outside official schools.[22] Apart from providing neutral literacy skills, this type of teaching was naturally linked to national agitation.

Conversely, the authorities in the Habsburg Monarchy respected 'local languages' – whether Czech, Sovak, Slovenian or Serbian – and allowed their use at elementary schools. Once Hungary became autonomous, in 1867, this linguistically tolerant approach was replaced by the policy of Magyarisation. When Romania declared itself independent in 1861, the government initiated Romanianisation policies in schools, whose aim was to impart national identity to the pupils in Wallachia and Moldavia – which had until then been independent – based on awareness of linguistic belonging. This shows that, in relation to modern nation-building, elementary schools may have been employed to strengthen identification with a nation, but were equally important as a means of assimilation or suppression.

Colleges and universities played a more important role from the point of view of national mobilisation. This was mainly because their curricula contained 'nationally' educational subjects such as history, literature and geography, all naturally unsuitable for the elementary schools, and because they were the institutions attended by the potential pioneers of national identity. The significance of 'national education' in the formation of national solidarity was appreciated by the French revolutionaries, the founders of the German national movement, and the leaders of the Czech and Norwegian national movements alike. It is irrelevant that some stressed the importance of learning about the national homeland's present while others favoured learning about its past – the role of school education was to prepare young people for life in a new national community. There was another, universally psychological factor, that was important for national mobilisation and that must not be overlooked: children do not become able to process and work with abstract terms, including 'nation', until the age of between eleven and thirteen. According to Gale Stokes, only those who had completed secondary schooling can develop an 'operational personality', and thus become able to participate in political and social activities in the interest of the higher community, which in our case translates into the ability to imagine a national community. It is thus essential to establish whether and how children from non-dominant ethnic communities gained access to secondary education, and what they were taught there.[23]

The difficulty lies in the fact that the function that schools fulfilled was determined by the interests of the state and by the practical needs of the parts of the population whose children attended them. The requirements by the state authorities were further modified in accordance with the nature of the state system. In Austria, emphasis was placed on fostering dynastic loyalty. The Danish, Swedish and Dutch authorities demanded that schools should also teach patriotism. French schools considered patriotic education to be a priority during the revolution, and continued to do so even after the revolution, despite accentuating different political factors. In contrast, many English secondary schools soon adopted 'merchant education'. In Portugal, nationally relevant subjects were only really regarded as suitable in the context of aristocratic education. After gaining independence, the new state-nations, such as Serbia, Greece, Romania and Bulgaria, made what were formerly church schools focus on education that would lead to national awareness.[24]

It was automatically assumed that secondary schooling would be conducted in the state language – which meant that, if members of non-dominant ethnic communities wished to retain their chance of being able to rise socially, they had to speak the language of state administration well enough to succeed in their studies. In addition, school education fostered love of the homeland, defined as a state. Attitudes and information that can be regarded as the nationally educational aspects of teaching had an integrating effect among members of state-nations, but proved ambiguous in the case of non-dominant ethnic groups. As national movements became more successful, the concept of loving the empire as one's homeland inevitably began to contradict the new national identity. Moreover, either traditional or newly implemented limitations existed in many places – for example, Tsarist Russia and Hungary, respectively – and were designed to prevent members of non-dominant ethnies from gaining access to higher levels of education.

In spite of all the variations in the systems of schools and the education they offered, it can be proved that no path to a modern nation was successfully concluded until a) the network of schools had been sufficiently broadened and school attendance increased, and b) the curricula had incorporated subjects that facilitated the adoption of national identity. This constitutes another factor that influenced the speed with which new national identities were adopted in different parts of Europe, within both state-nations and national movements. It appears that the outcomes of national movements were not affected by the fact that the language of education was the state language rather than the language advocated by their activists. Conversely, it was crucial that at some point the members of the non-dominant ethnies were enabled to regularly attend secondary schools, and possibly also universities, without having to assimilate linguistically or adopt the identity of the ruling nation.

A typology of national movements based on the way
they related to the process of modernisation

Modernisation changes and modern nation-building constituted a meeting of two uneven processes that combined and overlapped. Both democratisation and national mobilisation occurred in different countries at different times, but can we detect any degree of regularity between them that might lead to some general observations? Will new typological characteristics be revealed if we superimpose both processes and their milestones onto a time-line?

All nation-forming processes evolved through a stage when the leaders of a given nation made more or less conscious efforts to mobilise and integrate everyone they considered to be a member of their nation (phase B), and a stage that followed once this was achieved (phase C). The political concept of the nation and the political goals of the national movement were formed during these phases. When periodising nation-forming processes, another indicator – statehood – is employed as a criterion that differentiates between two fundamental types of these processes: those whose evolution towards a modern nation stemmed from an existing state-nation, and those in which statehood (or some degree of autonomy) was something that national movements strove for.

In state-nations, different aspects of modernisation assumed different positions on the timeline. In England, industrialisation came before democratisation was achieved, struggles for democratisation were initially connected with 'patriotism', and bureaucratisation followed even later. In France, by contrast, bureaucratisation occurred very early, even before the revolution; and democratisation, which was accompanied by national mobilisation, took place before industrialisation. In Sweden, bureaucratisation preceded both democratisation and national mobilisation, while industrialisation followed much later. In Spain, bureaucratisation also preceded gradual democratisation, and industrialisation gained ground mainly in provinces with a different (i.e. non-Castilian) ethnic background. In the Netherlands, attempts at democratisation, which was linked to national identity and did not prove particularly successful, date back to the second half of the eighteenth century – i.e. long before industrialisation and bureaucratisation. In Prussia, bureaucratisation was the dominant feature of the modernisation process, and very quickly combined with industrialisation in the western provinces; but the German national movement came into being and formed its political programme in the other, non-Prussian parts of the German territory before or during the arrival of Prussian bureaucratisation.[25] In other words, while it is true that in state-nations national mobilisation roughly coincided with modernisation, it is impossible to create a model of how it related to individual aspects of modernisation over time.

Although the relationship between national movements and the modernisation processes cannot be expressed by a single, generalising model either, it deserves a more thorough typology. This typology is acquired by bringing two sets of variables together and placing them onto a timeline. Firstly, four transformations are selected within national movements:

1. the beginning of national agitation (AB)
2. the transition from national agitation to a mass movement (BC)
3. the adoption and presentation of a political programme (PP)
4. the establishment of statehood or autonomy (NS)

Secondly, two transformations within the modernisation processes, which can be roughly dated, are added to this selection:

5. the arrival of democratisation and constitutionality (BR)
6. the beginning of the industrial revolution (IR)

The way in which these variables related in time can be expressed by means of a schematic table, which reveals the basic developmental types:[26]

1. nationally unifying movements
   (Germans, Italians)
   AB – PP – IR – BC – NS/BR
2. integrating national movements
   (Norwegians, Hungarians, Finns)
   AB – PP/BR – BC – IR – NS
   (Czechs)
   AB – IR – BR/BC – PP – NS
3. delayed national movements
   (Slovenians, Lithuanians)
   AB – BR – PP – BC – IR – NS
   (Latvians)
   AB – PP/BR – IR – BC – NS
4. insurgent movements
   (Serbians, Greeks)
   AB/PP – NS – BC – BR – IR
   (Irish)
   BR – AB/PP – BC – NS – IR
5. disintegrated movements that have succeeded
   (Catalans, Flemish, Basques)
   BR – IR – AB – PP – BC

6. disintegrated movements that have not yet succeeded
   (Galicians, Bretons)
   BR – AB – IR
   (Welsh)
   BR – IR – AB – (BC?)

The Czech and Hungarian national movements reached phase B while the old absolutist regimes were still in existence, with strong relics of feudal obligation. Their success and transition into the mass phase C coincided approximately with democratisation – i.e. the establishment of constitutionalism and principles of civic society. In Finland and Estonia, phase C was reached even earlier, before the 1905 political revolution. What was the significance of this sequence for the national programme?

National movements which defined their national identity within the framework of the old regime naturally aimed their efforts against the system of political oppression and Estate privileges. While it was unimportant whether this was thematised by only a few or many of the national programme's creators, it was crucial that they considered the principles of civic equality to be intrinsic to the national goals they pursued. The national movements' political programmes were formed in the context of political revolutions, and their aims were automatically integrated into the national programme. This occurred either at the beginning of phase C, as was the case with the Hungarian, Czech and Estonian movements, or already during phase B, as in Norway. Whether or not and to what extent democratism and anti-aristocratism prevailed among the leaders of the national movements, as they did among the Norwegians, Czechs and Estonians, will have been determined by other circumstances, perhaps including the ethnic group's social composition.

Movements that entered their phase B while the old regime was still in existence but whose transition to a mass movement (succeeding in national agitation) followed with a delay, were typologically different in the way they related to modernisation. Consequently, they reached the mass phase C only once a constitutional regime had been established, or once industrialisation began to spread to the territory of the non-dominant ethnic group. There were various causes for this 'delay'. Slovak national agitation started promisingly in the 1860s, but the movement was subsequently impeded until

World War I by forceful Magyarisation. The Lithuanian national movement faced tsarist persecution, and its early stages were complicated by the slow process of defining Lithuanian national identity against Polish in the second half of the nineteenth century. In some cases – those of the Slovenians, Latvians and Croatians, for example – we can hypothesise that the delay stemmed from the low levels of social communication, resulting from the underdevelopment of the mostly agrarian territory.

The leaders of 'delayed national movements' did not usually start striving to win supporters of the new national identity until constitutionalism and civic society had been established. However, the civic societies were represented by the elites of the ruling nations, and these delayed national movements were thus seen as standing in opposition not only to the ruling nation but potentially also to civic society. They could therefore be categorised as 'anti-modernist' movements, as a consequence of which the civic elements of their programmes were temporarily overshadowed by national demands.[27] This should be kept in mind when we examine the formation of their political programmes.

'Insurgent movements' can be found primarily within the territory of the Ottoman Empire, where national agitation gained the support of the popular masses, at least in some parts of the ethnic territories, before the political system was modernised. The outcome of these national movements was dependent on armed conflicts that bore strong resemblance to peasant wars against undisguised oppression – especially in Serbia and Montenegro. It was only after these conflicts celebrated their first successes – i.e. at the time of rising constitutionalism – that the leaders of Serbian, Greek and Bulgarian movements began to strive to implement the principles of civic society, which they had verbally embraced, into the day-to-day lives of their national states. The Serbian, Macedonian, Albanian and Montenegrin national struggles had had very little theoretical practice – they had almost entirely lacked the scholarly phase A. Domestic scholars turned their attention to studying the past, codifying the language, determining their own national identity and defining it against the neighbouring peoples after the national state had been established or the mass phase of the national movement had begun. Therefore, the basic characteristics of the term 'nation' were sought only once the spheres of science and education had come to be dominated by 'national interests', which hindered independent and objective scientific study. The creation of national culture as an instrument of national agitation followed a similar path.

'Disintegrated national movements' occurred under reversed circumstances. In states in which mostly liberal political systems prevailed, national agitation did not take place until civic society had formed. This was the case of the Breton and Provençal movements in France, the Scottish and Welsh movements in Great Britain, the Flemish movement in Belgium, and the Catalan, Basque and Galician movements in post-revolution Spain, in the last decades of the nineteenth century. This type of movement thus took place within west European multi-ethnic states. In all these cases, the advocates of the new identity had some difficulty in getting it adopted by the members of their own ethnic group – and, in some cases, even in defining it. It was not always clear from the outset whether their movement was going to be designated as national, regional or provincial. The leaders of these movements tended to be internally disunited and politically polarised, and they often failed to win the trust of the masses, and especially of industrial workers. Consequently, the transition to a mass movement was either markedly delayed or did not occur at all. The main difficulty that the leaders of national movements faced was in finding their niche among the domestic political powers, whose programmes were already polarised. This meant that their national goals could only be defined 'in the shadow' of the established political programmes and parties, or later on as a part of them. Whether the goals were initially mostly cultural (as in the Welsh, Flemish and Catalan national movements) or political (as in the Scottish movement) was unimportant.

The typology of how national movements related to modernisation changes serves its purpose in enabling us to place individual movements more precisely within the context of society-wide changes. This in turn allows us to achieve a better determination and comparative assessment of the limits and possibilities of the various elements of patriotic activities, which did not enter a vacuum but a specific, socially defined space. These activities will be studied and interpreted in the second part of this book.

The modernisation processes that took place in European countries affected the economic, social and cultural spheres, and caused an upheaval in the traditional society. This led to a gradual destruction of the relics of the feudal system, a secularisation of thinking, and a desecration of political legitimacy, which in turn freed the individual – slowly or suddenly – from habitual bonds and stereotypes. A crisis of old identities ensued. The subsequent search for new certainties and a sense of belonging did not start 'from scratch'. It made use of a wide range of legacies from the past, the most significant of which were ethnic bonds, institutional relics and historical interpretations. Certain peoples communicated more easily among themselves – because they shared similar cultural characteristics – than with members of other peoples, and this distinction often corresponded with social differences. Some forms of collective memory differed markedly in relation to the social background of their bearers, and ranged from continuous historiographic tradition to folk epics and family myths. Although modernisation destabilised old bonds, it intensified contact among individuals and between the individual and the state administration, increased levels of education, and encouraged migration and upward social mobility. This in turn had an effect on the role of language as an instrument of communication, and on people's notions of where they belonged – and thus their collective identity.

This part of the book has focused mainly on ethnic characteristics, relics of the past, and the impact of modernisation from the point of view of their relevance to the process of seeking and forming new identities that were considered to be national. This might lead to the impression that this relationship represents an inevitability – the beginning of a process that predetermined the formation of each of the existing European nations. Such an impression would be misleading.

The era of modern nation-building was characterised by the presence of integrating factors, which we have dedicated most attention to, as well as processes that were disintegrating nationally. These, however, were absent in the case of state-nations such as France and Sweden, where 'being a nation' was an indisputable legacy of the past, and formed part of the state-nation's political heritage. Conversely, disintegrating factors can be found within nation-forming processes that I have termed 'national movements'. Examples of such factors are intensive communication extending beyond ethnic and historical borders (as in south Wales, Lusatia or the Basque provinces), severe political oppression (as in Belarus and Eastern Ukraine), and cultural pressures for assimilation (as in France). In some cases, attempts at national mobilisation were hindered by the fact the elites of non-dominant ethnic groups could gain advantages within the existing supra-national state (for example, participation in British colonial expansion and rule).

Developmental alternatives and unsuccessful national movements could be addressed separately in a self-contained monograph, which would reveal or formulate a mechanism explaining why they failed. However, here we concern ourselves with the interpretation of the successful modern nation-forming processes. While the possibility of their success is inconceivable without the three objective factors analysed above (ethnicity, history and modernisation), whether or not this possibility became a reality was determined by other, equally important circumstances. These circumstances represented the subjective, optional aspect of the nation-forming processes – the actual building of nations – and hence the focus in the second part of the book is on activities 'in the name of the nation'.

PART III

Acting in the Name of the Nation

Our main focus has so far been on the general preconditions of the rise and success of modern nation-building, making the process as depersonalised as possible. However, this approach alone is not enough. While a nation cannot exist without its members being aware of their nationality, the forming of a nation cannot take place without specific activities of groups and individuals. Even if we uncritically accepted Gellner's remark about nations being created by nationalism, we cannot see nationalism as an abstract spiritual force that determines people's fates without the need for conscious collaboration on their part. However absurd such a proposition may seem, numerous authors of the literature on nationalism engage in analyses that disregard people and focus solely on 'nationalism' – an abstract, socially unanchored term. It is also common to refer to 'nationalists', who are placed freely in time and space without any concrete social context, as if they were ready-made frames – mono-dimensional people whose only personality trait is the vague 'nationalism'.

The previous part of the book paid attention to those factors constituting the fundamental preconditions of modern nation-building, and whose effect was 'objective' – i.e. independent of the visions and goals of the 'creators of nations'. It also provided evidence that historians mostly agree on the fact that the legacy of the past, ethnicity and the modernisation processes that occurred within the economic and political systems combined to act as a general framework for the forming of new national civic societies. This is not to imply that nation-building was teleologically predetermined by 'the purpose of history'. The process was not 'a mere superstructure' or an inevitable result of the circumstances characterised in the first part of the book. It was the decision to define a new form of identity with a group designated as a nation and to offer it to the fellow citizens that made it possible to create such a society. Nevertheless, this decision signalled only a historical possibility and a beginning of efforts that, as has been mentioned already, were not certain to succeed. This is due to the fact that turning a vision into a reality depended not only on the devotion and inventiveness of the players, but also – and primarily – on the combination of circumstances that existed, regardless of their wishes.

This leads us to the role of 'subjective factors' – i.e. of people who take action and make decisions – and to a realm where individuality and chance play their part. Since it is not easy to reach a consensus when analysing what motivates human behaviour, many of the findings and conclusions that follow will be presented as partial observations, and lead to hypothetical generalisations. A further objective is to determine what existing research reveals about the conditions that gave rise to and motivated activities conducted in the name of the nations-to-be, which aimed to shape their future.

We are interested not only in political but also cultural activities, and in ascertaining the means by which national consciousness has been emotionalised and mythologised. Questions need to be asked about the interests that lay in the background of gradual national mobilisation – what people expected from adopting a national identity, and what goals were pursued by those who 'awoke' these people from their national 'unawareness', spoke in the name of a nation, and steered them towards its creation. Although this area of study contains many issues that are still open to further research, it should not limit us to producing merely a long list of the wide range of partial observations by different authors. Let us focus on those key spheres of national activities about which we have enough information to enable us to attempt a comparative perspective, with the aim of arriving at some more general findings. From the point of view of their content, we will look more closely into three spheres of national activity: first, the use of history to activate the nation; second, the role of linguistic and cultural demands and activities; and, third, the role of nationally relevant conflicts of interest, including competition for political power. As regards the methods employed in national agitation, attention will need to be paid to symbols, celebrations and cultural activities, and in particular their effects on national consciousness. All of the above activities were the result of human efforts.

CHAPTER 6

The Players:
Speaking in the Name of the Nation

The first question that needs to be asked is: who were the people who advocated the creation of nations, became their 'creators', and made national demands in their name? In seeking the answers, we are interested in the individuals' social background rather than their names, personality traits or distinct views. Two quantitative factors are particularly important, especially in the case of national movements: what was the agitators' professional composition? And which sections of the population in a given country supported the national identity during the studied period?

Differentiation needs to be made with regard to chronology (according to the different developmental phases) as well as typology (whether the case in question is a state-nation or a national movement). In addition, allowances must be made for having to rely on estimates in some cases, while having precise figures only for certain national movements.

As we have seen, in most premodern European countries the term 'nation' had referred merely to those with political power – mainly to the privileged aristocratic classes. The terms *Natio Hungarica* and *Natio Polonica* are good examples of this, as is Luther's appeal to the nobility – the members of the *Teutsche Nation*. Similarly, the term *die Nation* was used in some lands of the Holy Roman Empire when speaking of assemblies of the Estates. According to Montesquieu, *la nation* gathered in the Estates-General – by which he meant nobles and bishops.

The difficulty lies in the fact that in some situations the reality differed from this simple model. Today it is very difficult to draw a clear line between an awareness of belonging to a premodern 'nation' in the sense of a 'state-nation' and to a group defined in ethnic terms, possibly in combination with religion or social standing. The participants in the Hussite movement, for instance, considered themselves to be 'true Czechs', based on religious and linguistic criteria, irrespective of whether or not they were of noble birth. The 'right' religion was an important identifier, but in order to understand this factor one needs to be equally aware of the fact that the society in question was one in which towns already possessed a significant share of political power – held not only by patricians, but also by artisans.[1] The Flemish townsfolk, who rose against the French king at the Battle of the Golden Spurs a century earlier, represent an even older example of this, as the strong awareness of 'national' belonging, which they retained for a long time, rested partly on ethnicity. Similarly, both high-born and low-born 'French' were mobilised in situations of extreme danger by the movement led by Joan of Arc, no matter how blurred by myths it later became. The sixteenth-century revolt against Danish rule by Gustav Vasa's rebel force was led by aristocrats, but free peasants' participation in it was conscious and active. Although further such examples can be found, on the pan-European scale they tended to be exceptions and anomalies rather than the rule at that time; and, as we have seen, it is highly debatable whether the participants' group identity can be designated as 'national' in the modern sense of the word. While in some cases it was an expression of self-identification with a particular ethnic group, in other cases it was simply a fight in defence of one's 'homeland', which was later – once a nation had been fully formed – reinterpreted by observers and historians as their nation's struggle.

The State-Nation

Determining the social base from which nations were built seems a relatively easy task in the case of state-nations. It can be reduced to a simple formula: the decisive role was played by those who led the struggle that sought to achieve a political transformation of the old regime and pave the way for civic society. The French case is the most famous: the Third Estate rejected the idea that the nation should be formed solely by the two privileged Estates, refused to remain 'the people', and elevated itself to the status of a nation. Discussions have taken place about whether the Third Estate was mainly represented by the 'bourgeoisie' or by a group of intellectuals, with a special role played by lawyers and members of independent professions in general.[2]

National slogans were most keenly received in Paris and in several other large towns. The idea of the nation was naturally also adopted by volunteer soldiers in the Revolutionary Armies and their officers, who remained loyal to the nation even after they were promoted to generals under Napoleon's command and became part of the empire's elites. Even as equal citizens, members of the upper and middle classes thus continued – except possibly during the Bourbon Restoration – to be the main force behind the French ideas of the nation and of 'nationalism'. However, organised state efforts towards national education for the French, which according to some authors led to 'integral nationalism', only began to take place during the reign of Napoleon III, and it was not until then that the whole of French society started to integrate into a nation.[3]

While in France the idea of the nation turned against the old regime's ruling classes in the eighteenth century, 'national' integration in England occurred in several stages, the first of which culminated in the conquering Norman aristocrats' integration into the Anglo-Saxon environment. Due to the fact that all townsfolk had belonged among the privileged since Magna Carta, the fundamental dispute over 'the nation' during the revolutionary seventeenth century was not dictated by a conflict between the aristocracy and the Third Estate, but by a conflict between the parliament and the power claims of the monarch.[4] The Glorious Revolution was a point after which Tory patriotism and the reformist patriotism of the Whigs merged together – which of course did not prevent internal political conflicts. Unlike France, Great Britain conducted its eighteenth-century wars not as wars of an absolute monarch, but as wars decided upon by the government and the parliament. This made it possible to cultivate the myth of parliamentarianism, in which the nation is built and decisions about it are made by the representatives of the people. The commonly presented reservations about the representativeness of the electoral system at the time do not alter this fact.[5] We may disregard the issue of an internal tension between British (imperialist) and English (national) identities – a consequence of the creation of the United Kingdom.

Denmark followed a different path – first dismantling imperial identity, and then establishing national identity. Danish Enlightenment reforms, which modernised the society in the second half of the eighteenth century, were based on patriotic efforts by the aristocracy. However, it must be remembered that this patriotism related to a state entity that was far from a nation: it was a multi-ethnic empire in which aristocrats were the bearers of imperial identity, irrespective of their ethnic origin. It was not until the Danish minority in Schleswig began to assert its rights in the first half of the nineteenth century that attempts to establish an identity for the linguistically and culturally defined nation as a civic society started to gain ground. The active force behind this transformation from imperial to national identity was the business bourgeoisie and independent professionals in Copenhagen, who were soon also joined by the royal court and the key section of the aristocracy. The experience of wars in 1848–49 and 1864 resulted in the process of national integration of the popular masses being very fast.[6]

To summarise, political modernisation within state-nations came in two forms, depending on whether it was revolutionary means or reforms that predominated. This meant that the leading role in the newly formed national community was played either by the Third Estate or by its coalition with the old system's ruling classes. With time, political leaders in all state-nations were sooner or later part of the wealthy elites among state officials, academics and entrepreneurs. This did not exclude the possibility of the rise in populist and aggressive nationalism 'from below' during the period of mass democracy.

The transformation of state-nations into modern nations, whether it occurred through revolution or reform, was closely connected with power struggles among the political elites. Its advocates only concerned themselves to a very limited degree with a rapid national mass mobilisation. They possessed sufficient intellectual and financial resources to take control of the public space, and to allow them to win acceptance for the idea of a single nation without needing to offer alternatives. This aspect of modern nation-building was markedly different in state-nations from its counterpart in multi-ethnic empires, especially in activities designated as national movements.

National Movements

The social composition of national movements was considerably more complex. Unlike in state-nations, in which cultural and

scientific activities were associated with state institutions, universities and the ruling elites, phase A of national movements was a
matter of personal interest and the scholarly zeal of individuals. In
areas where the majority of educational activities were controlled by
the church, the core scholars comprised members of church institutions and orders and their former pupils, even during the
Enlightenment. This was especially true of the Catholic countries. In
Protestant countries, and also in areas where phase A commenced
at a time when the Catholic Church had lost its monopoly, the
leading role was played by secular scholars – university professors,
state officials and private researchers employed by the aristocracy.
For the phase-A activities to be successful, it was crucially important
that the findings of scientific work could be published, which in turn
required a certain degree of freedom of printing and of technical
development. The printed word was an essential go-between, not
least because many scholars worked in the empires' metropolises and
thus outside the territories of their own ethnic group. This fact alone
may explain why phase A of national movements in the Ottoman
Empire and the Orthodox countries within Russia occurred only
marginally, and very late.

While the social base of phase A was relatively narrow, large
numbers of participants were an essential prerequisite for phase B.
The ruling elites of a given multi-ethnic monarchy were rarely at the
forefront of the national movement, simply because ethnic groups
seldom had a complete social structure. There is also empirical evidence against the assumption that national movements were
invariably movements of outcasts and the lower classes. Based on a
comparative analysis of the social structures, it is possible to establish
in general that the leaders of national movements comprised mainly
members of the most prestigious and lucrative professions and social
classes, whose ranks either contained or could repeatedly be joined
by members of non-dominant ethic groups.[7] In simple terms, it was
primarily the best-educated members of these non-dominant ethnic
groups who formed part of the leadership of national movements
– i.e. individuals classed as members of the so-called intelligentsia.[8]
But this social class was internally very diverse and, consequently,
what mattered most were the ethnic group's social composition and
the specific social and cultural circumstances under which a given
national movement took place – in other words, at what point and

to what extent it became a possible and common occurrence for members of non-dominant ethnic groups to rise socially.[9]

In two national movements – Magyar and Polish – the leading role was indisputably played by the aristocracy – the land-owning aristocracy as well as intellectuals of aristocratic origin. For instance, between one-half and two-thirds of the participants in the Polish revolt of 1831 were aristocrats (both with and without wealth). In the Kingdom of Hungary, a small proportion of the Slovak patriotic intelligentsia naturally came from the ranks of the minor aristocracy. Similarly, only a small part of the aristocracy participated in the Croatian national movement. In the Serbian struggle for national freedom we come across tribal chieftains (*knezes*), who were a similar category to the aristocracy, but it was the tradesmen living within the Hungarian territory whose participation (supported by individual aristocrats) was more active. The phanariots – the Greek equivalent of the European aristocracy – played their part in the Greek revolt, and participants of aristocratic origin were also present in the Basque movement. Other higher social classes were well represented, for example, in Norway, where the national movement was led by an elite of high officials and wealthy tradesmen, and later also by members of independent professions. The Catalan national movement eventually evolved along similar lines, and in the Balkan national movements tradesmen also gradually grew in importance. In theory, the fact that the aristocracy and middle classes participated in national movements meant that these movements had enough financial resources to develop cultural activities and more sophisticated forms of national agitation. This was not always the case in practice. As we will see, what proved more important was the correlation between entrepreneurial circles and the middle classes participating in phase B and the structure of the movement's programme. This is thanks to the fact that these people were responsible for quickly introducing political goals into this programme, which sooner or later included demands for statehood.

The members of independent professions were a small but influential elite among Czech, Slovenian, Lithuanian, Finnish, Irish and Flemish patriots. They were naturally also present among the leading advocates of national policies in the Greek and Bulgarian movements, but were outnumbered by the other, lower categories of intelligentsia, whose members had a much greater influence on the day-to-day running of the national movement. Independent professionals played a particularly important role in laying down the national movements' fundamental principles and requirements, and in presenting the movements to the outside world. That said, these requirements were not formed on the basis of the specific interests of independent professions but were modified according to whether or not the national movement was led by members of entrepreneurial and landowning elites. In the Polish and Hungarian cases, most independent professionals were directly interlinked with the aristocracy. It was thus not accidental that, during phase C, independent professionals were the cadre that the nation's political representatives were drawn from within the representative bodies.

The lower intelligentsia was by far the largest group among the movements' main players, and consisted mainly of the clergy. Although the catholic clergy rarely affected the setting of the movement's goals so directly, as in the case of Slovene priests, they were often the most numerous among the 'ordinary' patriots during the phase of national agitation. This was the case with the Catholic clergy in the Czech lands, in the Flemish and Croatian national movements, and later also in the Lithuanian and Irish movements. In the Slovak national movement, the Catholic clergy shared influence with Lutheran pastors. The Uniate (Greek Catholic) clergy played a major role in the national movements of the Ukrainians-Ruthenians in eastern Galicia and the Wallachians-Romanians in Transylvania. Protestant pastors were a significant group only in the Finnish national movement, in Wales, and under specific circumstances in Slovakia. Orthodox clergymen had a strong presence in all national movements in the Balkans, but especially in the Serbian and Romanian movements.

When assessing the role of the clergy, the specifics of different religious denominations need to be taken into account. The attitudes of the Catholic clergy were largely dictated by the church's discipline. In areas where territorial claims or the national movement's scope more or less corresponded with the territorial framework of the church organisation, the Catholic hierarchy's stance on the clergy's participation in the national movement was benevolent, and in some cases – including the Czech, Croatian, Flemish and Irish – even supportive. In places where the national movement interfered with the territorial units of church organisation – such as in the Slovak efforts in relation to the Hungarian Empire or Lithuanian efforts in relation to the Polish church hierarchy – the clergy initially had difficulties participating in the movement. Conversely, the Protestant pastors' participation in national movements was much more dependent on personal choice – in other words, on their ethnic roots and relationship with the parish; hence the difference between the active role of pastors within the Finnish territory and the almost complete absence of such a role on the part of (German-speaking) pastors within the Estonian and Latvian territories.

The Orthodox Church in Russia was organised according to the principle of 'official nationality', which prohibited the participation of its clergy in the Ukrainian or Belarusian national movements. In contrast, the Orthodox Churches in the Ottoman Empire let their own ethnic orientation guide them; the struggle to free the Bulgarian clergy from their dependence on the Greek Church, for instance, constituted the first stage of the Bulgarian national movement. Nevertheless, this type of merging of clerical and national interests was specific to the Balkans rather than a general rule, which was one of conflict or tension between the liberal-secular and religious components of national agitation, such as among the Flemish, Slovenians, Slovaks and Lithuanians.

As regards the officials, their involvement was dictated by the degree to which participation in a national movement was tolerated by a given multi-ethnic empire. The degree of tolerance was relatively high in the Habsburg Monarchy (especially after 1861), but even there the number of officials employed in private services (patrimonial and municipal) was much higher among patriots than among those serving the state. The participation of officials was also widespread in the Flemish and Finnish movements. On the other hand, there were naturally no officials among the leaders of national movements in the Ottoman Empire – nor in the Baltic region, where German bureaucratic elites were drawn strictly from among the Germans. The lowest category of intelligentsia – teachers and petty clerks – was the largest and most significant segment, particularly among the Estonian, Macedonian and, to a lesser degree, also Latvian patriots.

It was very rare for the urban lower middle classes, especially artisans and small tradesmen, to be found among the national movements' activists. Their presence was most noticeable in the

Czech national movement and less so in the Slovak, Bulgarian and Slovenian movements. Small tradesmen and entrepreneurs were also of some importance in Riga, the centre of the Latvian national movement.

While peasants always constituted the core of the non-dominant ethnic groups, they were rarely found among the leaders and organisers of phase B of national movements. The only example of this was probably Lithuania, where the specific factors of political oppression and a lack of professional teachers resulted in the peasants' accomplishment of national agitation largely through their own efforts. In most cases, the better-educated peasants decided to participate actively in national movements at a later stage, and it was primarily national mobilisation in the countryside that enabled these movements to reach their mass phase C.

From the point of view of gender, national movements – particularly in their first two phases – tend to be seen as an exclusively male affair. Admittedly, there were only a handful of female authors, who the patriots valued. The percentage of women who helped finance and supported patriotic activities was also very small in many national movements. Women did not run patriotic institutions or journals and seldom participated in laying down the national programme, which meant that their direct influence was very limited. Some of the national programmes already called in phase B for the emancipation of women, but they had no chance of success. Although the discourse of the time permitted and even welcomed the involvement of women in national agitation, it was expected to be conducted by men.

Despite this, it does not follow that the role played by women in modern nation-forming was insignificant, or that they were altogether absent in national movements. Their involvement in modernising state-nations and in national movements was primarily indirect, and involved 'internally orientated' activities. Women became instruments of national education, and often also the symbol of national virtues. As a guarantee of the nation's existence, they were the object of both agitation and adulation. This specific role of women will need to be considered carefully when we examine the issues of emotional manipulation and the 'complementarity' of national symbols.[10]

The Social Origin of the Patriotic Intelligentsia

There were major internal differences within the 'intelligentsia' – the social class that played a decisive role in all national movements – which means that we cannot limit ourselves to differentiating according to professions alone. Questions must be asked about the status of this class in the overall social context, which provided the conditions for the development of an intelligentsia in the true sense of the word.[11] We therefore need to examine the social background from which patriotic intellectuals originated, and in which they grew up. Heuristic exploration of the intelligentsia's social origins is very demanding, and still to be conducted in the case of most nations – unless we are content to be limited to the biographies of the handful of leading figures.

Certain general findings can be drawn from the typological differentiation among nation-building processes and from what we know about different countries' educational systems. It suffices to consult university registers to reach the reasonable assumption that the majority of educated people in state-nations – such as the English, French, Swedish and Spanish – came from families of wealthy bureaucrats, large landowners, dignitaries, and so on. In these countries elites were replaced from their own ranks. The same hypothetical assumption can be made about the leaders of the German, Italian and Norwegian intelligentsias; and a majority of the educated leaders of the Hungarian and Polish national movements were also connected with the aristocratic environment. Conversely, Estonian, Lithuanian, Latvian and (western) Ukrainian patriots in phase B came primarily from among the peasantry. It is noteworthy that older historiography mistakenly assumed that Czech and Slovak patriots were also of peasant origin.

Let us attempt to verify these assumptions in several cases by employing empirically quantifiable data – which can be readily obtained, in particular, for the (probably decisive) segment of the university-educated national intelligentsia. Such data are available for the social origins of the German, Czech, Norwegian, Slovak, Finnish, Lithuanian and Estonian intelligentsias, and can be presented for easier orientation in Figure 1.[12]

Figure 1

Social origin	Germans	Czechs	Slovaks	Norwegians	Finns	Lithuanians
Large landowners, high officials	30	1	2	10	5	0
Entrepreneurs, large tradesmen	15	1	0	25	3	0
Independent professions	15	3	2	10	5	1
Officials and petty clerks	12	15	2	10	20	2
Evangelical clergy	12	-	18	20	35	-
Teachers	2	3	10	2	1	1
Army officers	2	-	0	10	8	-
Artisans, shopkeepers	8	50	35	5	10	2
Peasants	3	20	25	5	10	90

Between one quarter and one third of the German and about one tenth of the Norwegian intelligentsia came from the ranks of high officials (or large landowners). This category amounted to less than 10 per cent among the Finnish patriotic intelligentsia, and was absent or almost absent in all the other national movements.

Almost one-fifth of German and one-tenth of Norwegian students came from families of independent professionals, while this figure was just 5 per cent among the Finnish, and even lower in the Czech and Slovak cases.

Only around 10 per cent of the university-educated among the Germans, Norwegians and Czechs came from the families of middle and lower officials or employees (petty clerks). The same category among the Finnish patriots amounted to 20 per cent.

More than one-third of the Finnish and almost one-fifth of the Norwegian patriots were from families of Evangelical pastors, and the figure was also 20 per cent in the Lutheran part of Germany.

At least one-quarter of Estonian and Macedonian patriots came from families of teachers, as did one-tenth of Slovak patriots, while the proportion of this category in the other national movements was well below 5 per cent.

Between 10 and 20 per cent of the German university-educated intelligentsia, and a full quarter of their Norwegian counterpart, came from the ranks of entrepreneurs in the sphere of commerce and production. In contrast, an entrepreneurial background was present in less than 5 per cent among the Finnish and the Czechs.

Artisans (both urban and rural) and small tradesmen formed the family background of approximately one-half of the Czech, more than one-third of the Slovak, and one-tenth of Finnish patriots. It was under 10 per cent in the German environment, and even less in the Norwegian.

A large majority of Lithuanian patriots came from peasant families, as did two-thirds of Estonian patriots – but only one-third of Slovak and a little more than 10 per cent of Czech patriots were peasants. In the Finnish, Norwegian and German cases the proportion of the intelligentsia from a peasant background amounted to approximately 5 per cent, or less.

Based on the data above, we can state that there were marked differences between the national movements in terms of the social origins of patriotic intelligentsia, and that three types can be differentiated:

1. The leaders of the movement had been raised by families belonging to the upper-middle or middle classes. The German and Norwegian cases prove that when the ethnic group had a complete social structure, the national intelligentsia was drawn mainly from among the wealthy entrepreneurial and educated elites. A specific subcategory of this type are national movements whose patriotic intelligentsia came primarily from an aristocratic background, even though in terms of profession they could be regarded as members of the middle classes. Good examples of such situations are the Polish and the Hungarians.
2. The predominant force among the advocates of the national movement were the petty intelligentsia, who came mainly from the peasantry and the countryside, such as peasants and teachers among the Estonians, Lithuanians and Macedonians.

3. The leaders of the national movements originated from the lower-middle classes, mainly from the urban environment, but also from rural areas. The urban classes were more prevalent among the Czechs and the Catalans. The Czech intellectuals included a significant proportion of sons of the artisan middle classes. Elsewhere, such as among the Slovenians and Slovaks, patriots from the countryside predominated, and there was a large proportion of sons of pastors among intellectuals from the countryside among the Finnish.

All of this confirms that the professions with the strongest presence among the national movements' activists were those that could be continually joined by members of non-dominant ethnic groups, without their having to undergo assimilation. Therefore, the deciding factors were the social structure of the ethnic group and the opportunities that presented themselves to the members of individual classes and social groups at a given time in terms of upward social mobility and access to education. In cases where the ethnic group's social structure was primarily agrarian and where access to education was limited or costly, activists were drawn mainly from the ranks of the lowest sections of the rural intelligentsia (for example, the teachers among the Estonians and Macedonians). In Catholic countries, where theological education was financed by the church, patriots also included the clergy. In places where the ethnic group consisted of both agrarian and urban populations and where a degree of 'democratisation of access to education' had been accomplished, it was the educated secular intelligentsia who constituted a significant proportion of advocates of the national movement.

What is the significance of this examination of social origins for a deeper analysis of nation-forming processes? It is not merely an intellectual exercise with words and figures. While there is general agreement among researchers that nations were created not as a result of an anonymous natural force but through human efforts, opinions diverge on how influential agitators' personal inventiveness was, and on the significance of the social circumstances from which these players had risen. Reasonably enough, the arguments the protagonists employed in national agitation bore some of their distinctive cultural and social features, which reflected their experiences and social background. This in turn may have affected their national demands and ideas about what national values were, and thus also about the content of national consciousness – 'nationalism'. Moreover, the forms of social communication and activities in favour of the nation varied greatly. We can reasonably assume that the social communication that took place in an aristocratic environment would have been very different from its equivalent in peasant settings. We also know that both celebrations and symbols assumed different forms, depending on whether they had originated in a peasant environment or in that of towns and their educated elites. Many of the socially based national stereotypes, which came into existence during national agitation, were also manifested at later stages, including the mass phase of national movements, as a consequence of which they are often encountered to this day.

Being familiar with the lower social classes, having an understanding of their needs, and being willing and able to approach them are all factors that in most cases distinguished leaders of national movements from the elites of state-nations. This is easily verified by examining their willingness to make democratic principles part of national programmes, and by the intensity with which they sought to win the support of the broad masses for the idea of the nation. It also manifested itself, for example, in their choice of literary works – in the themes and the social environments they covered, both past and present. It would be beneficial to attempt to discover the extent to which social settings affected the way history was perceived, and thus the specific national historical consciousness and collective memory.

The social base of the national movements' leaders must also be taken into account when we consider the interests that lay in the background of national mobilisation – or, more precisely, what motivated the leaders to spread a new national identity. Social analysis will also lead to revelations about these agitators' ability to make use of such relationships and views during phase B as were favourable for the national mobilisation of the members of their ethnic group.

CHAPTER 7

Nationally Relevant Conflicts of Interest

The process of modernisation brought about a number of fundamental changes to the social and political spheres, which in turn had an impact on group interests in societies with a developed division of labour. The aim of this chapter is to study the importance of changes to the relationships among people and states, new conflicts, and different types of conflicting situations for the creation of modern nations. This question also cannot be explained merely by referring to an omnipresent or universally influential 'nationalism'. As before, a differentiation will be drawn based on the fact that the relationship between the interest and power spheres on the one hand, and nation-forming and national consciousness on the other, took on different forms in state-nations and in the context of national movements. This difference is made no less relevant by the truth that the sphere of 'material' interests and the sphere of interests defined as 'national' were both partly a power struggle. 'National interest' had a very different meaning for politicians in state-nations than in multi-ethnic empires, and the struggles for power also differed both in content and form in these two entirely different types of situation. Social and class conflicts within the society of a state-nation that was undergoing modernisation and was ethnically almost homogenous had the potential to act as a disintegrating force in relation to national identity, and to interfere with the unity of the nation. Their effect within multi-ethnic empires was very different.

Struggles for a Place in the Sun: Fighting for Political Power

As had already been stated, most authors refer to nations as political or state entities, or communities that strove to achieve statehood. Although all forms of statehood and politicisation are the outcome and simultaneously also the starting point of a power struggle, very few studies of individual cases of nation-forming, and very few 'theories of nationalism', have concerned themselves with the issue of power. There have only been occasional references to power interests – for example, by Gale Stokes, for whom the key question was how nationalistic rhetoric had made use of people who strove for and had succeeded in gaining power,[1] and by Wolfgang Kaschuba, who considers the 'national construct' to be primarily a political strategy of power and rule.[2] That said, both of these authors merely hinted at the matter. Although Michael Mann addresses the issue of the relationship between a nation and power systematically, he bases his work on the category of social power – an important but only a partial aspect of nation-forming. He states that four elemental sources of social power gradually combined in a nation: ideological power, which predominated in the proto-national phase; commercial capitalism, which encouraged the great powers in pursuing particular economic interests; militarism, with the help of which 'proto-nations' become confident and competing nations; and industrial capitalism, which completed the development and gave rise to economic power struggles.[3] This characterisation is only partially satisfactory, since it is limited to state-nations and gives no consideration to the nation-forming processes of nations without a state. Moreover, it disregards the category of power in a narrower, individualised sense of the word.

Michael Mann is among the few authors whose analysis of power reflects awareness that different social circumstances affected the ways in which it was used. Power had a very different appearance when feudal society still rested upon privileges and repressive regulations, compared to after this society had disintegrated. Civic society opened new possibilities and offered new forms in which power could be employed, especially once the secularisation of public spaces had taken place.

Many authors have refrained from using the term 'power' simply because it has negative connotations and evokes associations with *Machtbesessenheit* and *Machtergreifung* – i.e. it corresponds roughly with Lord Acton's view that 'power tends to corrupt and absolute power corrupts absolutely'. They have avoided the term so as not to offer an implicit negative evaluation of both the process of forming and the very existence of modern nations. However, it is the ambiguity of the term that constitutes a far more important difficulty, together with the fact that, despite its frequent use, attempts to define it have been very rare. The definitions of 'power' provided by the social science literature diverge substantially, which makes it hard to apply them in the context of national issues.[4] In this respect, parallels can be drawn between the terms 'power' and 'nationalism'.

It is not the aim of this chapter to conduct a terminological analysis of how the categories of 'power' and 'nation' mutually relate; let this task be left for a future generation of social scientists. The intention is to draw attention to the importance of this subject and, among existing works, seek those theoretical concepts that help us understand and analyse the conflicting topics lying at the roots of nation-forming processes. Although Max Weber employed the concept of power repeatedly, he considered the term 'amorphous', and preferred the words *Herrschaft* and 'authority'.[5] Nonetheless, his definition of both these terms was too atemporal to make them applicable to nation-forming processes – which, admittedly, he addressed only marginally.[6] Indeed, as far as I am aware, Weber's *Herrschaft* and 'authority' have also not yet been employed by any of the 'theories of nationalism'.

It is easier for historians to work with concepts that take into consideration the varying uses of power over time, such as Popitz's differentiation between five levels of power. The 'sporadic power' of a robber in a forest progresses through the level of 'normative power' towards the creation of a 'power apparatus', and, eventually, 'state power', which claims a monopoly on setting the norms.[7] While we can discuss and apply this model to developments that occurred in the context of the modernisation of state-nations, its applicability to national movements is limited. That being said, not all dimensions of power are relevant to nations and nationalism.

In national communities, power did not gain ground by resorting to repression or force, but rather through 'conditioned power' (John Galbraith), which induced a change in the thinking and decision-making of individuals. In some cases it combined with 'compensatory power', which achieved submission of the members of the nation by offering advantages as compensation.[8] This corresponds with Etzioni's concept of 'persuasive power', exercised not by means of violence but by acting upon emotions, manipulating symbols, and propagating national values.[9] Consideration could be given to whether or not this type of power fits in with Popitz's phase of normative power, since it was not until later that power was institutionalised, incorporating great-power interests in the superior, national or state-national framework.[10] In Marvin E. Olsen's words, this was when the 'overall settings' were being determined, which included the parameters and conditions for further uses of power.[11]

This does not exhaust the issue of the use of power in the national context. Once a stable allocation of positions within the national government is achieved, it opens up the opportunity to exercise another level of power – effective control of state power, i.e. a 'non-decision-making' power, established at the outset, which is a priori opposed to calls for change and even obstructs the adoption of certain decisions.[12] In the circumstances of nation-forming pro-cesses, this form of power hinders the very vision, the idea, of alternative national movements or similar centrifugal processes (as seen from the imperial and state-national perspectives). We are familiar with such applications of power from the attitudes of the governments of state-nations, such as France, or empires, such as Russia and England.

The concept of power addressed so far is that which focuses on individuals and their efforts to assert themselves, institutionalise certain positions and make others follow their will. In addition to this, it should be remembered that power is also a collective and institutionalised phenomenon. In fact, some authors research power as exclusively or predominantly a collective matter. These include Hannah Arendt and, in particular, Michael Mann, for whom social power is chiefly about the relationships between interest groups. Similarly, Karl W. Deutsch characterised power as an 'interaction of organisms' – i.e. as the ability of a certain group of people to impose their will upon others. This is usually related to situations of conflict, when an established system is confronted with forces that are in pursuit of their own interests, seek power, and thereby cause 'dis-order'.[13] This characterisation is just as applicable to internal political struggles within state-nations as to national movements that threaten the existing 'order'.

Steven Lukes took the phenomenon of collective power to the level of mutual interests; the relationship between an individual and collective power struggle is expressed by the question of who repre-sents the interests of the group and what this individual can offer or gain. The term Lukes uses in this context – the 'service conception' of power – is of key importance in the study of nationally motivated power struggles. An individual who seeks power wishes to serve the interests of the group or, in other words, self-identifies with a group and presents his interests as the interests of the whole group.[14] In our context, the service conception of power would have meant a struggle for power that would be used to benefit the interests of the nation or national movement. It did not necessarily imply particular material demands as, according to Niklas Luhmann, a community of interests may be expressed simply, with the help of universally accepted symbols. This enabled a group to draw the same conclusions about the consequences of their attitudes and actions towards new challenges and, in this manner, power became a code for this group.[15]

The group's attitude to power had another specific dimension in the framework of nations. In those cases where a nation had been formed – whether within a state-nation or during a national movement – self-identification with the nation was accompanied by the understanding that the nation had a distinctive personality and specific interests. This personified nation thus responded like a person – i.e. asserted 'its' interests as though they were the interests of individuals of each among its members. In other words, an increase in power or prestige of a nation was meant to be felt by each of its members as an increase in their personal power and prestige. The difficulty is that, in the same way as an individual's power is unthinkable without the presence of other individuals who are subjected to it, the power of a personified nation cannot exist without other nations, similarly subjected to its will. We need not explain that this was an illusion, and that it was the members of political and economic elites who defined 'national interests', based on what the national interests appeared to be to them from their perspective. The assertion of one's power over others in the form of 'national interests' and the subjection of other nations to the will of one's own nation was logically only possible in situations where one entity considered itself to be stronger than another that is, or gives the impression of being, weaker. It was the intertwining of the two concepts – a collective struggle for power on the one hand and the personification of a nation on the other – that later gave rise to aggressive, militant nationalism. This type of nationalism was primarily the product of politicians who headed nation-states, and it was unimportant whether these nation-states had emerged from premodern state-nations or from successful national movements.

This leads us to the question of what role power struggles played in national movements, since we have so far chiefly considered the situation of state-nations. The fundamental difference between the two types of modern nation-forming will also become evident in this respect.

Struggles for power occurred along two axes: horizontal and vertical. The former involved those who regarded themselves as the qualified or traditional holders of state power, i.e. the ruling classes. The latter was a struggle 'from below' – a struggle of reformers, rebels and revolutionaries against those in power. The 'vertical power struggle' predominated in national movements, placing them alongside reformist and revolutionary struggles. It was not until phase C that power struggles in national movements also began to occur along the horizontal line, and even then it was more of a struggle among the potential rather than actual holders of power.

The need to self-identify with a new type of a social group (usually called a nation) and the desire for power can be identified as two anthropological constants, whose paths crossed at the start of the development towards a modern society. When this crossing and intertwining took place in the circumstances of a premodern state-nation, the power struggles sooner or later resulted in the state-national society (the hierarchically ordered feudal society or society of estates) transforming into the civic society of a nation-state. Conversely, when the two constants met in a situation of an ethnic community within a territory of a multi-ethnic empire, it led to more or less severe, open-ended clashes. A nation-state was only one of the possible outcomes of the vertically orientated power struggle.

It would be a large oversimplification if all conflicts arising from national movements were immediately and unreservedly ranked as power struggles. The vast majority of national movements at first – i.e. in phases A and B – pursued cultural, linguistic and socially emancipatory goals. While these activities could not bring the leaders of national movements power over others, they could greatly increase their prestige and authority among those who embraced the identity of the forming nation. Of these two terms, authority is sometimes placed within the context of the struggle for power when it is seen as its weaker form: people follow authority because they agree with it and embrace the value system, which this authority offers as their own.[16] Struggles over linguistic and cultural programmes shaped leaders of the nation, who gained a monopoly of intellectual influence within their movement. They became prestigious authorities without immediately benefiting in terms of power or wealth. That said, as was noted by Antonio Gramsci, any earlier interest in achieving hegemony in the cultural and intellectual spheres was later followed by a leading position in struggles for political power.[17] There were only a handful of cases in which the vertical struggle for power emerged at the same time as the struggle for culturally defined prestige. This was found in those national movements that aimed to achieve statehood from the outset, primarily within the Ottoman Empire but also in Norway and Ireland.

All national movements eventually joined the world of power struggles by beginning to formulate political demands. The timing of this usually depended on a concurrence of several circumstances – changes to the political system of the given empire, to the social composition of the leadership of the particular national movement, or to the relationship between the number of the members of a state-nation and of the members of an ethnic group, and so on. The decisive factor was that any focus on a political programme was in essence always a struggle for equal civic rights for the members of the community that was at a disadvantage due to its inferior ethnicity, which makes it unthinkable to construct an opposition, a 'dichotomy', between 'ethnic' and 'civic' national movements. In central European settings, this contrast is derived from anti-Slavic attacks by German liberals. Friedrich Engels's famous critique also falls within this framework, and was made relevant to the east-European context at the turn of the twentieth century through the radical critique of national movements formulated by the leftist Social Democrats, such as Rosa Luxemburg. As an argument against this critique, it needs to be emphasised that the 1848 revolution, as well as the year 1905, witnessed a collision of two movements, both of which fought the old regime over the implementation of civil emancipation: one within the framework of the ruling nation, the other within the framework of the non-dominant ethnic group. The difficulty was that leaders of national movements in the Habsburg Monarchy regarded national emancipation as an integral part of civil emancipation. In the Russian revolution of 1905, the fighting front against the Tsarist regime contained three alternatives: a pan-Russian constitutional but nationalistic alternative; a pan-Russian class-emancipating, proletarian alternative; and a 'secessionist', nationally liberating struggle of the non-Russian national movements. Although the questions of how they interrelated and whether or not they overlapped are very interesting, answers to them will have to be the subject of a separate comparative analysis.

By demanding the right to participate, which can be seen as either the first step towards or a lower level of the politicisation of national movements, the leaders of these movements began to fight over political power with the existing system of power. Consequently, the attitudes of the ruling elites towards these leaders also changed. For as long as national movements remained focused on cultural and linguistic demands alone, they did not threaten the monopoly of power enjoyed by the elites of the multi-ethnic empires. This is the reason why the activities of such movements were often graciously tolerated by the ruling parties, whether these took the form of a surviving feudal regime, such as in Russia and Austria prior to March 1861, or a liberal regime, such as in Britain, Spain after 1873, or Austria after 1861.

As long as leaders of national movements were orientated to culture – and thus prestige – they did not jeopardise the monopoly of power of the empires' ruling elites. This is because prestige, constrained by the boundaries of one's own ethnic group, could be spread to other people almost limitlessly. It could also be increased without harming the interests of those who ruled the empire. Being graciously tolerated by the ruling parties usually came to an end once leaders of national movements had begun to call for partial autonomy or an opportunity to hold key posts – i.e. for a share of political power. It became evident that the powers-that-be would have to share their power with the leaders of national movements: political power cannot be increased freely within one and the same state entity, and positions of power have to be shared. An increase in the share of power in favour of these who had so far been powerless would lead to a decrease in the share of power among those who had enjoyed exclusive access to it.

The politicisation of national movements gave rise to two diametrically opposite viewpoints with regard to evaluating them: a perspective 'from above' and a perspective 'from below'. Designating either of them as 'nationalistic' will not help to analyse or understand them. The perspective 'from above' was the view of those who were interested in maintaining the status quo, and whose monopoly of political power in the state came under threat once a given national movement demanded that power be shared.

The perspective 'from below' considered a share in power to be of vital importance for personified nations that did not enjoy full rights but asserted their legitimate desire for life. This is the reason why their leaders perceived the refusal of 'national rights' by those in power as a threat to the very existence of the nation. The rhetoric of the time often presented this as a matter of (national) life or death, and although we can view such attitudes with a critical eye today, we must understand them within their historical context. We need to see them as an aspect of politics, while appreciating the overall context of the real distribution of strength by asking the questions: who was dangerous? Who posed a threat to whom? And who had to defend themselves? Undoubtedly, the Ruthenian-Ukrainian movement posed little danger to the existence of the Polish nation, just as the Czech and Slovenian movements did not jeopardise the existence of the German nation, the Slovak national movement to the Magyar nation, or the Finnish movement to the Russian nation. Conversely, the discourse of that time reveals that the national existence of ethnic communities was considered to be in real danger of assimilation. For the time being, let us put aside the question of whether or not such concerns were justified.

Although national movements threatened neither the national existence of state-nations nor, up to a certain point in time, the existence of empires, they did imply a threat to the state elites' monopoly of power. In Russia, Austria, Spain and Great Britain alike, the elites increasingly self-identified with the idea of a personified nation. When the ruling elites could not employ repression 'from above', such as in Tsarist Russia and the Ottoman Empire, they resorted to various forms of harsh struggles for power. One of the ideological instruments employed in the struggles over maintaining one's superiority of power was to accuse national movements of 'secessionism', undermining the integrity of the state, and egotistical nationalism. These accusations became a stereotype that has survived to the present day: national movements are described as mere regionalism, condemned for contradicting civic principles, being anti-liberal or 'ethnicist'.

Situations of conflict have escalated whenever the political pro-gramme of a given national movement was extended to include demands that the members (more precisely, leaders) of the forming nation be allowed to make decisions about their own affairs more of less independently of the central authority of the state or empire. A programme of autonomy thus came into being that was based on the belief that the political power of the centre should be minimised within a territory that national leaders had defined as belonging to 'their own' nation.

The difficulty was that, in the process of defining any of these potentially autonomous territories, the principle of the historical border collided with the reality of ethnic borders. No territory could be demarcated as compact, inhabited solely by members of one ethnic community. In the Czech lands as defined by the historical border, there was a large German minority; in the Kingdom of Hungary the members of the self-nominated ruling nation, the ethnic Magyars, were even a minority among the population. Similarly, there was a large Protestant minority in Ireland, a Serbian minority in Croatia, a Swedish minority in Finland, and a Castilian minority in Catalonia and the Basque country. Power struggles in autonomous territories were complicated by simple election arith-metic, which placed the members of the ruling nation in the position of a minority within these potentially autonomous entities. This inevitably led to the escalation of power struggles, and to defining of new political parties strictly according to the criterion of nationality. The only exception to this was the internationalist socialist move-ment, but even this exception was only temporary, and showed marked local variations.

Struggles over participation initially occurred primarily between the leaders of national movements and the central governments. Where the mass movements succeeded, the horizontal form of power struggle also tended to come to the fore. Although struggles among the leaders within national movements displayed similar character-istics to those among leaders within state-nations, there was an additional characteristic feature: when the conflict with the ruling elites escalated, national arguments also became an important ingre-dient of various ideologies during the power struggles inside the national movement itself. It became a part of daily political folklore to emphasise one's merit with regard to the nation and accuse political rivals of not being sufficiently devoted to the national interest. A common consequence was a nationalistic escalation of political rhetoric, as no one wished to risk losing their share of political power. Despite this, even in their phase C most national movements did not demand a complete secession and creation of their own national state until World War I. This empirical fact proves the fallaciousness of the stereotypical notion of most Anglo-Saxon authors who have been unable to imagine a 'nation' without its association with 'statehood'.

Political power struggles were thus a major aspect of conflicts of interest, which were made relevant by being turned into national conflicts and becoming a part of national emancipation. Disputes between states which are addressed in the next section, were also justified in national terms, but this by no means implies that nationally relevant conflicts can be seen merely as political struggles and struggles between states. Struggle 'for a place in the sun' could also procede as struggle for social, economic or cultural interests.

Conflicts Between States and Nations

Conflicts of interest that had existed between European states from the medieval to early modern periods are one of the historical legacies of our continent, and inevitably influenced international relations in the nineteenth century. Stereotypical images of enemies, expressed in 'national' terms, survived until the period of modern nation-forming. The situation is relatively easy to understand and describe for those authors whose scope of research allows for the 'modern nation' and the 'state' to blend into each other. According to Étienne Balibar and Immanuel Wallerstein, for instance, if a group at the head of a state needs to assert its interests against a group standing outside the state, it achieves this goal by deploying nationalistic sentiments. The instability in the hierarchical system of international relations has provided fertile ground for the search for an ideology that would justify efforts to maintain one's superiority of power over another state, as well as efforts to weaken such superiority. The ideology of nationalism has proved best suited to serve this need.[18] So-called nationalism is thus not the cause of conflicts, but a label referring to conflicting group interests. However, such a shift in the usage of the term was naturally only possible in situations in which nations were already in existence, whether in the stage of state-nations or nation-states.

The subject or source of nationally defined conflicts between states was not limited to endeavours to alter the international distribution of power to the benefit of some and the detriment of others. There were also territorial reasons: conflicts over borders, calls to revise them, and conflicts over positions in the colonies. That being said, conflicts over borders were initially not very common in Europe after the end of the Napoleonic wars, and became a source of nationalistically formulated conflicts only in two regions. In central Europe, these took the form Italian claims towards Austria and German claims towards France and Denmark (besides the already completed annexation of parts of Poland). In the Balkans, the non-existence of historical borders meant that territorial disputes became a source of conflict among all new nation-states. Although the twentieth century witnessed an increase in both the number and intensity of border disputes among nation-states, this occurred at a time when these states had already been established in most parts of Europe. Therefore, border disputes of the twentieth century cannot be superimposed onto the previous century as a factor that was relevant to modern nation-forming. This does not call into question their role in the escalation of nationalism in the twentieth century.

Conflicts over territory also arose between states without a common border within Europe, as in some cases the disputed territories were in the colonies. The roots of British–French disputes lay in colonial conflicts of the mid eighteenth century, while for a long time colonial interests dictated Spanish foreign policy. The 'belated' colonial expansion of Germany and Italy became a real threat to the stability of the hierarchical relationships among state-nations. Overseas expansion eventually became a factor in national mobilisation (but not in the nation-forming processes) in all of these cases.

The nation-forming function of inter-state conflicts is not only commonly associated with colonial expansion, but also chiefly with war. Charles Tilly expressed the relationship between 'war' and 'state' aptly: 'war makes the state and the state makes war'. The important role of war and international disputes in the strengthening of national identity is emphasised by many authors, including Linda Colley, Anthony Smith and William Bloom.[19] Their perception of war is that it was a factor that mobilised, rather than created, national identity.

A rather more radical view is advocated by several German researchers, in particular Dieter Langewiesche, according to whom a nation is always implicitly linked with war, since nationalism (as he understands the term) has always contained elements of hatred towards other nations.[20] However, this is a very one-sided view from the perspective of a great power, if not a specifically 'German' view, and it is doubtful whether such a connection is verifiable as a universally European phenomenon. One can hardly conceive of an attack by Norway against Great Britain, Estonia against Russia, the Netherlands against Germany, Portugal against Spain – and so on. Nonetheless, this does not change the fact that, even without real war conflicts, both the fiction of the 'age-old' enemy and the myth of a national threat had formed part of a reservoir of stereotypes and other emotional aspects of national mobilisation.

Scholars, who replaced the term 'nation' with 'nationalism', have been able to describe the relationship between war and nationalism as organic, or even inevitable, since nationalism manifested itself in all wars – not only in the ideology of the ruling elites but also in the mentality of ordinary soldiers. However, this relationship is indicative of the later consequences, and not the causes, of modern nation-forming, which are the subject of our analysis. It is another example of how misleading a mechanical and stereotypical use of the term 'nationalism' can be.

Admittedly, war played a role in the forming of several European nations, and thus deserves to be considered. The most significant factor for the nineteenth century was a change in the way in which wars were conducted. Until the end of the eighteenth century, wars were primarily waged by rulers and their states, which did not rule out the possibility of expressing the interests of the ruler or state in 'national' terms as the last resort, such as during the One Hundred Years' War in France, or the war against the Spanish threat in England in the second half of the sixteenth century. It was not until the French Revolution and Napoleonic times that a real shift occurred towards wars in the name of the nation. The French example inspired the ideology of the 'patriotic' war – i.e. a war in the name of the king and homeland – as was conducted successfully in Prussia at the end of the Napoleonic wars and unsuccessfully in Austria in 1808–09. The symptomatic difference was that the war waged in the name of the dynastically defined homeland was more easily transformed into a war in the name of the nation – or, more precisely, the nation-state – in the relatively ethnically homogenous Prussia. Such a change in perception was inconceivable in multi-ethnic Austria, as is well illustrated by the fact that World War I was still primarily a war 'for the Emperor' in the Habsburg Monarchy. Spain and Russia are other examples in which the shift to a 'national' war against Napoleon is commonly observed.

The notion that a war was a significant cause of nation-forming is far from universally valid. It applies to some state-nations (France) and to new nation-states, which characteristically emerged due to a war or, in some cases, a series of wars. Wars opened the door to Italian and German national unity, and brought an end to Ottoman rule over Greek, Serbian and Bulgarian populations. That being said, wars accompanied not the beginning but the end of the long process of the forming of the Italian and German nations, both of which had been fully formed as regards society and culture. Therefore, only wars in the Balkans were 'nation-forming' in the true sense of the word, and can thus be described as a specific form of mass national movement.

The empirical basis for the view that war was an inevitable cause of modern nation-forming is sparse. The process of modern nation-forming tended to occur by peaceful means, and a war with an external enemy only played a role in the cases mentioned above – i.e. on relatively rare occasions. References to the national ideology of the twentieth-century wars do not stand the test of scrutiny: as has already been stated, those wars were a consequence, not a cause, of the existence of modern nations. Although aggressive nationalism was undoubtedly part of the ideology of conflict in the nineteenth and twentieth centuries, using it to explain the general, binding causal relationship between war and nation-forming in such a manner brings no benefit, and is essentially merely a rhetorical gesture.

Similarly, we cannot draw simple generalisations when examining the influence of nationally motivated conflicts on the national mobilisation of the populations in the old state-nations. Although it holds true that British colonial expansion, as well as French revanchism against Germany, had a major impact on the national mobilisation of the respective peoples, does the same apply for the other state-nations? It is a known fact that the Cuban war had an impact on the crisis – i.e. mobilisation – of Spanish national identity. However, it is very unlikely that the loss of Belgium that resulted from the 1830 revolution was significant for national mobilisation in the Netherlands. While disputes with the Norwegians may have irritated the Conservative section of Swedish politicians within the union, they were of marginal importance in the context of all the Swedes. Conversely, the defeat in the war over the Schleswig-Holstein territory was an important, albeit not the sole, trigger for the transformation of Danish identity from imperial to national.

Besides the contradictory relationship between two equally powerful states or nations, we also need to take into consideration the relationship between a stronger state and its weaker counterpart. A threat from a more powerful neighbour influenced national integration by strengthening national identity.[21] This was manifest not only in the Danish case mentioned above, but also in Belgium, where the presence of a strong neighbour in the shape of Germany (and also France) brought about the need for cohesion. The Russian and Habsburg (or more precisely Magyar) proximity had a similar impact on reinforcing Romanian national identity after the influence of the Ottoman Empire had begun to wane.

It is no accident that debates aimed against 'secessionist nationalism' have argued that it involves entities that are not viable – i.e. not able to withstand an attack by a more powerful neighbour. This argument is characteristic of the nineteenth century in that it is based on the notion that attacking a weaker neighbour is a normal occurrence, and fits within the moral code of state-nations. Besides this criticism, there is also the view from the opposite perspective: while the formation or national mobilisation of a strong nation-state posed a threat to its weaker neighbours, the forming of a small nation-state posed no danger to its stronger neighbours. The problem more likely lay in the fact that the ruling state elites refused to accept that they should lose 'their' territories, and that they feared that the new small state would become an instrument or a satellite of someone stronger. Whatever the truth, it is certain that the term 'nationalism' is applicable to all types of contrary attitudes in this context, which will be of little help in allowing us to differentiate and develop a typology of national identities and activities. One solution may be to adopt a narrower definition of nationalism, such as the one employed for instance by John Breuilly, according to whom nationalism is 'a political movement seeking or exercising state power'.[22]

On the basis of all this, we can conclude that it is vital not to fall victim to the misapprehension that has plagued many researchers, and perhaps the entire mainstream of the so-called theories of nationalism – the idea that the modern nation is a consequence of wars due to their connection with aggressive nationalism. Empirical data show that the relationship between these two entities needs to be differentiated. Whereas wars may have led to a stronger sense of internal cohesiveness within the populations of state-nations, and thus strengthened their national identity, this was rarely the case in ethnic communities. If a war occurred at all within the framework of ethnic communities, it was logically only as a consequence of successful nation-forming. In these circumstances, war indeed helped create a few nation-states – primarily in the Balkans. While it undoubtedly also reinforced nationalistic stereotypes, it was not primarily a nation-forming factor.

Uneven Development

The struggle for one's 'place in the sun' also involved struggles over social and economic positions. Therefore, let us turn our attention from inter-state relationships to an analysis of the conflicts of interests within the societies of individual states and empires. We are chiefly interested in those conflicts that played an important role in the national mobilisation of ethnic communities. Conflicts arising from state-national and imperial interests were irrelevant for national movements. Nationally relevant conflicts need to be sought outside the sphere of international relations.

A macro-analytical view was presented by Stein Rokkan, who incorporated nation-forming processes in his complex model of modern state-building. The relationship that is fundamental to this model is found between the centre and the periphery, which exists owing to four ties: the economy, culture, the legal system and the system of political power. In ethnically homogenous settings, the relationship between the centre and periphery acted as an integrating force of a state-nation. Conversely, situations where the periphery was ethnically different from the centre led to tension between the two. The process of nation-forming in the periphery was more intense (and more successful) where it was more interconnected with economic ties (in particular with towns) and culture or, in some cases, with the Church.[23]

While Rokkan's very abstract concept has itself had little influence on empirical research, it can be regarded as the general framework within which a great many authors have made interpretations based on empirical research. Debates about 'internal colonialism' as a source of nationalism, as formulated by the sociologist Michael Hechter on the basis of analysing England's relationship with the other parts of Great Britain, also fall into this framework. According to Hechter, the evolution towards capitalism was accompanied by the creation of an internal unevenness, owing to the division of labour along a cultural line, which had existed between the centre (the core) and the periphery. People in the British periphery were consequently assigned a social role that they perceived as inferior. In addition to this, their local cultural traditions were weakened by the culture of the centre spreading to the periphery. This in turn hindered the homogenisation of the state territory as it strengthened local, ethnically different, cultural policies, and in some cases centrifugal 'nationalisms'.[24]

Many authors embraced this concept, and some also applied it to 'external colonialism', as a factor which reinforced and justified nationalistically expressed resistance to colonial power. The British historian Tom Nairn evaluated this particular role of nationalism as positive.[25] The relationship between the core and the periphery is also the focus of Wallerstein's model, which sees it as the dominant relationship in the capitalist globalising society. Wallerstein and Balibar have advanced the rather thought-provoking thesis of colonialism being a key moment in the nation-forming process: all nations are a product of colonisation, as every one of them either colonised or was colonised by another.[26] The term 'colonisation' of course needs to be understood in this context as a metaphor for a relationship of dependency.

The critique of Hechter's concept was much more fruitful. Although A. W. Orridge, for example, agreed that conflicts of interest played an important role in national mobilisation, he was critical of mechanical explanations based on a lack of development in the periphery. In support of his argument, he pointed out that in many cases the peripheries that became nationally mobilised were those that were the most developed in the context of the whole multi-ethnic state, such as Catalonia and the Basque country. Orridge also proposed that nationalism was not merely a protest against subjection and inferiority, but also an attempt to construct a specific type of a political 'other', which cannot be explained by the relationship between the centre and the periphery.[27]

Based on an extensive comparison of ethnic conflicts, Donald Horowitz warned that nationalism is supported by disadvantaged groups in the underdeveloped periphery as well as by more advanced groups in more developed regions. Agreeing with this, Hechter modified his theory, defining the key conflict of interest as one that led to a situation in which people supported a nationalist alternative as an outcome only when they expected that their position in the labour market would be enhanced by the creation of a nation-state.[28] Hechter's attempt to use the theory of rational choice in helping to explain nationalism was not generally accepted.

The relationship between the centre and the periphery had a political as well as a social aspect. Alexander Motyl places an emphasis on the power struggle between the political elites who hold power in the centre and the local elites in the periphery. He believes that the bond between the periphery and the centre will remain politically intact as long as the elites at the centre continue to have something to offer to the periphery. In other words, the elites in the periphery will embrace 'secessionism' only once they discover or believe that the centre cannot or will not offer them anything any longer.[29] However, this model assumes that the periphery corresponded with the territory occupied by the ethnic community.

How strong was the motivational potential of the periphery in relation to national mobilisation? It is important to remember that state-nations also had their centres and peripheries, and that the periphery was characterised by a slower national mobilisation in France, England, Denmark and Sweden. At the same time, it must not be overlooked that even peripheries that were occupied by non-dominant ethnic groups always contained regions that were nationally more active, more involved in the national movement, and regions that were nationally more passive. Analyses of the unevenness of the territorial distribution of national activities have been relatively conclusive about the fact that regions participating most actively in national movements in phase B were those with a denser network of schools, stronger and more intensive market ties, and comparatively higher living standards. Conversely, neither the proximity of an ethnic border nor of an industrial or administrative centre appears to have played a nationally mobilising role.[30] We cannot infer a causal relationship between economic underdevelopment and a lower level of national mobilisation. There were many factors at play, and while a higher level of economic development proved integrating in some cases, it was a disintegrating factor in others.[31]

A sense of provincial inferiority had a nationally mobilising effect mainly in those parts of the territory of a given ethnic community that were less peripheral – i.e. in those which formed the 'core' within this provincial territory. This is understandable, since such a position made it possible to state the rights of the province and strive for its emancipation from the centre. Specific reflections on the provincial position and its national interpretation have varied in time and space. National movements that in their phase B focused on cultural demands tended to accept their inferior political and administrative position in the periphery. This changed with the emergence of a mass movement and adoption of a political programme, which called to a greater or lesser extent for equal rights for the province and the centre. The prevailing idea was that a degree of autonomy combined with democratic political participation would reduce the dependence on the centre. Although this programme was gradually adopted by most national movements within the Habsburg Monarchy, it was only partially implemented in the Czech lands, Galicia, Carniola and Croatia once Magyarisation had begun in Hungary.

Unlike in the Habsburg Monarchy, where all the national movements initially accepted the dominance of the political centre, which was simultaneously also dominant both culturally and economically, the situation in Tsarist Russia was more complex. Although Finland and the Baltics respected the centre's superiority in power, they were not among the economically backward parts of the empire, and were relatively successful in overcoming the political aspect of their provincial position. To an extent, their situation was helped by the fact that both Finland and the Baltic governorates were culturally and economically at a higher level than the average reached by the (Russian) centre. Prior to March 1848, the north-Italian provinces of the Habsburg Monarchy showed a similar cultural, and partly also economic, superiority in relation to the Austrian centre. From the beginning, the Catalan and Basque national movements both occurred within a more developed, richer province against the less developed centre. In contrast to these, Hechter's model of internal colonialism does apply to the Irish national movement, whose position was not dissimilar to that of a colonised province, and where the dominance of the English centre was indisputable in all respects.

The position on the periphery did not always have a nationally mobilising effect, as was the case in numerous instances, especially those where a part of the original periphery had become integrated into the centre. Examples of these include south Wales, south Scotland, the Bilbao region, Upper Silesia and, to an extent, Moravia. It must also be remembered that the situation of a region in the periphery could serve as a nationally mobilising factor only when national agitation had achieved a certain level of response from the members of the non-dominant ethnic community. In other words, people needed to become aware of their provincial position before they could understand its 'translation' into the language of a national movement.

In situations of mass national movements, calls for the need to overcome provincial inferiority usually became a political demand: dependence on the centre was to be reduced in the name of civic equality and justice. At the same time – and understandably, in psychological terms – efforts continued to come to terms with being in the position of a province that was weaker, or even failing to develop. Weakness and remoteness were idealised and seen as idyllic. 'Small but pretty' is how one patriotic song describes the Czech homeland, and many other national movements contrasted the unspoilt rural province with the morally corrupted centre. This brings us to the topic of stereotypes.

Conflicts Stemming from Modernisation

Having examined conflicts that arose from struggles over political emancipation and the assertion of civic society, I will now address those nationally relevant conflicts that originated in changes within the social and economic spheres. To what extent were national demands in tune with the struggle for the removal of feudal privileges? To what extent were they inspired by the emergence of new forms of economic and commercial activities, accompanied with an increase in social mobility and the democratisation of education?

It can be theoretically assumed that the conflict between peasants and their landlords – in other words, the drive to emancipate peasants – only became an important factor in nation-forming under particular circumstances. It was chiefly in situations where large landowners and their officials used a state language that peasants could not understand, regardless of whether they were subjects or serfs. It also had nationally integrating consequences in state-nations. The French National Assembly's disposing of feudal obligations is symbolic proof that the implementation of modern national solidarity was inconceivable without the principle of citizenship – i.e. without eliminating privileges and emancipating the peasants. Although such a harmonious concurrence was rare, it can serve as a model: neither political emancipation nor the transformation of an absolutist state-nation into a modern nation could be realised without freeing the peasants. This is not to imply that, by being freed, peasants were automatically fully integrated into the national community. Although they were aware of belonging to a state-nation, this did not automatically lead to their cultural or political self-identification with the nation and its interests. As has already been pointed out, peasants were not among the 'key players' of public life in state-nations until much later, when they often stood in opposition to the increasing power of the state and to modernisation.

Although the conflict between peasants and their landlords had a very different impact in the context of national movements, it cannot be claimed that it had a nationally mobilising effect in all of them, or from the outset. The peasant uprising in the Czech lands in 1775, for example, presented no national or ethnic demands, and involved both Czech- and German-speaking countrymen. The unrest of Estonian serfs at the end of the 1850s had only social goals, and there were similar tendencies in Latvia. Although Ruthenian peasants in eastern Galicia murdered many Polish aristocrats during the uprising in 1846, their motivation was social and lacked a national ideology. Viewed from the opposite perspective, the Hungarian aristocrats, who around 1790 demanded that Magyar be the official language, also protested against the abolition of serfdom.

The Polish national struggle in the first half of the nineteenth century paid only marginal attention to the economic situation of Polish peasants, or to bringing them freedom and political emancipation.

This situation changed with time. Leaders of national movements eventually realised that their success was dependent on gaining the support of the peasantry, which formed the core of the non-dominant ethnic group. At the Hungarian Diet in 1827, the patriotic magnate István Széchenyi urged that the peasantry should be freed and given equal civic rights. Czech patriots called for the abolition of serfdom in the 1840s, and by 1848 Czech village petitions included linguistic as well as social and political demands. By then, purposeful efforts at mobilising the Ruthenian (Ukrainian) peasants had commenced in eastern Galicia, and were to prove fruitful within a few decades. The national movement with an anti-Polish orientation presented itself as representative of peasant interests with success. The speed with which Estonian national agitation succeeded during the 1870s is often attributed to the fact that the radical wing among the patriots made the freeing of the peasants from rule by German landowners the priority of the agenda. At the other end of Europe, Irish national agitation managed to win mass support only when demands for Home Rule were included in the programme, addressing the plight of impoverished Irish tenants.

In some cases, other interests can be found behind the national mobilisation of the countryside. The central role that Lithuanian farmers played in the national movement tends to be explained by their resentment towards Polish-Jewish towns (and towards their economic superiority) rather than towards the Polish aristocracy. Similarly, the national mobilisation of Slovenian peasants was mainly motivated by their aversion to the German towns. Finnish farmers were personally free, and the most likely trigger for their national mobilisation was their antipathy towards the Swedish-speaking administration. Characteristically, however, when the Finns sanctioned the introduction of Finnish into schools in 1863, they also sanctioned the abolition of feudal privileges.

Where towns were the epicentres of national agitation and national life was orientated towards the model of an urban life-style, leaders of national movements found it difficult to gain the support of the peasants, particularly when these were not dependent on foreign landowners. For decades, Norwegian farmers were hesitant towards the 'national policy' implemented by state officials and tradesmen. The Flemish national movement did not win the farmers' support until the interwar period; the Croatian, Slovak and initially also Irish national movements also had difficulties. Often, much depended on the attitude adopted by the Catholic clergy towards the national movement.

Which nationally relevant conflicts mobilised people in those national movements in which the urban environment and urban middle classes played the decisive or important role? In this context, the willingness to embrace a national identity was influenced by the conflict between emerging industrial production, which was accompanied by the pressures of a large market, and the interests of traditional crafts and small-scale local trade. This conflict was particularly manifested in the attitudes of Czech artisans and shopkeepers, who felt under threat from the large German-speaking market and the growth of large-scale industrial production. During phase B, this conflict also made itself felt, albeit to a lesser degree, in the Latvian, Slovak and Flemish areas. The mobilising force that manifested itself in such attitudes was thus more of an aversion towards modernisation. With the rise of a mass movement, this conflict of interests transformed into a conflict between Czech, Latvian, Estonian and Slovenian small-scale production – i.e. the small bourgeoisie – and wealthy entrepreneurs, who mainly identified themselves with the ruling nation. This type of tension formed part of the conflict between the economic centre and the less advanced, but modernising province.

A new nationally relevant conflict of interest stemmed from the fact that modernisation created a need for an educated labour force. Although this need was met by broader access to higher levels of education, it was hindered by the fact that upward social mobility continued to be difficult. The new conflict was thus between the opportunity to be educated to a higher level and the chances of social success – i.e. of being able to rise socially. Despite the fact that the democratisation of education occurred with varying degrees of intensity and at very different times across Europe, it always enabled members of the lower classes to gain access to education. It meant that, in multi-ethnic states, secondary and university education became available to members of the non-dominant ethnic groups.

This is a general assumption, based on a comparative analysis of the intelligentsia's social background (see Figure 1).

Nationally relevant conflicts of interest arose whenever the new intelligentsia's endeavour to succeed professionally caused social difficulties. Norwegian patriots expressed concern in 1814 about officials from Denmark and Sweden continuing to take posts in Norwegian administration, thereby crowding out local applicants – graduates from the newly founded university in Oslo. In the 1830s, Czech university graduates made complaints about their difficulties in securing appropriate positions, caused by their being Czech. At the end of the 1850s, after the children of Estonian and Latvian families had been granted permission to study at the university of Dorpat (Tartu), there were growing numbers of university-educated Estonians and Latvians who, unable to earn a living at home, were forced to move to distant Russian towns to find work. Lithuanian university graduates were in a similar situation. The complaints presented by the Flemish movement in 1859 included objections to the unequal footing of the Flemish in relation to gaining posts in state administration. It is understandable that such situations opened the hearts and minds of young intellectuals to national agitation, which offered a new national identity, in the name of equal rights, to the members of all nations.[32]

In this context, the democratisation of education can be regarded as counterproductive from the point of view of the old regimes and their elites. As access to education was extended to members of non-dominant ethnic groups, the numbers of university-educated intelligentsia grew. However, since the ruling elites continued to be replenished from within their own ranks, the new intelligentsia was appointed to inferior, less well-paid posts or none at all. Unsurprisingly, demands for a fair allocation of posts of authority and an introduction of the non-dominant group's language into the state administration had already been incorporated into the national programme during the phase of national agitation. Later, during the mass national movement, these demands acquired a distinctly political charge.

Last but not least, we need to address the role of class conflict, of which, in a capitalist society, the classic case is considered to be the conflict between workers and entrepreneurs. This topic has been studied extensively in literature and, for the purposes of this book, it suffices to note only its main characteristics. In a state-nation, the workers' movement was understandably a threat to its internal stability – a 'national enemy' – whose existence was often not foreseen by the ruling elites in the process of nation-forming. In contrast, in a multi-ethnic empire the conflict between the worker and the entrepreneur could become nationally mobilising if the latter belonged to the elites of the ruling nation. Social Democratic Internationalism, which was based on the idea that workers of different nations were closer to each other than to their respective 'national' bourgeoisie, did not become part of practical politics, and encountered long-term success only within the programme of the Bolshevik Party.

The degree to which workers were open to adopting the national identity – i.e. the speed with which they were incorporated into the national community – depended on whether the national movements attempted to integrate them before the rise of the Social Democratic movement. Leaders of workers who had become politically self-aware before the workers were integrated into a national movement adopted internationalist attitudes much more readily, and consequently often found themselves in conflict with their own national movement (Latvian, Finnish or Basque, for example). In contrast, the influence of internationalism was much weaker where leaders of national movements had engaged with the workers before the workers' political movement emerged (such as in the Czech lands and Ireland). The acknowledgment of national distinctness gradually permeated most workers' parties, and their leaders accepted the notion of national emancipation by the time of the Second International. In areas that continued to be unaffected by industrialisation during the mass phase of the national movement, internationalism had no significant influence on these movements, remaining the preserve of small groups of intellectuals.

In conclusion, it can be stated that nationally relevant conflicts of interest were among the fundamental prerequisites for national mobilisation, and were the main driving force behind nation-formation under the conditions of national movements. These conflicts were not necessarily verbalised and many of them were presented under a 'false label'. However, those concerned gradually became aware of the correlation between their social standing and their national or ethnic difference. This is why a system of transmission was created through which conflicts of interest or social and political tensions were articulated within the language of national demands and national interests. Since this transmission usually involved no feedback, the 'national version' of the conflict of interest was eventually able to break away from its original economic, social or political context and stand alone. This in turn led to national stereotypes, and to 'national interests' being made sacred, regardless of how realistic their background was.

Nevertheless, with the possible exception of political power struggles, the impact of nationally relevant conflicts cannot be studied as something inevitable and automatic. Their effectiveness was dependent on a whole range of other circumstances – in particular, the crisis of identities that combined with critical developments in the social, economic and political spheres. Other relevant factors were the level of intensity of social communication, without which the 'national versions' of the conflicts of interest would not have spread, and certain basic political conditions, which needed to exist for this spreading to take place. Conflicts also combined and accumulated: several nationally relevant conflicts – besides the ubiquitous struggles for prestige and power – can be detected in all nation-forming processes. I venture to formulate the preliminary hypothesis that the greater the number of nationally relevant conflicts that accumulated in the setting of a national movement, the faster the success of national agitation.

As stated at the beginning, the national relevance of conflicts of interest differed in state-nations and in national movements. Social conflicts, which could prove nationally mobilising in the circumstances of national movements, could have the opposite effect in state-nations by threatening their national integrity. This holds equally true for efforts to free the peasants and for the workers' question. Limited opportunities of upward mobility among the intelligentsia could be presented as a national conflict in the Czech setting, whereas in France the effects of this same issue could be political and social, but not national. Conflicts that were more likely to be internally divisive in relation to the national society of state-nations served as a nationally mobilising factor in the circumstances of national movements.

With some exaggeration, it can be said that social and sometimes also regional conflicts slowed down national integration in state-nations, whereas they achieved the opposite within national movements. When these conflicts occurred, the circumstances of national movements offered more favourable conditions for national integration than those of state-nations. It is also in this context that we need to seek explanations as to why national mass mobilisation in France and Sweden, for instance, required significantly more time than in Norway, the Czech lands and Serbia.

There is another side to this issue. With regard to nationally relevant conflicts in state-nations, national integration was dominated by their relationship with other states or nations. In state-nations, political power was held by groups and individuals, who justifiably considered it necessary to ensure national coherence. This is one reason why national education and other activities fostering national confidence received extensive support from the state power during modernisation reforms. They admittedly also possessed greater power and financial resources than members of national movements. This is also why state-nations emphasised the moments of an external threat to national existence more often than national movements. This form of national mobilisation tended to be accompanied by aggressive nationalism, and sometimes also by the politics of war.

This differentiation is not meant to produce a dichotomous, value-laden distinction between two types of nation-forming: the peace-loving approach of national movements and the expansive, aggressive approach of state-nations. Firstly, such a dichotomy would be far from the truth, as was demonstrated by the bloody conflicts connected with the forming of nation-states in the Balkans. Secondly, it would disregard the evolutionary nature of national movements – i.e. the differences in the mentalities and the forms of national struggles between the agitation phase B and the mass phase C. Oppression by the ruling state-national apparatus encountered political resistance only after struggles over power had come to the fore – i.e. during phase C. This is also the moment when conditions had become suitable for aggressive nationalism. The closer a national movement came to achieving national autonomy, let alone statehood, the greater the tendency to imitate the forms of national agitation employed by state-nations. This manifested itself in copying their forms of organisation, symbols and celebrations, as well as in adopting their self-confidence and aggression.

CHAPTER 8

National Myths and the Search for a Common Destiny

A national history was one of the main arguments commonly used in the nineteenth century to achieve mobilization (and civic education) of one's national group, and to justify one's ethnic group's right to exist as a nation. Despite this, opinions about the significance of history for modern nations and nationalism differed greatly.

There was agreement on the 'perennialist' idea of a nation, and that the past was thus the decisive criterion of a nation's existence. An important question is what this past entailed. When history stood for political history, as was the prevailing tendency within traditional historiography, the existence of state-nations was easily explained by the continuity of their political history. From this perspective, the French, Swedish and Dutch nations existed simply because they each had their own state-national history. The German nation 'obtained' its history by means of adoption, or, rather, national adaptation of the Holy Roman Empire (of the German Nation). 'Having one's own history' meant existing as an indisputable entity in a historical continuity, and this concept did not originate in modernization. It was clearly a relic of the premodern, feudal mentality, according to which the right to anything rested on old privileges. The older a state, a dynasty or an aristocratic family was, the more prestigious or noble it was considered to be.

Another acceptable argument in favour of a nation's existence was its former, medieval statehood, which had only recently been interrupted by external circumstances. This, however, posed difficulties in deciding what lapse of time and what degree of loss of independence were admissible. The circumstances under which the given medieval state had lost its sovereignty came to be seen as crucial.

This traditionalist approach gave rise to the already-mentioned differentiation between 'historical' and 'unhistorical' nations during the mid-nineteenth-century struggles for national demands.[1] The existence of historical nations was justified by a history of statehood (albeit limited), which made them historically legitimate. Unhistorical nations lacked a political tradition, and thus also a 'history'. The historical argument was accepted by international public opinion especially in the case of Poland, which was being destroyed by its neighbouring powers. Discontinued statehood was also regarded as a viable argument in the struggles over the formation of the Hungarian and Croatian nations. In contrast, the continuity of statehood was usually called into question in the Czech case (the Lands of the Bohemian Crown had been part of the Holy Roman Empire) and in the Scottish case (due to the Union of 1707). On the other hand, statehood could not serve as an argument employed by political history in places where nation-forming took place within ethnic groups with no adaptable state tradition, such as the Finns, Latvians and Slovenians.

It is true that most scholars nowadays no longer share the opinion of the German (and not only German) Liberals of the 1848 revolution that only 'historical nations' have the right to be generally recognised. However, present-day 'Western' research still sometimes continues to indicate latent doubts as to whether the formation of the nations, which had once been labelled 'unhistorical', was truly legitimate and 'organic'. To this day, it is relatively common to ask whether the existence of several nation-states was the 'necessary' outcome of historical developments or merely a random coincidence. It is almost as though 'small nations' were contrary to the general progression from a state to a nation. This subtly sceptical factor tends mostly to appear in works addressing 'east-European' nations.[2] It also used to be the implicit outcome of older comparative works and overviews of European nations and their creation, in that they automatically limited their scope solely to 'historical' nations.[3]

Political history – the state's history – is seen as crucially important especially by authors who define a nation by reference to the state, and thus understand nationalism to mean a struggle for an independent state or a strengthening of the state. Breuilly's basic typology is based on differentiating between the forms of state that 'nationalism' originated in. In relation to the past, he then contrasts the English and French 'national ideology' with the 'unification nationalism' of the Germans, Italians and the Polish, and the 'separatist nationalism' of the Czechs and Hungarians (Magyars).[4] According to Rokkan, a state-nation emerged from a historical core, which retained its privileged or more advantageous position over the other inhabitants of the state province even after the civic society and state were formed.[5] Josep R. Llobera and several other authors also stress the significance of the political development of a state, albeit in close connection with other factors. Even Frederik Barth's emphasis on the importance of borders reflects a state-historical angle.[6]

Admittedly, political borders are only one of the factors that Barth employs in his ethnically (and historically) based definition of a nation. Moreover, the prevailing belief today, among non-historians in particular, is that nation-forming processes were affected not only by political history but also by social and cultural history, together with so-called value systems. Indeed, it was this concept that served as a foundation of Friedrich Meinecke's differentiation between 'state' and 'cultural' nations at the turn of the twentieth century, and of Otto Bauer's construct of the elemental stages of the evolution towards a nation – from a nation of knights to one of townsfolk and scholars, all the way to the socialist nation of the future. Lamprecht's understanding of the evolution of national consciousness also dates back to the same period.[7]

Since the mid twentieth century, numerous scholars have stressed the importance of national consciousness and 'nationalism', and have consequently broadened their perspective by also including the 'unhistorical nations'. The idea that modern nationalism is a natural outcome of the evolution of nationalism since ancient times is characteristic of Hans Kohn. It proved influential and was shared by many other authors at the time. An interest in ethnic groups and 'small nations' forms an organic part, if not the starting point, of Anthony Smith's theories.[8] Adrian Hastings, like Smith, considers nations to have their premodern roots in a broad range of traditional attitudes, and criticises authors who associate 'nation' and 'nationalism' almost solely with the nineteenth century.[9] The view that modern nations are a result of the evolution of societies and cultures (and therefore also of ethnic groups) since the Middle Ages is used as a methodological starting point in most attempts to construct national histories, evidence for which is presented in the second part of this chapter.

Since World War II, and especially the 1970s, the concept of the importance of history has shifted from 'objectively existing' historical events, institutions and traditions to memories of the past and 'invented traditions'.[10] In the context of this concept, it is essential to distinguish between two versions.

One assumption is that modern nationalism developed, with a greater or lesser degree of continuity, from premodern memories of the national past; the past continued to live primarily as a collective memory, often connected to particular locations.[11] This memory was a continuation of even earlier manifestations of identification with a nation, which some authors refer to as 'protonationalism'.[12] Whether there was continuity within this development, or whether awareness of it was interrupted in the early modern period, remains a subject of discussion. A popularly held view is that the nationally defined historical consciousness of the late medieval and early modern periods had a very limited social base – the aristocracy everywhere, and townspeople in some areas.

The other assumption, which has gained ground in recent years, deploys Ernest Renan and Eric Hobsbawm's term 'invented tradition', and states that the advocates of modern nationalism 'invented' the histories of their nations in a way that suited their ideas about national characteristics and the nation's interests. This concept makes historical reality redundant, and what becomes decisively important are the ('nationalistic') intentions of the historian who 'creates' the nation by telling stories about its past. Historical narrative was often reduced to 'myth' – an instrumentalised use of history for the purpose of educating and disciplining one's own nationals, and potentially also as an argument against the national enemy. Nevertheless, it should be borne in mind that some authors use the term 'myth' synonymously with 'historical narrative'.

The next part of this chapter will focus mainly on the aspect of 'collective memory', which characterised determined efforts linked to the concept or construction of national histories. The term 'national myth' is used in this book to refer to the narrating of the one story that played a crucial role in national identification, with no attempt having been made to confirm its veracity. The term 'construction of national history' will be used in cases involving a comprehensive approach – i.e. narrating the nation's history from its formation to the present day. History was employed in searching both for a common origin and for connections, which had not only bound the members of a nation together in the past but were able to appeal to them in the present. Expectations of what image the forming nations had or should have, and ideas about the nation's interests and national enemies, must have been important. The historiographical tradition – the manner in which earlier interpretations of the past had, with more or less continuity, depicted the 'national' history of a given political entity, ethnic group or nation until the nineteenth century – was another influence.

Historical consciousness formed a bridge between the search for a nation's past and the realities of its current life. This term is used here to encompass all the visions and knowledge of the past that formed part of the thinking of the members of national groups at the time, and which lay (or oscillated) between two extremes. At one end of the spectrum there were myths and notions about the past that were vague, uncritical, often unverifiable, and usually undated. At the other end of the spectrum lay critical knowledge that aimed to present the national entity's past as systematically and truthfully as the historical science of the time allowed. For our purposes, this polarity can be seen as a tension between scientific narratives (attempts to construct national histories by means of critical scientific research and conclusions) and mythology (the purposeful adoption and creation of national narratives).

Some scholars draw attention to the semantic and rhetorical legacies of the past. The term 'nation' acquired a positive connotation and a mobilising quality during the early modern period, especially in state-nations (such as England and Holland) when they faced external threat.[13] As has been noted, modern national consciousness had also been historically affected by *patria* – the term for homeland, which had become a normative category by the late medieval period. It took on a new meaning during the Enlightenment, when patriotism in England, Holland and Germany became the forerunner of struggles for reforms aiming to implement civic principles, which later characterised the understanding of the term 'modern nation'.[14]

Scientific History as an Argument

Work on national histories was dictated by two key transformations that occurred in Europe in the nineteenth century, mutually influencing each other. One of these transformations constituted a social process – the forming of a modern nation – while the other affected the sphere of intellectual production and witnessed the birth of scientific historiography. Present-day observers tend to regard the developments of the medieval and early modern periods as distant 'prehistory' but, for the main players in national struggles and historians of those times, events from this distant past formed an organic part of their present and, conversely, their present was an integral part of history.[15] This was a typical and, to some extent, inevitable perspective both among the members of state-nations and among the advocates of national movements in ethnic groups that either already had or were developing an awareness of a common origin.

However, the importance of history in nation-forming did not reside solely in this sense of immediate historical continuity (the extent to which it was fictitious is irrelevant at this point). It had deeper causes in the general context of the evolution of people's ideas about the world and the transformation of value systems. Let us start with the generally accepted fact that the nineteenth century was a century of historical science – i.e. a century during which historical truth stood at the forefront of the widely accepted value system. It was expected that a correct and accurate understanding of past events would acquire generally accepted authority, and would thus serve as an effective argument for the present. This authority was represented and maintained by an area of study that was professionally qualified and 'predestined' to pursue historical truth: history; and, with it, historians.

By the early nineteenth century, many scholars and members of the elites agreed that everything that existed – all entities, institutions and even visions, that demanded general recognition – had to express and justify their right to exist (i.e. their right to be recognised as viable) by means of history. Such superiority of extant 'rights' was not a new phenomenon, but a modification of the legacy of the old feudal society's regulations.

It must be remembered that history possessed another instrument that inspired human activity: the ideas and value systems of Greek and Roman antiquity popularly adopted by scholars. The successful rise of humanistic grammar schools during the nineteenth century, and the knowledge of classical languages, made topics from antiquity part of European scholars' everyday lives. Antique virtues – which included not only bravery and truthfulness, but also the love of the motherland and a willingness to die for it in the way Greek and Roman heroes had done – inevitably pervaded their thinking and sense of morals.

All this did not mean, however, that history was the exclusive domain of conservatives endeavouring to preserve the old order. All movements that in their essence sought to dismantle the status quo and move beyond the old order sought their own historical legitimacy. This was the case of national movements, which concern us in this book, but also of revolutionary and social movements – one need only consider the Jacobins' adaptation of antiquity or the central role of the historical argument in the *Communist Manifesto*, claiming that 'all history is the history of class struggle'. The importance of historical argument, and thus also scientific history, for national movements was predetermined by the primordial and perennial concepts of the term 'nation'. If a nation had existed since at least the Middle Ages, even if it happened to have been suppressed, subdued or divided, its very existence was an embodiment of history. The older the nation could prove to be (with the help of its historians), the greater its prestige and the weight of its demands.

Where the modern nation was formed within a stabilised state-nation that had existed continuously since late medieval times, such as France, Sweden and England, the correspondence between the 'age-old nation of the past' and the 'civic nation of the future' was regarded as valid in its entirety, and not questioned. The situation was more complex where nation-forming occurred by means of a national movement, and a modern nation was created from a non-dominant ethnic group. In these circumstances, the national movement needed to prove its nation's age-old existence – hence the already mentioned mid-nineteenth-century dispute over 'historical' versus 'unhistorical' nations.

Even though the terminology has changed, this disagreement lives on, as can be seen from the lack of understanding and dismissive attitudes among members of 'historical' nations towards the demands and objectives pursued by nations 'without history', both in the past and, in some cases, still today. Admittedly, not all 'historical' nations' histories were seen as equally important or valuable and, moreover, the growing influence of the constructivist concept of the term 'nation' fostered the idea that the construction of national histories was merely an instrument of political interests, and that its 'scientific' ambitions served as a disguise for these interests.[16]

In order to appreciate fully how significant, and simultaneously misleading, this requirement was in order to prove the 'historical' nature of a nation's existence, we must remind ourselves, once again, of the fact that, throughout the whole of the nineteenth century, the vast majority of historians and the 'public opinion' of European society equated history with political history. Statehood, or the existence of at least some forms and manifestations of political life and public activity, therefore constituted history's main content, and political developments were thus the prime, if not the only, object of historical knowledge. Political history bore witness to the fortunes of the given people's nation (and, in a figurative sense, their personal fates), which were not necessarily the fortunes of a triumphant state – i.e. a state-nation making a claim to be a super power, or to political, military or other achievements. Both victorious battles and tragic defeats could have a nationally integrating effect; past national failures could become a challenge for the present.

For the successful and powerful state-nations, 'national interests' soon grew to encompass the vision of the (French, British, Spanish or German) 'civilisational mission', both as an integral part of and an excuse for expansion. In some cases it became a recurrent theme within the national history – as is evident in German historiography, for example, which not only in the nineteenth but also in the twentieth century advocated the notion that the Germans were (and still are) the 'bearers of culture' among the Slavic peoples in Eastern Europe.[17]

National history also assumed a very different form by depicting the plight of the members of a nation that had been defeated, oppressed and stripped of its 'rights', whose history was dominated by the theme of defending itself against an external, more powerful enemy or struggling for the rectification of injustices. Logically, this alternative could only be employed by the leaders of national movements if 'their' statehood had been interrupted or disrupted by adverse circumstances, such as in the Czech, Hungarian, Norwegian and Croatian cases.

When national movements had no political history to turn to, attempts soon emerged to replace the absence of political history with themes related to cultural history; national identity was interpreted as a result of achievements and innovations in the cultural sphere. Social history was used in the construction of national histories mainly in places that had developed a distinctive system of (positive or negative) social dependences that could be given national attributes. These included anything from the social oppression of the Estonian serfs by the German aristocracy to the free Finnish peasants struggling against the harsh Nordic climate.

Everyday political experiences in the nineteenth century taught citizens (historians included) that no nation existed in isolation – i.e. isolated from other nations. Consequently, learning about one's national history could not be limited to one's own nation alone. National histories were written in relation to the histories of the neighbouring nations, particularly those to which a given national historical argument made references, serving as a justification for the national programme. This applied not only to the 'large' nations, where this aspect of national histories was represented mainly by their foreign policy, expansion and war, but also to the nations that had only just embarked on defining their 'historicalness' and its recognition. English history defined itself primarily in relation to French history, similarly to the way in which German history repeatedly related to France as the main source of threat. Correspondingly, Czech history was inevitably interlinked with German history, Finnish with Swedish (and later Russian) history, Slovak with Hungarian and Czech histories, and Ukrainian with Polish and Russian histories.

There were two approaches to placing a given national history in its wider context. The first approach involved comparing the nation with those nations considered 'typical' at the time, and thereby ascertaining the extent to which its national evolution was distinctive. In the second approach, national history was compared with the accepted set of attributes that characterised a nation – i.e. with an ideal type of national evolution, which could only be constructed on the basis of the knowledge of at least several other national histories. The two approaches overlapped, and both aimed to reveal the distinctive features, as the fundamental argument in favour of a nation's right to exist was its historically proven distinctness.

A number of more general modernisation changes affected social thinking, and added to the significance of national histories. It was mainly the historicist revolution – a consequence of a fundamental shift in the way society and its evolution were viewed – within which the Enlightenment notion of society proved most influential. It saw individuals and groups as outcomes of sequences of events that were inevitable, and therefore foretold further developments. From this point of view, the forming of modern nations was an inevitable progression.

Another general prerequisite for the historical argument to produce an effect and be convincing was peoples' ability to make sense of information about history – i.e. the transformation from 'people without history' (Claude Lévi-Strauss), as was the case in traditional, premodern societies, to 'historical people'. Immediate personal experience of historical change was the most significant factor enabling and reinforcing the ability of the popular masses to develop a concept of history. In France (and some other regions in its close vicinity) it was the Revolution that brought about such experience, while in central Europe, for example, it was the Napoleonic wars, disintegration of the old Empire, and the reforms of Enlightened Absolutism. Awareness of current changes and developments eventually extended to include awareness of changes in the past, giving rise to historical consciousness.

This brings us to the important question of how different societies responded to the construction of national histories. Their response was largely determined by the above-mentioned ability to be aware of and develop a concept of history, which was not commonplace and depended on a certain level of education. Here we have to consider the ways in which historical consciousness spread. School education and the reading of fiction, which is addressed elsewhere in the book, played a major role in this context. The integration of state entities was in most parts of nineteenth-century Europe accompanied by civic education, and history thus gradually became one of the main school subjects, and its textbooks centrally important. That being said, scientific historiography was neither the sole nor the immediate source for schools' decisions with regard to teaching history. Since the majority of schools were state schools, it was the government and its policy that determined the selection of facts and the outline of national history, which was defined as state history.

It should be taken into account that the subject of national history occupied a very different position in schools of state-nations, on one hand, and those of multi-ethnic empires, on the other. The backbone of history taught at schools in France, Holland and Sweden, for example, was formed by the histories of the respective state-nations. This reflected their need to bring up conscious citizens who would self-identify with their state's present as well as its past, which corresponded with the past of their nation. In contrast, the central governments of multi-ethnic empires ensured that histories of ethnic groups that lived within their territories were incorporated into the history of the relevant empire as its constituent parts – whether they were referred to as countries or regions. The rise of national movements consequently led to a tension between the officially presented 'imperial' (state) history of the whole entity, and the unofficial regional or 'national' histories of the provinces. In more general terms, there was tension between the system of historicised political dominance of the central elites and the national histories, which was to benefit the elites of the forming provincial ('unhistorical', 'non-state') nations. This occurred not only in the 'Eastern' but also in the 'Western' empires, such as Spain, Denmark and Great Britain.

Despite this dichotomy, the belief that prevailed in nineteenth-century settings was that national history was the only context within which history could be written. Moreover, it was assumed that the basic general framework used by the recipients of history – i.e. its readers – to process further historical information was also based on national indicators. Indeed, it is hard to imagine that any non-national ('supra-national') history could have existed at the time. Various publications, proudly labelled *Weltgeschichte*, *Histoire général* or *Modern History*, were (and often still are) essentially collections of the histories of individual nations – mainly the 'big' ones that could point to their historical statehood.

What did 'having one's own national history' mean to the members of the forming nations? The reasons why the concept of national history was crucially important for national confidence can be summarised in the following four points:

1. If we consider 'collective memory' to be intrinsic to the structure of human behaviour, then historical consciousness relating to national groups represented an important aspect of nation-forming: it reinforced self-identification with a nation.

2 In the nineteenth century, national histories legitimised national existence. Just as there could only be one nation that was 'one's own', there could only be one national history, which precluded alternative dimensions or any overlapping with other national histories. The nation's present was seen as the outcome of the national group's linear historical development since medieval times.

3. National histories offered personal certainties as a substitute for immortality. They allowed individuals to feel that they shared their ancestors' lives and were part of the nation's past ('We are . . .', 'We won . . .', 'We have suffered . . .'). In addition to this continuity with the past, the histories of personalised nations also provided individuals with a 'perpetual' future in the form of their merging with their nation.

4. National histories served as a starting point when forming the concept of national values and creating collective value systems. History proved the most suitable source of these value systems because 'historical experience' provided the foundation for the construction of specific examples of moral standards for both (nationally) positive and negative behaviour. Ambitions and aspirations for the future of the nation and the ideal character-istics of its members were reflected in narrations of the past as well as in the selection of model examples.

The Construction of National Histories

What form did the process of searching for – or, according to some authors, 'inventing' – national histories take? What materials did historians make use of when (re)constructing them?[18] The tradi-tional notion of the nineteenth century presents us with an image of a historian in dialogue with the past in order to 'uncover' the history of his nation. If we disregard the semi-educated dilettantes (mostly from the ranks of journalists), political agitators and a small group of deliberate fabricators, the vast majority of historians did not falsify history. They were genuine and honest in their efforts to discover the truth about their national past and to present the conclusions of their research to their contemporaries. It was understandable that they highlighted the events and processes they saw as significant in the context of the history of the nation with which they self-identified.

These typically involved the positive aspects of the nation's past and, whether intentionally or not, this construct of the national history strengthened national confidence and offered arguments against the nation's critics and enemies (both real and imagined). Inadvertently, a 'database' of stereotypes and moral standards was created and built up for future generations of the nation once it had been established. National history was thus also shaped by the authors' concept of the nation at the time.

In most cases, the 'construction' of national history occurred in three stages – or, rather, within three types of approaches – which came into existence one after the other, but would later coexist and enrich each other. The first stage corresponded to romantic historiography, the second stage to scientific 'positivist' history, and the third stage to 'revisionism' – i.e. critical historical science. The aim of the latter was the systematic 'dismantling of myths', which did not exclude the possibility of creating new ones. In general terms, it holds true that, once scientific historiography gained ground, the construction of national history had to respect a number of principles fundamental to critical science. It was not possible to violate the principles of logic, invent historical events or figures – least of all to invent national history where there was none. While historical narration could not 'go against' existing and critically verified sources, it did not prevent the 'nationalisation' of past events. Nonetheless, this nationalisation by and large tended to take on the form of a selective approach to historical data, and at times also a one-sided causal interpretation of the relationships between events. It was not, as is claimed by some present-day incompetent non-historians, conducted by means of falsifications and inventions. Historians have always been expected to (re)construct history using only verified historical data.

National history entered the nation's day-to-day life as an elemental part of historical consciousness, which brought with it the opportunity to instrumentalise the outcomes of scientific efforts. That being said, scientific historiography could rarely foresee such instrumentalisation, let alone its political effects, and in some cases it was even so certain of the weight of its arguments that it unwittingly engaged in the historical justification of concepts that had been tainted by national interests. Due to the fact that the perennialist and personalised conceptions of nations dominated the nineteenth century (and beyond), it can be claimed with a degree of exaggeration that historians constructed national histories as a form of collective memoir. Since most historians self-identified with the nation whose history they were writing about, their work – while respecting all the principles of modern science – bore the clear marks of memoir. Consequently, when dealing with this type of information, similar criteria to those employed within the traditional methods of historical science must also be applied to national histories.

There are rules that can be followed when comparing the ways in which different historians selected and organised data. Our premise is that the construction of national histories involved certain basic elements, which need to be monitored throughout this comparative analysis. First, there is the geographical aspect of national history: in which territory it takes place, what borders demarcate this territory from the outside world, and how the territory is structured internally (regions, metropolises, the centre as against the provinces). Second, there is the temporal aspect: where in time the origins of national history are placed, which events are used to periodise national history, and which events are seen as marking its greatest and darkest periods. Finally, there is the social aspect: those who – which historical ethnic and social groups – are considered members of the nation, and what value is given to their role in national history.

As I have said, attention must be paid to the wider context of relationships with other nations, within which different national histories were placed. It is already clear that the history of a nation without its own state formed part of the history of the imperial state within whose territory this nation existed, and which would have marginalised – if not altogether negated – this nation's national history. In this situation, national history took on the shape of the history of the rising ('revived') nation's struggle against the ruling nation, whose historians, however, saw it as a component of their own national history. An important factor was the extent to which different nations' constructions of national histories overlapped with regard to territories and historical figures. For instance, the Holy Roman Emperor Charles IV was (and still is) regarded as a significant national ruler by both the Czech and German nations. The social situation at the time also needs to be taken into account. The readership for whom history was being written varied in terms of its historical education as well as its social structure. Similarly, there were differences between the authors and their political and social backgrounds.

The different historical starting points noted in the previous chapter make it obvious that national histories were not (and could not be) constructed according to the same model. Fundamental variations were determined by the relationship between the premodern reality and its objectively existing institutional legacies (relics) and the circumstances in which modern nation-building took place. This perspective allows us to distinguish four ways in which national histories were created:

1. National history emerged as the history of the state-nation, whose existence and deep historical roots were unquestionable. In this situation, national history was constructed as a 'natural' continuation of the state's development since medieval times. The territory of the historical state was seen unreservedly as the national territory, and national history was thus essentially the same as the history of the state. It is noteworthy that this type of national history had a particular characteristic – in most cases there was no generally binding 'metanarrative' ('master narrative'), i.e. no single consensual version of national history. From the very beginning, at least two basic concepts commonly contended with each other, which roughly corresponded to the state-nations' internal political and class differentiations. The Tories and Whigs competed in their approach to history in England; in France the division lay in the attitudes towards the Revolution and the *ancien régime*; and there were divisions within Spanish and Dutch historiographies. Another characteristic feature was the already-mentioned tendency to include the histories of ethnic groups, which were already asserting their right to exit as distinct nations, in the state-national history. Finnish history was made part of Swedish history, Catalan and Basque histories were integrated into Spanish history, the histories of the Baltic States and the Ukraine continued to be seen as part of Russian history, Lithuanian history as part of Polish history, and so on.

2. National history lay claim to historical statehood, which largely corresponded to the ethno-national reality at the time of the

emerging national movement but which had been discontinued during the previous centuries. Since this statehood continued to live in more or less powerful institutionalised relics, national history could assume the form of political history. National identity was demonstrated by pointing to various historical state formations, whose borders, however, usually differed from the ethnic ones. This complicated the issue of self-identification for minorities, and affected the way in which national history was approached by the Czechs with regard to the territory of the Lands of the Crown of Bohemia, the Polish with regard to the territory of Rzeczpospolita, the Magyars with regard to the territory of the Kingdom of Hungary, and also the Lithuanians, the Greeks and the Basques.

3. Medieval statehood, to which national history could lay claim, had been destroyed so thoroughly that proof of it only existed in the written sources of the time, and it survived merely in mythological 'memory'. In such situations it was very difficult to establish where the borders of the claimed historical territory should lie – or, indeed, to define a basis for the notion of the historical continuity of the national entity. The consequence of this was a considerable overlapping of theories that different national movements adopted as 'their' historical space. This was the case of the Balkan nations, and also of the Ukrainian and Belarusian nations.

4. Some national movements had no historical continuity with any historical political unit to point to; nor could they construct a tradition of national statehood on the basis of mythological 'memory'. Here, national identity was based on the collective memory of the common fate of an ethnic group, defined by language and culture. This in turn predetermined an ethnic definition of national borders, which usually did not contain compact settlements of foreign minorities. History played a lesser role among the arguments employed by these national movements, and the historical argument mainly referred to the group's collective suffering and work under foreign rule.

In addition to these four types, there were also several transitional cases. For the Germans, for example, the tradition of statehood referred not to a single state but to the many German states joined together within the Holy Roman Empire, which became a substitute for German national history. The fact that it disintegrated before the construction of national histories took place did not pose any problem. In the Catalan case, it was the tradition of autonomy rather than of statehood that was considered of national value. Finland gained political autonomy in 1809 – shortly before the emergence of the national movement – which did not leave enough time for national history to be constructed on the basis of statehood.

We will now move from general observations to the empirical sphere. No work on national histories can be conducted without monographic scientific research dedicated to specific topics. Such research – the formulation of its objectives and the selection of its subtopics – was, to a greater or lesser extent, inspired by the consensual image of national history and, conversely, any construction of national history had to be (and must be) guided by the conclusions of these partial studies. It is rather unfortunate that, while there has been an increase in the volume of partial studies relating to the various ways in which individual national histories have been approached, the growing number of empirical findings has not been matched by attempts to organise them by means of comparison. The previous chapter presented general observations based on implicit comparison, but it should – in the future – be modified by explicit comparison, so allowing a systematic analysis of the synthetic constructions of national histories. The best way to achieve this may be by comparing the analogous historical circumstances in which the initial steps towards the creation of modern nations took place – i.e. the emergence of civic societies in state-nations, or phase C of national movements. In addition, this comparison could be based on a systematically assembled 'questionnaire', such as the one presented in Figure 2, covering all the aspects of the constructing of national histories that have been mentioned thus far (and some additional ones). This would undoubtedly entail some degree of simplification and omission of detail, but would, in return, make it possible to provide convincing empirical evidence of the true specifics of individual national projects, as well as a typology of the ideas about national history and its role in modern nation-building.

<u>Figure 2</u>

National History: Construct and/or Reality?

1. *The definition of the nation's 'own' history:*

Territorially, the national borders were defined by:
A pre-existing state – 'historical borders'
The ethnicity of the inhabitants
Older regional units
The internal structure of the national territory was perceived as:
National centre(s) versus the provinces
Different historical and/or geographical regions
Chronological dimensions:
When did the nation start to exist?
Where were its origins placed in time?
Where did its members come from?
Was there continuity or discontinuity of national history?
What were the moments of national integration and/or disintegration?
The system of national values:
Why were some periods and events seen as times of glory and others as times of decline?
Among the heroes who were representative of national values, which ones were regarded as positive and which ones as negative?
Was there a stable system of positive and negative values, seen as intrinsic in the nation's 'own' history?
Unity and diversity within the concept of national history:
Master narratives
Alternatives and competing concepts

2. *National history in the European context:*

'We' and Europe:
How strong was the interest in non-national (European) history?
Did historical thinking encompass the idea of the general development of the entire continent? Of the whole of humanity?

What historical hetero-stereotypes of other nations were there?

What was considered the most common type of mutual relationship with neighbours (for example, war, trade, culture) in national history?

Which aspect of the nation's 'own' history was seen as specific, and how frequently was it contrasted with the history of the 'others'?

Reflections on uneven development:

Were comparisons drawn between national history and the general situation across the rest of the continent, or the history of certain nations?

Were certain countries (including the nation's own) perceived as either more or less developed (underdeveloped), and were there attempts to understand and explain it?

3. Social factors:

Who were the most influential authors of master-narratives?

What was their social background, profession, education, and political and cultural engagement?

Who were the addresses of national history?

How was information about national history spread among the population?

4. General problems and interdependences:

Myth and reality in understanding national history:

What was the relevance of scientific argument in the search for the 'purpose' of national history?

What was the status of historical truth as the final criterion?

National history and the process of nation-forming:

National history as political and national argument

Increasing interdependence between politics and national history

It is no coincidence that the calls for the re-examination of the romantic version of national history made by some historians during the era of so-called positivism in historical science were based on results of rather partial archive studies. While it would be interesting to compare the various roles of these 'revisionists' in the context of individual national cultures, such a study has yet to be carried out.

The relationship between national history and the national audience was reciprocal – the construct of national history was only acceptable if it was compatible with a general historical awareness among the population to which it hoped to appeal. If this was not the case, it passed unnoticed and ceased to exist, as demonstrated by the failure to construct an Austrian 'national history' at the turn of – and then again in the middle of – the nineteenth century, to encourage the non-Magyar population to adopt the concept of Hungarian history in the late stages of Dualism, and to achieve a single concept of Czechoslovak history in the interwar period. This is because a certain rudimentary 'mythological' awareness of the common past, if not of a common origin, of the given group's members had already become intrinsic to both the forming of a nation and the existence of an ethnic group.

Characteristically, in extreme situations both in the context of national movements and in state-nations, national histories began to be drawn up and accepted as evidence of the real or apparent 'age-old' threat to national existence. They came to be perceived as authoritative proof that not only national values and interests but also the nation's 'age-old enemies' were historically anchored. This was then only a step away from the adoption of the decidedly nationalistic concept of a nation's special historical mission, and the view that such a mission legitimised expansive policies and superiority over anyone who was weaker or 'underdeveloped'. Subsequently, a fallacious conclusion was made in historiography that one's own national history held the key to understanding universal history – that general contexts can be evaluated according to the criteria of national history, and thus also according to national interests. It is self-evident that this combination of stereotypes, with its marked potential for aggression, was particularly dangerous when – but not only when – large, powerful state-nations were involved.

National History in Myth and Tradition

The scientific construction of national history could only fulfil its national role if it succeeded in becoming part of the historical consciousness of those to whom national agitation tried to appeal. It may seem that this was easily achieved with the beginning of newspaper and journal publishing, combined with fictional adaptations of history, poetry and theatre, and also with the existence of history textbooks at schools. But the difficulty is that this progression cannot be seen as a simple technical reproduction or a mechanical 'transmission' of the scientific interpretation of national history. Each such transmission did not only entail further distortion and simplification. Even more importantly, once an image of the past was communicated to the wider masses, it mixed in people's minds with their pre-existing mythologised historical awareness – with ideas of the past that they had received through family traditions (as part of a 'lay collective memory'). In short, the more closely connected the spreading of the scientific view of national history and the forming of the national memory were with agitation (the national movement), the greater was the shift away from the critical approach of science to mythologised historical awareness. The popularisation of national history went hand-in-hand with the creation of national myths.[19]

This leads us to the role of myths in the forming of national identity. Not all narratives whose aim was to popularise history can be regarded as national myths, but only those that were purposefully placed within the context that provided the foundations for and gave rise to the notion of a common fate uniting all members of the nation. Unlike in the construction of national history, these were not synthesising narratives but separate stories and accounts of episodes. Since they rested in the surviving spontaneous (eventually non-verbalised) collective memory, they were easily utilised in national education and national agitation.

One precondition for the creation and effectiveness of national myths was the *primordial* (perennialist) *concept of a nation*: since nations were communities that had always existed, ancient myths were equally relevant to the nations of present day. Another prerequisite for a national myth to be effective was its widest possible (general) acceptance, and a form of sacralisation – i.e. its becoming a 'sacred text'.[20] It was thus indisputable, inviolable, and beyond any type of criticism. The myth not only served as an instrument of national agitation; it also became a sign, with the help of which members of a national group communicated, a code that allowed them to orientate themselves, and the foundation for the symbols of national existence.

National myths had several functions, which makes it possible to differentiate between them. In its basic form, it was primarily a means of enabling a national group to become self-aware by allowing a consensual acceptance of attributes and stories that generated certain values. In so doing, the myth defined the group and facilitated communication and solidarity among its members. Simultaneously, it made possible a change in the hierarchy of identities – i.e. a shift in favour of the national identity. As a bearer of memory, a myth was one of the pillars of the continuity of national existence.[21]

The position occupied by national within the composition of historical consciousness reveals that they were not entirely bound by scientific data about past realities. They were part of the reality of their time, not of the past, and thus subjecting them to historical critique and 'disproving' them would be meaningless. Myths must, above all, be assessed in themselves and in terms of their social function.[22] It was not uncommon for members of national groups to adopt as the symbol of their identity myths that they themselves did not believe in, and which had already been refuted by historical research. The efforts made by some contemporary authors to disprove national myths in the name of historical truth are therefore often pointless.

At the other extreme there is the view that there is no need whatsoever to approach myths critically, since they are pure fiction. However, there is a reason that warrants a critical comparison between myths and their historical realities. In order to be able to interpret their variable functions, attention needs to be paid to the ways in which they process, alter or fabricate aspects of the narrative about the historical events to which they relate, what they add, and, most importantly, what they leave out. The needs of different times and advances in historical science meant that over the course of time myths 'discovered' and integrated new aspects of national history, while 'forgetting' others.

Myths should not be equated with traditions, despite there being a large overlap between these two approaches towards the past. In contrast to a myth, a tradition seeks continuity with the past – it is not a memory of the past, but sees itself as its organic continuation. It may have been based on a myth and, just as in the case of a myth, we are mostly interested in the role it played in the context of its time. Only secondary to that is the phenomenon of 'invented traditions', which tends to be overplayed and distorted when reinterpreted. It should be stressed that the author of the term, Hobsbawm, does not classify all traditions as invented. He distinguishes between 'invented' and 'genuine old' traditions, of which the latter can be found in all societies, while the former are mainly characteristic of situations that involved swift social changes.[23]

Critics of the constructivist concept of tradition point out that, since all traditions (invented ones included) appeal to people, who have certain attitudes towards and ideas about the past, they have to respect and fit within the existing (given) framework of value systems. The Scots would not have adopted the 'clan' kilts if they had not considered themselves to be a distinct group, and if they had not attached a symbolic value to them in relation to their clans – something that existed objectively. Even an invented tradition cannot completely disregard a link between the past and the national myth.[24]

Modern national myths often built upon older, medieval and early modern myths, which were addressed in Part II. Some went back to even older, premodern and already forgotten myths. Old myths were modified rather than adopted in their entirety, especially *the myth of origin*, as the age of a 'nation' had already been a commonly employed argument in premodern times. For example, when the Humanists discovered Tacitus's description of the lives of the Germanic tribes, this image was incorporated into the modern myth of origin of the German nation, together with the cult of the Cheruscan (Saxon) chieftain Arminius (Hermann). The Germanic myth gained significance due to its interaction with the myth about the blood lineage between the Germanic tribes and the German people.[25] The medieval myth about France arising from Gaul and Francia was updated and, by the end of the eighteenth century, the Third Estate emphasised its Gallic (Celtic) roots as against the 'conquering' Frankish aristocracy. In the nineteenth century, the invasion of Gaul by the Franks was used as a metaphor to explain the marked social class differences within French society: the aristocrats were the descendants of the Germanic Franks, the common people of the Celtic Gauls. Vercingetorix became the national hero in this context. Towards the end of the century the myth was modified, and the joining of the Gauls and the Franks came to represent (republican) national unity and integration.[26] The Czech medieval myth about the original Czechs being peaceful migrating farmers transformed into a myth about the 'dove-like' democratic personality of the Slavs. In this respect they stood in direct opposition to the authoritarian and aggressive Germanic people.[27] The myth about the origin of the brave and fearsome Magyars continued to evolve in a parallel manner.

The myth of the Golden Age – a memory of the old times, when the qualities and virtues of the nation were still unspoilt – occupied a specific place among myths.[28] In this vein, Kievan Rus was celebrated (in relation to the orthodox tradition) by the Russian Slavophiles from as early as Peter the Great's times, early Christian Ireland by the Irish patriots, and the era of the independent Grand Duchy by the Lithuanians. The notion of the Golden Age was often linked to the myth of origin. For the Latvians, their Golden Age corresponded with their early times, before the invasion by the Teutonic knights, when the people lived peacefully and were led by their elders. For the Ukrainians, the roots of the nation dated back to Kievan Rus, when the first steps were taken towards being seen as different from Russia, and this tradition persisted during the times of the Kingdom of Galicia and Volhynia, until about 1300. After that, it was the Cossacks of the sixteenth century who came to be seen as the new beginning of the Ukrainian nation.[29] According to the Romanian myth, the Romanians originated from the Dacians, who had lived in the territory of modern-day Wallachia, Moldova and Transylvania, and been Romanised while under the rule of the Roman Empire.[30] Even the modern Turkish construct of national history sees the Golden Age as pertaining to pre-Islamic and pre-Ottoman times.

In Great Britain, the myth of origin was strongly linked to race. Whereas 'Englishness' was based on the image of Anglo-Saxon ancestors, Francophone Normans were considered to be a foreign element. In Scotland, the contrast between the Celtic and Anglo-Saxon races was regarded as representative of the differences between the sexes, the former being the embodiment of female virtues (togetherness, sensitivity, closeness to nature), while the latter stood for male qualities (placing importance on organised society, reason and culture).[31] An additional set of opposites, which was updated and politicised in England, was an earlier contrast between Anglo-Saxon democratic principles, already embraced by the revolutionary Puritans and later by the Whigs, and the Norman principle of authority.

In the nineteenth century, the myth of origin was employed by a new sphere of activity – the study of prehistory. *Archaeological research* made it possible to search for the roots of one's own nation, and even race, in prehistoric times – and, more importantly, in trust-inspiring authentic relics.[32] However, the strength of national interest in prehistory varied, partly in relation to circumstances at the outset of the nation-building processes. Relatively low levels of interest in 'national' prehistory were displayed in England, and initially also France, where it was not until the experience of the empire and the year 1870 that steps were taken towards nationalising the study of the Gallic and Roman eras. Similarly, scientific archaeology in Denmark was not influenced by national factors until the late 1860s – i.e. after the defeat in 1864, when the need to redefine Danish national identity involved a search for its ancient origins. In Portugal, the role of archaeology was limited by the fact that attempts at anchoring the Portuguese nation in prehistory were not supported by national myths placing its origins in the Middle Ages. In addition, the archaeological argument was altogether absent in some cases, such as the Slovenian national movement.

In contrast to this, Celtic prehistory became one of the key components of the Irish national movement, and archaeology also played an important part in Scotland in defining Scottish identity against that of the English. The idealisation of Germanic prehistory had initially been justified by non-archaeological means in German countries, but archaeology was eventually used to support national and even racist arguments, mainly under the influence of Gustaf Kossinna. After the loss of statehood, the gathering of ancient relics that would prove the Slavic nature of the land became the national cult in Poland, where archaeology provided national arguments by studying the prehistoric differences between the Slavic and Germanic peoples. Although the Lithuanian national movement was largely based on the myth of the 'Golden Age' having been the era of the pagan Grand Dutchy, until the interwar period archaeological research within Lithuanian territory was in the hands of Polish and, to a lesser extent, Russian archaeologists, which meant that their findings were not very helpful for Lithuanian national purposes. Czech archaeology in the nineteenth century focused mainly on research into Slavic relics, aiming to extend the continuity of the Slavic settlement as far back into the past as possible, while disregarding relics from the times of Germanic settlement.

National myths that related to history can be broadly divided into three basic types: first, significant battles and war missions; second, the principal positive, progressive transformations of the national state or national community; and third, important cultural and intellectual achievements by an eminent figure seen as a member of the nation.[33]

First, the large extent to which national myths pertained to wars and battles[34] was undoubtedly a reflection of the mentality of the time, but also an expression of the fact that national communities ('we') define themselves mainly against others ('they'). It is thus logical that battles, both victorious and lost, became part of national myths. The Battle of the Teutoburg Forest marks the beginning of German history. The Greeks were able to claim even older famous battles, especially those during the Persian wars. The Battle of Mortgarten of 1317 and the Battle of Sempach of 1386 opened the doors to independence, and thus national existence, to the Swiss, as did the Reconquista, and especially the acquisition of Grenada in 1492, to the Spanish. The Battle of the Golden Spurs of 1302 should have become the Belgian state-national myth, but was 'seized' by the Flemish national movement. There were several other battles that helped protect national independence. For Poland, they were the 1410 Battle of Grunwald, in which they fought off the Teutonic Knights, and the Siege of Jasna Gora (the Battle of Czestochowa), which – with the help of the Virgin Mary – resulted in a reversal of fortunes in their near-defeat to the Swedish king in the mid seventeenth century. The victorious sea battle against the 'Invincible Spanish Armada' in 1588 and the Battle of Trafalgar in 1805 were of similar significance for England, as was the freeing of Vienna from the Turkish siege in 1683 for Austria, or the Hussite victory over the crusaders and the saving of Prague in the Battle of Vitkov Hill in 1420 for the Czech lands. The Battle of Nations at Leipzig in 1813 was 'reinterpreted' as a German national victory during the second half of the nineteenth century.

Another group of battles is formed by those that had tragic consequences for national destiny – permanent or temporary. A good example of a battle with a permanent effect is the Battle of Kosovo of 1389, in which the Ottomans annihilated the main Serbian army and thereby brought about the subjugation and destruction of Serbia.[35] Another example is the Battle of Mohacs of 1525, which not only provided a route for the Ottomans into the Hungarian Empire, but also (as a result of the young Ludwig Jagellon dying in the battle) enabled the Habsburgs to accede to the Czech and Hungarian thrones. Prior to that, the fall of Constantinople brought down the Byzantine Empire, which the Greek national movement considered to be the Greek state of the Middle Ages. The Battle of White Mountain of 1620 severely disrupted Czech statehood, and subsequently also Czech culture. The Siege of Alesia also qualifies, to an extent, in which Julius Caesar defeated the Gauls led by Vercingetorix. Of all the remaining battles, those that became part of the world of myths were mainly those with dramatic, poignant plots, such as the defeat and death of Ottokar II of Bohemia in the Battle on the Marchfeld in 1278, the death Gustavus Adolphus of Sweden in the Battle of Lützen in 1632, the defeat of Charles XII in the Battle of Poltava in 1709, or the fall of Tadeusz Kosciuszko.

Numerous other defeats became part of the world of myths, encouraging contemplation as well as contradictory views, which aimed to assess the meaning of national histories. Hence the French interpretation of the 1870 defeat: the nation was paying for its sins and, using Zola's metaphor, was 'crucified' so that it could rise again. This metaphor had been used much earlier within Polish Messianism in the first half of the nineteenth century: the Polish nation may have been defeated and 'crucified' but, in return, humanity would be saved. In Denmark, the defeat of 1864 led to the rethinking of Danish national identity, while the Battle of Hastings in 1066 opened the doors to the one-hundred-year rule of the Normans over England. Another example is Messolonghi, during the Greek revolt in 1826.

Among the myths of the nineteenth century, it is worth noting those that were associated with wars of conquest and battles abroad. As a general rule, it was much easier for battles (both victorious and lost) to enter the national 'hall of fame' if they formed part of defensive efforts to save the nation or its interests. Therefore, the conquest of Jerusalem by the Crusaders in 1099 as part of the Belgian myth, colonial conquests overseas as part of Spanish and Portuguese myths, the Viking conquests as myths of the Nordic nations, and the conquests by Alexander the Great, which old Greek and new Macedonian myths compete over, are all relatively rare.

Second, myths that were founded on *important milestones in national histories* tend to be divided into two 'agglomerations', one being placed between the early phase and the height of the Middle Ages, and the other at the turn of the nineteenth century. The construction of the mighty Danevirke fortifications at the beginning of the historical era, during the Viking Age – later reinterpreted as anti-German – and the 'national' flag with a white cross, which was seen as a gift to the Danes from God during the conquests in Estland in the thirteenth century, occupy an important place in the Danish national myth. To the Magyars, the national state was founded by the king and national saint Stephen I. The legend of the Czech Duke and national saint Wenceslaus proved contradictory, as its national aspect was damaged by Wenceslaus's voluntary surrender to Henry I the Fowler, and thereby to German rule. The issuing of Magna Carta in 1215 is seen as the beginning of the modern parliamentary system in England, just as the oath taken in Rütli in 1307 by the representatives of three cantons is seen as the origin of the Swiss state.

In this category of positive myths there are also several medieval and early modern uprisings, which sought to 'better society' – for example, the rebellion led by Engelbrekt Engelbrektsson in Sweden, the Hussite revolutionary movement in the Czech lands, the revolt of the Comuneros against the rule of Charles V in Spain, and the revolt in the Netherlands against Philip II of Spain. Whereas the Puritan revolution of 1640–60 was a source of contradictory opinions within the English discourse on national history, the myth of the Glorious Revolution of 1688–89 was generally accepted.

The legacy of the French Revolution, particularly its Jacobin phase, which became a controversial topic during the nineteenth century in France, leads us to a further wave of nation-forming events – namely, the time of civic revolutions and reforms. While the first phase of the French Revolution gradually gained general acceptance in France, the Jacobin myth as the democratic revolutionary alternative was never widely adopted. The reforms, which were regarded as crucial for the transformation towards modern society in Denmark, were those implemented by the 'patriotic aristocracy' at the end of the eighteenth century. The Polish myth of the Constitution of 3 May 1791 celebrates an attempt to bring about such changes, which was thwarted by magnates whose intervention resulted in the constitution being revoked as soon as it had been passed. For Norway, the event that marks a revolutionary change was the assembly of the people's representatives in Eidsvoll, which led to the adoption of the constitution in May 1814. The Belgian revolution of 1830 stands at the beginning of its statehood. German history sees the roots of a turn towards national statehood in the patriotic movement against Napoleon in 1813, although the key event was the proclamation of the German Empire in 1871. Garibaldi and his 'Thousand' are the most noticeable heroes in the struggles for a united Italy, but the beginning of the Italian state is associated with the deal between the king and Garibaldi in Teano in 1860.

Famous *historical figures* were another factor that entered the national context. All European nations pride themselves on the fact that their leaders have revered important figures from 'their' past. The broad and rich range of these figures comprises national heroes, outstanding artists, scientists and philosophers, but there is no need for an exhaustive list. For the purposes of this book, it is of greater interest that some regularity can be detected in the types of individuals who were nationally celebrated. Although efforts were made to exaggerate the importance of some of these people, they could not be totally invented. Therefore, the cult of political and military national heroes can be found primarily among state-nations, and then among those national movements that could lay claim to a tradition of statehood.

National heroes commonly originated from the context of profound changes within national histories, and from times when the nation was under threat or expanding. Frederick I Barbarossa was the embodiment of the great expansions of the 'Germans' abroad, and also of the missed opportunity to create a centralised German monarchy. Gustav Vasa was designated the founder of the modern Swedish state, while his earlier contemporary, Matthias Corvinus, was celebrated as the national king of the Magyars and, later, William of Orange as the securer of Dutch independence. Alongside these men, William Wallace was celebrated as a fighter for Scottish independence, Jan Hus as an exemplary fighter for freedom of conscience and the rights of the Czech nation, Mikael Agricola as the founder of Finnish national literature, and Tadeusz Kościuscko as the tragic hero in the struggle for Polish national independence.

Characteristically, it was very difficult to reach a consensus about the ideal of a national hero in places where two different concepts of national history collided, such as in France. There were also numerous important historical figures who had little chance to become the heroes of national myths – especially members of the Habsburg dynasty and, to a degree, those in their service, such as Eugene of Savoy. The attempts to integrate the Austrian multinational monarchy around the cult of the Habsburg dynasty foundered on nationalist German, rather than Czech, opposition.

The cult of famous Renaissance and early modern artists bolstered primarily the Italian and, to a lesser degree, also the French and Spanish national consciousness. Fine artists of the Italian Renaissance and members of the French literary and theatrical tradition were part of national myths in the nineteenth century. However, the further north and east we progress, the more we find that the focus of national memory lay on important scientists and philosophers, ranging from John Locke to Leibniz, from Linnaeus to Lomonosov.

Some famous historical figures became the subject of fruitless, nationally motivated disputes over which nation was entitled to incorporate them in its pantheon. As many as three nations – the Bulgarians, Greeks and Macedonians – have fought over the 'European saints' Cyril and Methodius, the Germans and the Polish over Nicolaus Copernicus, and the Italians and the Spanish (Catalans) over Christopher Columbus. Similarly, the Norwegian-born Danish playwright Ludvig Holberg is also claimed by two nations. In contrast, a double identity did not become a source of conflict when there was no discord between the national groups involved. For example, the image of Charles IV as an important Luxembourger easily coexisted with that of Charles IV as the Czech 'father of the homeland' – not least because he was not classified a 'German' ruler within the Czech historical context.

Historical consciousness, upon which national groups' collective memories rested, was one of the factors that supported self-identification with one's nation, and thus the nation-building processes everywhere in Europe. When Bauer emphasised a hundred years ago that a 'common destiny' was a precondition for national existence, he was referring to historical reality. Although we know today that this togetherness was just as easily rooted in discourse, fiction and myths as in reality, the difference is unimportant from the point of view of its nation-forming function. It is significant, however, that all attempts at national mobilisation within nation-states and all national movements employed the instrumentalisation of the common past as an argument to support their claims to national existence, and as a platform from which to make demands 'in the name of the nation'. The historical argument made use of critical science, journalism and school history, as well as fiction, poetry and other types of art. Depending on which of these tools were favoured by the collective memory, this instrumentalisation of national history was dominated by either the more mythological or the more critical elements of historical consciousness.

The process of searching for a common fate and giving it in the form of national history always involved construction, but it would be misguided to equate construction with calculated untruths and label national histories as purposefully invented or falsified. This approach only became possible during the postmodern era of disrespect for critical reason and the truth. But this did not apply in the nineteenth century, during which there was a consensus that historical truth could be discovered, and when its authority was enforced. Although historical science served the 'national interest', in most cases it did so not by means of fictitious inventions but by being selective about historical facts and biased in its interpretation of objectively existing written and printed sources. Václav Hanka's forged manuscripts, which are a popular reference made by authors who wish to cast doubt on all historical research, are an exception to the rule. The basic instrument of manipulation in any construction with a national bias was not the use of untruths, but rather selective work with historical truths – or, more precisely, with findings considered to be truthful. Part of the ethics that governed the activities of scientific historians, as well as those who popularised historical findings, was to make it known when they were leaving scientifically verified data in support of myths – usually for nationally educational purposes. Moreover, even if we overplayed the significance of myths and regarded them (mistakenly) as the historical base of the reinforcement of national identity in the course of the nineteenth century, it would not call into question the legitimacy of the very process of modern nation-building.

CHAPTER 9

Fighting for National Language and Culture

Opinions about the role of language and ethnic identity in the nation-forming process are often controversial. This corresponds to the diametrically opposed views on what defines a nation and nationalism, and what their characteristic features are. It is understandable that authors who use statehood to define a nation attach little or no importance to the role of ethnic and cultural factors in nation-forming. In this context, it suffices to mention names such as Rogers Brubaker, Charles Tilly, Michael Mann and John Breuilly. When the significance of the language cannot be completely refuted, many authors, including Eric Hobsbawm and Juan Linz, categorise it as an 'artificial artefact' or a myth, which is primordial and thus damaging rather than beneficial.[1] Ethnicity shares a similar fate. Ernest Gellner considered ethnic circumstances – i.e. belonging in linguistic terms – to be a neutral fact, which in itself did not necessarily lead to nationalism. In his line of thinking, the language could not give rise to nation-forming. It is also not uncommon for critical views of the role of language in the past to reflect the authors' political opinions about the role of ethnic identity and linguistic requirements in the present. This applies to Hans Kohn, whose disdain for the ethnic definition of a nation during World War II was an expression of his opposition to German racism and chauvinism. Similar politicisation can also be found among contemporary authors. For instance, Liah Greenfeld sees orientation towards language and ethnicity – especially within the forming of the German nation – as the herald of reactive and anti-democratic nationalism.[2]

It appears to me that empirical historical findings support the view that regards ethnic identities and cultural bonds as important, if not inevitable, precursors to a modern nation. This observation, which was common among the German authors of the first half of the twentieth century, was later presented in a balanced manner by Eugen Lemberg. The most influential contemporary author appears to be Anthony Smith, who regularly returns to the re-examination of the role of ethnicity. His differentiation between 'ethnic categories' and 'ethnic communities' has enriched the terminological repertoire employed in empirical research. According to him, the journey from an ethnie – or, rather, an ethnic community – to a nation was a process of politicisation, mobilisation and new imagination, encouraged mostly by the intellectuals.[3] Language occupies an important place in Smith's concept of ethno-symbolism, although it is rather overshadowed by his reinterpretation of the symbols of past values.[4]

The ethnic roots of national existence tend to be seen as an important research subject by social scientists rather than historians. The anthropologist Thomas Hylland Eriksen focuses on the identification role ethnic bonds have played in times of insecurity, chaos and political change. These upheavals increased the chances of ethnic identity being transformed into nationalism, and Eriksen thus draws a distinction between ethnic identity, which dictates an individual's loyalty to a group, and nation, which, in keeping with the Anglophone linguistic tradition, he understands to refer to a *political* community.[5] In addition, ethnic roots can influence the nature and programme of national identity, and opinions about this interrelationship are polarised. While Walker Connors recommended as early as 1974 that 'ethno-nationalism' be respected as a positive correlation between modernisation and ethnicity, other authors (mistakenly in my view) place ethno-nationalism in opposition to 'civic nationalism', and at times even alongside racism.[6] In the context of the French language, the term *nationalité* is sometimes employed to refer to cultural and linguistic interrelationships which were a natural starting point on the path towards 'nation-formation'.[7]

The argument that the development towards a nation stemmed – at least in the case of some European nations – from the circumstances of a given ethnic group was reflected in the large project titled 'Comparative Studies on Governments and Non-Dominant Ethnic Groups in Europe, 1850-1940', organised by the Strasbourg-based European Scientific Foundation in the 1980s. Despite the fact that its findings were published in several thematic collections, it appears that the majority of later researchers remain unfamiliar with them.[8] However, it is legitimate to enquire into how ethnicity was related to the linguistic demands that were fundamental to most national movements. While this chapter focuses mainly on language as an aspect of ethnic identity, this is done with the awareness that similar consideration could, at least in some cases, be given for instance to religion.

Non-historical thinking, and a failure to differentiate between the role ethnicity played in the past and the role it plays in the present, leads to many complications. Nowadays, the linking of national and ethnic identities – placing emphasis on the ethnic community as a nation-building factor – is often (and rightly) considered a sign of primordialism, which is unsuitable for the needs of the civic society. The negative effects of present-day ethnically defined national demands are often mistakenly incorporated into interpretations of historical developments, and cause terminological confusion. Generalisations about the 'ethno-nationalism' of current times are mechanically employed in critical assessments of the development from an ethnic community to a modern nation that occurred in the past.

Another methodological problem stems from the existence of subjective and objective identifiers of ethnic groups. Many researchers differentiate between the objective role of ethnic and linguistic relationships (among other things as instruments of social communication) and their effect on the subjective feelings and sense of belonging of the members of the group.[9] John Edwards adds that, even though the socialisation of cultural models may not be the same for all generations, the subjective sense of group ties remains.[10] References to the interplay between ethnic and other group identities are significant. According to Walter Freeman, there is a correlation between the social structure of an ethnic group and the importance of ethnic bonds among its members: the more homogenous the social structure of the group, the stronger the ethnic identity of its members.[11]

There appears to be a general agreement about the need to combine the study of the objective functions of ethnicity and of linguistic relationships with research into how people actually perceived their ethnic difference. Therefore, it is essential to analyse not only the ways in which structures work, but also how people make sense of their own attitudes and behaviour. Anthropologists in particular are aware that people's words and deeds do not always correspond.

Joshua Fishman, a sociolinguist, who laid the foundations for the study of the social functions of language and its relationship with nationalism, distinguished between the conscious symbolism of a language and its unconscious 'primordial ethnicity'. In a sense, he anticipated Smith's view that the symbolisation of language and culture is a fundamental nation-forming factor.[12] Both the social function of linguistic relationships and the symbolic value of the language in the process of nation-building are subjects whose conclusions remain open. However, it is useful to pay close attention to them.

National Culture as an Instrument of National Mobilisation

In this chapter the term 'culture' is not used in the sense given to it by current cultural anthropologists and sociologists. It carries the same meaning it had during national movements. At that time, it was primarily understood to mean 'high culture', and thus referred to works of literature, music and fine arts – although, admittedly, popular culture was also taken into account and seen as a specific aspect of national culture. The need for a common national culture in this sense of the word was, therefore, mainly felt by members of the 'national elite' – i.e. the bearers of the nation-forming process. They perceived it as an expression and proof of national distinctness, and it is understandable that the elites of state-nations considered national culture to be a natural part of their lives. This is perhaps the reason why present-day researchers from these nations tend to see national culture as consisting of the symbols and activities that popularised the works of high culture. Conversely, researchers who emphasise the importance of national culture for the existence (coherence) of each particular nation mostly come from the ranks of the 'small nations'. Neither literature nor any other of the arts constituted a readily available heritage from premodern times that the elites of these forming nations could deploy, which is why they regarded the arts primarily as an instrument of national (and civic) education.

Given this fact, a chapter about the forming of national culture must take into consideration the typological dichotomy within nation-building in Europe. Indeed, this may well be the area in which the differences between the two types of development were most marked. The fight for the national language and the creation of a distinct national culture were truly specific to national movements, distinguishing them from nation-forming within old traditions of state culture and language. This is not to say that 'high culture' did not play an important part in the forming of state-nations. Culture was of great significance both as a symbol and as tangible proof of national existence in the case of the 'unification type' of nation-forming (that of the Germans, Polish and Italians). In fact, culture played such a central role in the building of the German nation that, to this day, many authors use the term *Kulturnation* to refer to the premodern era.

Struggles to establish distinctive national cultures initially came in the form of efforts to break free from Enlightenment cosmopolitanism, embodied in the French culture then dominant throughout the continent. The quality of local cultures was assessed by comparing their works with the French models. From the beginning of the nineteenth century, there was a gradual shift towards a conscious emancipation of national cultures, which is commonly associated with Romanticism replacing Classicism in all the arts. Although this is oversimplified, it is clear that Romanticism was compatible with the modern idea of a nation. They both originated under similar circumstances – an atmosphere of intellectual uncertainty and crisis of identities. A nation was one of the certainties that some Romantics were able to find amid the general lack of certainties and fluctuating values.

National culture cannot be looked upon as a relationship between two abstract terms – 'culture' and 'nation'. In common with all forms of art, it concerned a mutual relationship of three tangible elements – the author, the work and the audience. Each of these was able to function independently in the context of the day-to-day life of the nation, and each reflected national aspects of culture. Most authors adopted the stereotypical notion of the time that they not only ought to but also wanted to benefit their nation through their work – both by celebrating its existence and by encouraging its intellectual and moral growth. Their activities also involved constructive criticism aimed at their own ranks. In state-nations the authors were able to build consciously on the continuity of the old domestic tradition, which included the use of the state language in literary work. This also applies to the 'cultural' non-state nations – the Italians and the

Germans. In contrast, national movements usually lacked this inherent awareness of cultural continuity; their leaders strove to restore continuity where possible. Attempts were commonly made to convince authors from multi-ethnic empires to realise that their true cultural home was the nation arising from the ethnic group they originated from.

It would be both belated and misleading to judge works of national culture by absolute artistic criteria. Although these works claimed to belong to 'high culture', they were not of the same quality. The works of the newly forming literatures in non-state nations seldom reached the aesthetic standards of culture found in state-nations. However, the relevant factor in the context of this book is that these works were the outcome of efforts that national movements made gradually to attain a comparable level with the established developed national cultures.

A certain regularity can be exemplified: the building of national cultures tended to start with literary and theatre productions. The leaders of national movements initially questioned what function the newly forming national literatures could serve. One possibility was that they would enable the people of their respective nations to gain a sense of the achievements of the more evolved literatures within Europe. Their other purpose was to create a distinctive national literature (and subsequently other forms of art) that lived up to high aesthetic standards. At first all national movements adopted the former, educational alternative, but most of their leaders eventually replaced it with the determination to focus on the demanding task of creating their own national culture. Their success was dependent on the presence of authors as well as on the support the new works of culture received from their audiences.

The function of the new works was not necessarily firmly set. They existed in their own right, and they often proved to play a different role in the life of the nation from the one intended by the authors themselves. For example, the fact that the author's main intention was to depict a beautiful landscape was unimportant – the work itself could easily become a symbolic construct, an apotheosis of the 'national' landscape.

The crucial factor with regard to the effectiveness of any piece of work was its reception by the audience. Although the main and decisive consumers of culture in the context of the social settings at the time were educated, the professional structure of these consumers varied greatly. In state-nations the consumers of culture roughly corresponded with the intellectual elites and ruling classes of this nation. In contrast, the consumers of culture were yet to be found in the settings of national movements, and often rose from a completely difference social background into the elites of state nations. Our findings about the key 'players' in the life of the nation, and the differences in their social composition and social origin, also apply to the consumers of national culture, as they usually comprised the same circle of people. While the variations in the social anchoring of the members of the cultural audience in different national movements may have influenced the form and content of the new cultural works, they would not have changed the fact that these works were being created consciously within a national context.

In the nineteenth century, the adjective 'national' came to signify quality. National distinctness, expressed chiefly by language, stood for the quality of the work (without excluding such a possibility), which was a reflection of the Herderian dream that the purpose of all national cultures is to enrich the culture of mankind as a whole: each work of a nation would be a contribution to the culture of all mankind. The degree of emphasis differed, however. The French cultural world, for instance, had such a high level of inherent confidence in being the most evolved national culture in the world that there was no need for cultural production to reflect its relationship with the nation. This held true to such an extent that even anti-traditionalist tendencies, which in some cases criticised nationalism, were essentially French. The same applies to English cultural production.

The German and Italian cultures, on the other hand, were much more explicit in emphasising that the national culture ought to be of a high standard, and ideally comparable with the artistic level of French culture. These cultures also contained clear expressions of national, patriotic, or, as some might say, 'nationalistic' nature, both within literature and elsewhere. It is not an accident that great opera composers such as Richard Wagner and Giuseppe Verdi were not only seen as the key figures of the German and Italian national cultures respectively, but were also later interpreted (either in positive or negative terms) within the context of radical nationalism.

This is one of the features that the German and Italian cultures have in common with the national cultures that originated from national movements. Bedřich Smetana, often criticised as a Wagnerian, became the creator of the Czech national opera, Stanisław Moniuszko of the Polish opera, Edvard Grieg of Norwegian national music, and Jean Sibelius of the Finnish equivalent. An awareness of being 'behind', and a resulting determination to catch up with the more evolved cultures, motivated the development of the older national cultures of the Germans, Italians and Polish, as well as the emerging national cultures of ethnic communities, such as the Norwegians, Czechs, Magyars and Finns. A necessary condition for this was a sufficiently large and interested audience. It is noteworthy that the national movements, which succeeded in attaining a high level of national literature and culture by the turn of the twentieth century, had all reached their mass-movement phase during the nineteenth century and possessed, in terms of their social composition, a wealthy middle class and educated elites.

Literature was naturally the most significant means of spreading national identity. Growing literacy and reduction in censorship led to greater numbers of readers, while reading societies and the creation of communal, municipal and private lending libraries played an important role in facilitating communication and awakening awareness. Collections to finance the publication of books[13] and build lending libraries became a major instrument of national mobilisation. In some national movements, a book written in the national language became a symbol and a 'code' of national belonging.

Theatre served as an aspect of national culture on two levels, both of which were rooted in the past. On the one hand, there was the 'big' theatre, which was a platform where the members of the elites of state-nations met and demonstrated their erudition. Although this theatre in state-nations maintained its traditional links with the Estates for a long time, in its essence it gradually became the expression of a modern national culture. Conversely, theatre could perform a similar function in national movements only once they had reached their mass-mobilisation phase – i.e. when it could serve as a 'shrine' to the national spirit and language, a place where the nation's cultural public opinion was formed.

On the other hand, there was also folk theatre that built on the tradition of travelling theatre groups, and was a complementary means of national communication among the social strata that could not overcome the social and wealth barriers keeping them apart from those who attended the 'big' theatres. In other words, big theatre mainly played a nationally uniting role in state-nations, while folk theatre (including amateur theatre) had a similar function in national movements, especially in their agitation phase. That being said, almost all national movements strove to create a permanent and truly representative 'national' theatre – the Czechs, for instance, achieved it by the early 1880s, and the Estonians at the turn of the twentieth century. However, especially in the provinces, amateur theatre retained its nationally educational function even after 'bricks-and-mortar' theatre had been established.

The so-called folk culture constituted a specific aspect of national culture. In the true sense of the word, it was a 'discovery' of the Romantic era, but its status and role differed in relation to the type of national culture that pertained. In state-nations it acted as an embellishment and a rarity, which was applauded but remained on the periphery of interest. In contrast, in national movements folk culture acquired a role that – strictly speaking – it was not entitled to: it became a symbol of the nation's 'perennial existence', and a proof of the advancement of the national genius. The weaker the inherited literary tradition was, the more emphasis there was on folk culture. Although in some cases folk art served as a source of the central national myth (for example, the Finnish *Kalevala*, the Estonian *Kalevipoeg*, and Serbian heroic songs), in most cases it was an inspiration and a symbol. For many decades, the national construct of 'folksiness' within the art of these nations stood for value, and provided important, if not normative, foundations for national art, whether these were works of literature, music or 'national' architecture.

Linguistic Demands of National Movements

While views on the importance of language in ethnic identification vary greatly, it is clear that the players in most nation-building processes used language not only as a means of communication but also as an identification code and instrument of national mobilisation. The idea that a single nation or nation-state would not be united in linguistic terms was inconceivable to most nineteenth-century intellectuals – whether they were active patriots or not. This was partly a legacy of Enlightened Absolutism and its efforts to achieve uniformity and linguistic homogeneity. It also stemmed from the idea that a nation was an entity whose integrity was, among other things, reflected in its use of a single language.

As I have noted, there was a latent internal conflict between two motivations: the need to create a single state language and to provide all ethnically defined nations with a literary language. Whereas these two goals were compatible in state-nations, the opposite was true in national movements – the fact that multi-ethnic empires each had a unified state language ruled out the possibility of national movements using their own languages. Let us put aside this conflict and its impact on politics at this point, and instead look closely at the linguistic efforts made in the context of modern nation-building, which display (albeit with a delay) a number of common traits. I will disregard the developmental type of nation-forming, but pay close attention to the phase of national movements or nation-building in which linguistic demands were made.

Language-related demands and attitudes can be divided into five levels or segments, which occurred in sequence and were cumulative: as the linguistic demands became more complex with time, they built on the earlier elements and presupposed their existence. This internal differentiation will enable us to place language policies within specific social contexts, and analyse the social background of each of their segments.

In defence and celebration of language

The defence of language was by no means peculiar to national movements. The aesthetic value of language, its history and ability to express complex thoughts and feelings, were already being emphasised in Italy, France and England during Humanism.[14] Cases of the celebration of a language and of a longing for its fame have been sporadically documented since early medieval times.[15] Understandably, efforts to preserve a language soon became integrated into phase A of most national movements. Celebration of the German, Magyar and Czech languages dates back to the eighteenth century. Arguments in defence of the Dutch language, which were employed in the Austrian Netherlands in the second half of the eighteenth century, attacked the French language.[16] In the first half of the nineteenth century, celebrations and defences of the national language were published in Norway, Finland, Croatia, and later also Catalonia.[17] The arguments employed in defence of the language involved references to its aesthetic value, its glorious past and the practical relevance of its usage. Although these celebrations tend to be associated with the influence of the ideas of Johann Herder, it should be remembered that this was not always the case. Some were created earlier, and some authors were unaware of Herder's work. The erroneous conclusion that national movements concentrated on linguistic demands as a result of Herder's influence is a popular stereotype and a legacy of the earlier research tradition.

Celebration of language was common among arguments employed by most national movements in the context of national agitation, although its role was now quite different. During phase A it had primarily aimed to appeal to intellectuals and the ruling elites, rationalising the distinctness of a non-state language and justifying it to those who made decisions about its usage and recognition. During national agitation it became a patriotic argument, which mainly addressed the members of the same ethnic group and urged them to cherish their mother tongue as one of the fundamental bonds guaranteeing their national identity. This argument was common to all national agitation, irrespective of when or where in Europe it took place.

The Czech journal *Čechoslav*, for example, updated and re-ran its article on the defence of the German language from Hormayr's *Archiv* in 1824, which among other things states that 'he who does not love his mother tongue is not a friend of the homeland'.[18] Some seventy years later, the founder of the Basque movement, Sabino Arana, wrote that 'if you do not love the language of your homeland, you cannot love your homeland either'.[19] The motto that one of the founders of the Finnish national movement, Johan Vilhelm Snellman, created in the 1840s claimed that 'without Finnish we are not Finns',[20] and a similar notion was voiced in Catalonia some fifty years later: 'language . . . is the spiritual foundation of our existence'. At the beginning of the twentieth century, the Catholic Belarusian patriots even approached the Pope in their determination to defend their language.[21] By no means can this be accounted for by a mere mechanical reference to 'cultural transfer'.

In connection with this new focus on the celebration of language, we must touch upon the recipients of national demands and national activities in general. The leaders of national movements pursued their demands in two directions:

1. 'Outwardly' – approaching the state administration, local authorities, ruling intellectuals, nobility, government, and so on, with the aim of obtaining approval and support for their linguistic and other goals.
2. 'Inwardly' – turning to their own ranks in efforts to mobilise the potential members of the rising nation for the adoption of a literary language and participation in patriotic activities.

Endeavouring to codify the language

The long journey from a spoken dialect (vernacular) to language codification was a reflection of the need for modernisation and an essential element of cultural standardisation.[22] It must be remembered that its timing was markedly different in state-nations than in most national movements. In state-nations, efforts to establish a civic nation were preceded by successful attempts at codification of the language – in France, for example, from as early as the seventeenth century.

In some national movements patriots were able to build on the language of publications dating back to the early modern period, and they served as a source and foundation of linguistic norms. In other national movements, linguistic norms were founded upon dialects, and in others upon translations of official documents from the language of the state elites, upon the terms used in the economic sphere, or upon religious life and the like. Joshua Fishman uses the term 'language planning' to denote the parallel existence of three processes: linguistic organisation, popularisation and standardisation. All of these processes were present in decrees from the time of the French Revolution, and concerned themselves primarily with a consistent usage of the newly codified language for the purposes of education and agitation, rather being quests for a linguistic code and codification.[23]

It should be noted that the role of 'language planning' went beyond standardising the culture and popularising the language. When the leaders of national movements defined a nation in terms of language and culture, they had to determine where this definition finished – i.e. where the nation started, where its boundaries lay, who belonged to it and who did not. The search for a linguistic standard was the only means of drawing a clear and comprehensible border between the in-group and the out-group.[24]

It was usual for educated discussions about grammar and spelling to have already taken place during phase A, and to have led to the publication of dictionaries and grammar books. However, the findings of individual researchers did not always correspond to generally accepted linguistic norms. Discussions about language codification tended also to continue during phase B, as a result of which they were increasingly affected by agitation as well as linguistic factors. Finding the 'right' linguistic norm – unless its foundations had been laid during phase A – became a national goal. This gave rise to the persisting belief that there is a constant need to nurture and perfect the standard language – a need for the so-called 'protective approach' to language.[25] This nurturing involved attempts to cleanse the national language of foreign elements, tending towards linguistic purism, the effectiveness and rationale of which are a subject of discussion up to the present day.[26]

Individual paths towards linguistic codification were asynchronous, which corresponded with the overall asynchronicity of the nation-forming processes. They also varied greatly from the point of view of the linguistic circumstances in which they arose, and in terms of the selected principles. In simple terms, almost all national movements in phase A were confronted with two options:

1. Take advantage of the older tradition, preserved in the form of 'printed language' or medieval literary language, the success of which was largely determined by the strength and continuity of this linguistic tradition.
2. Build upon the current spoken language, in which case the success was mainly dependent on the ability to resolve the issue of different dialects.[27]

The process of creating modern Czech is a classic example of language codification based on an older tradition of a literary language, despite its not being entirely free of friction. The search for a standard norm in Catalan was able to draw on a similar advantage. In contrast, endeavours to build on an older literary language in Wales, and particularly in Ireland, were met with great difficulties, while the return to medieval literary Norwegian was never even considered by the Norwegian national movement, and remained a dream of a handful of individuals. The Norwegian approach to continuity with a standard language was indeed unique, in that it adopted Danish, the language of the ruling elites, and modified it to suit Norwegian pronunciation. It was not until phase B that a movement formed, advocating a new language that had been created by combining different dialects. This movement was only partially successful, as a result of which both linguistic norms continued to exist side by side.[28]

National movements that took place within the territory of the Eastern Orthodox Church had to deal with the fact that the only literary language that could be claimed as a bearer of the national cultural tradition was Old Church Slavonic, albeit modified in relation to local linguistic circumstances. In the Serbian national movement, voices demanding the use of the Serbian form of Old Church Slavonic remained restricted to only a section of the clergy, and played a marginal role. The supporters of Old Church Slavonic in the Bulgarian national movement were able to take advantage of its being a symbol of resistance to the Greek language, and of Greek domination of Bulgarian church life. However, the plans to return to this dead church language were abandoned after discussions that had begun in the 1840s. The tendency to build upon the tradition of Old Church Slavonic was the longest-lived in the Ukrainian national movement, where some patriots were convinced that it would help bridge not only the marked differences in dialects but also the differences stemming from the political divisions of the territories in which these dialects were spoken.[29] In all these cases, a focus on the spoken language eventually prevailed. In Greece the conflict between the advocates of the old literary language of Katharevousa and supporters of the modern linguistic norm of Dimotiki culminated in the two norms coexisting until the twentieth century. In this sense, there is a parallel between the unusual two-track language codification in Greece and Norway.[30]

The codifying of the national language on the basis of a living, spoken language was confronted with the difficulty of deciding which of the dialects represented the desired, pure 'core' of the language. While the journey from a spoken to a standard language was relatively straightforward in a few cases, it proved especially compli-cated in areas where the dialects were markedly different.[31] The search for the norms of the national language concerned primarily those national movements that could not build on an older tradition of their own literary language.[32] Language codification was a long process, in which opposing views clashed but which simultaneously helped eliminate concepts that were contrary to linguistic and social realities.[33] This needs to be taken into account when reading present-day contemplations of languages being arbitrary creations and 'artificial constructs' that somehow originated by chance.[34] It holds true that the success and speed of modern nation-building – within state-nations as well as national movements – was partly dependent on how fast a general consensus was reached on the issue of codification of the national language, and how fast the linguistic norm spread. However, there were cases where national mobilisation was successful despite linguistic instability, such as in Norway, the Ukraine and Slovenia.

From the point of view of the recipients, activities related to lan-guage codification typically tried to appeal to the members of the forming nation by offering them a cohesive, modern literary lan-guage. The effectiveness of this offer was much less to do with the 'agitators' themselves than with the extent to which their linguistic construct was in tune with the language (and social) circumstances and social communication needs of the time.

Intellectualising the national language

A codified language could become a living language only if it proved that, in the context of cultural life, it was capable of expressing a wide range of themes, reaching beyond the day-to-day topics of conver-sation. The term 'intellectualisation' is used in this book to refer to this process. A brief examination may lead to the impression that language intellectualisation was specific to national movements that could not make use of an older tradition of literary work. But a more accurate statement is that attempts at the intellectualisation of the language in state nations was a serious task, which fell into the cat-egory of state-national cultural policies.

While it would appear logical to assume that standardisation of a language was a precondition for its intellectualisation, this was not the historical reality. Linguistic norms were often only established in the process of creating literary works. Perhaps the most famous example of this is the role of Alessandro Monzani's novel *The Betrothed* (*I Promessi sposi*) in finding a resolution to the conflict between the tradition of the Tuscan literary language and the North Italian literature over which it was the binding version of standard Italian.

It was not within the power of educated discussions about grammar and orthography to stop patriotic writers from publishing their creations. However, it is also true that literary work sometimes developed with a marked delay, which corresponded to the asynchronous nature of nation-forming processes, and often greatly influenced scientific discussions about linguistic norms and decisions pertaining to whether or not a particular dialect was accepted.

Independently of this asynchronicity, it can be said that all national movements gradually embraced efforts to develop the newly established (revived) standard language of their emerging nation in various literary genres. In this context, we can differentiate six groups of activities, which generally followed one another:

1. Newspaper reporting and educational reading for ordinary people usually constituted the earliest form of intellectualisation. Newspaper and magazine publishing stood at the outset of phase B of most national movements (in some cases it had already been established in phase A), and through their function of agitation and communication they enriched and developed the rising modern language.

2. The gathering, adaptation and imitation of folk poetry and folk culture in general was deployed at the beginning of all national movements, but played a major role in those where patriotic scholars had had a very limited opportunity in phase A to build upon an older tradition of a 'printed language', such as in Finland, the Baltics and the Ukraine. As has been noted, folk poetry served as a source of inspiration, temporarily even as a substitute for a nation's own literary work, and as a source for the rudimentary elements of historical consciousness (for example, the Finnish *Kalevala* and Serbian heroic songs).

3. The nation's original poetry, as well as translations and paraphrases of works of poetry from developed literatures, initially

acted as means of enhancing and advancing the emerging languages, and as proof of their level of development. They also conveyed attractive pieces of writing that sought to raise national awareness. Patriotic poems were recited at every occasion, and their texts were set to music as patriotic songs.

4. Short narratives and stories were originally created chiefly for the purposes of patriotic magazines, and formed most of their content. The writing of novels tended to follow later – the main reason for this delay being that, if these larger versions of fiction were to be published in book form, a market of readers needed to emerge first, creating the necessary demand. This was a question of wealth as well as of the level of education among the readers within the non-dominant ethnic group. A hypothesis offers itself here that the attainment of the whole spectrum of genres in literature, including novels, falls approximately into the same period as the achievement of a complete social structure within the emerging nation. Only then did the category of writers, as state-nations had known them for a long time, emerge: independent authors who made a living from the sales of their own literary work.

5. Theatre plays were, in some national movements, one of the very early genres in which the new language found its use, provided that at least wandering and amateur theatres were allowed the political and material circumstances to exist. Theatre performances had the specific role of spreading the knowledge of the standard language, and often also of its correct pronunciation.

6. Scientific research was confronted with the arduous task of creating its own terminology. Only those national communities that comprised sufficient numbers of university-educated scholars and possessed scientific institutions could call for the creation of their own national scientific language. In this respect, individual national movements varied greatly.

As has been noted, discussions took place within some national movements over the purpose that the 'revival' of a given language should serve. In the Estonian national movement of the 1870s, for instance, consideration was given to whether it would suffice to stop at translations from developed literatures. As late as 1905, a number of leaders in the Ukrainian national movement recommended that the newly codified Ukrainian language be used primarily when writing educational literature for ordinary people, newspapers, and light fiction.[35]

National language in schools

If the standard language was to fulfil its social and communication functions, it needed to be learned and adopted by as many citizens as possible – ideally, all of them. While this was a natural assumption for both enlightened reformists and revolutionaries from the second half of the eighteenth century, the question remained as to how it could be achieved. The state lacked the money, and often also the inclination, to implement consistent general school education. Therefore, knowledge of the standard language continued to remain part of the social barrier and a symbolic code of the social classes who monopolised access to education, which signified power. This was as true of the members of the German *Bildungsbürgertum* as of the English aristocracy and the university elites or the French notables. In state-nations, calls for equal education in the national language were almost Jacobite in their essence, and could be carried out only once advanced levels of democratisation had been reached within the educational system.

What was an expression of democratic radicalism in a state-nation represented existential inevitability in a national movement. The new ('revived') language was not viable until it became the language of schools. The language first needed to find its 'consumers', even though external circumstances tended to fall short of 'market' conditions. Endeavours to make it the language of schools were directed both 'outwardly' (to state and local authorities) and 'inwardly' (to one's own ethnic group). State authorities were requested to support schools in which pupils would receive education in their mother tongue, and would be taught this language. Simultaneously, parents were asked to send their children to these national, patriotic schools – provided they existed and the parents had a choice.

Fighting for the opportunity to attend a national school became an effective tool of national mobilisation, both within national movements and state nations, which also needed citizens who spoke the state language and embraced the national culture. Children's attendance was not the sole objective; school attendance strengthened bonds that connected the members of forming state-nations as much as they connected participants in national movements. Besides facilitating communication, language education at schools principally created a 'consciousness of common belonging' – within both ruling nations and national movements.[36] At schools pupils learned not only the literary form of their mother tongue, but also to observe, describe, understand and interpret reality through identically defined terms, and thus in a similar manner.[37] The question of the extent to which this identical viewing of reality also affected people's national identification has yet to be analysed in depth, and is an important research task.

Whereas state-nations gradually achieved a substantial increase in school attendance, the success of the struggle for national schools in the context of national movements depended on the state school policy of the multi-ethnic empire in question. These policies varied greatly between empires, and changed in relation to their internal developments. A further factor to be considered is that variations existed in individual state policies with regard to the different types of school attendance.

In those areas of the Austrian Empire that were ethnically diverse and lacked a pronounced ethnic consciousness – for example, some of the Slovenian and Slovak regions – school education was bilingual. Linguistic tolerance was also present in the Baltics and in Finland, within Tsarist Russia. Conversely, Lithuanian, Belarusian and Ukrainian schools had to teach in Russian, and it was not until the revolutionary year of 1905 that important lasting changes were achieved by the national demands of the respective national movements.

However, authoritarian enforcement of the state language at schools was by no means peculiar to multi-ethnic empires of the Russian and Austrian types; parallels existed especially in France and Spain. Pupils in Alsace and in Brittany were penalised for using the local vernaculars (*patois*) as late as the turn of the twentieth century. The rise of the national movement in Wales at the beginning of the 1840s was triggered by a parliamentary proposal for English to be the compulsory language of teaching, in the interest of raising the population's living standards. In contrast, the Prussian school policy was based on a proven concept that teaching the youngest children at schools in the language of a non-dominant ethnic group provided a favourable basis for Germanising the pupils later. For practical reasons, primary schools in all multi-ethnic empires (with a few exceptions within Tsarist Russia) were eventually allowed to teach in the mother tongue.

The teaching of a codified national language at primary schools posed difficulties not only in the context of national movements. Even in parts of state-nations, where people spoke dialects different from the state language, children from ordinary families experienced a 'cultural shock' on joining a school. They had to learn a language they had come across before but which was not necessarily easy to master – for example, in southern France, in several parts of Spain, in the southern and some of the northern provinces of Italy, and also in the Catholic regions of Germany, where Luther's German was not automatically part of parish life.

The situation was very different at secondary schools, which educated the potential elites of state-nations and multi-ethnic empires. It was therefore in the state's interest not to allow tuition to be conducted in anything other than the state language, least of all the language of a non-dominant ethnic group. Throughout the nineteenth century, the higher levels of education in state-nations were almost entirely monopolised by the intellectual elites, for whom the standard language and the 'mother' tongue were one and the same, and for whom mastering the state language was thus not an issue. The same was true of the Italian intellectuals and the German *Bildungsbürgertum*.

By contrast, all national movements struggled to include the local language as one of the school subjects, let alone make it the language of education. National movements pursued two sets of goals: while their most basic agenda was for the national language to be a subject taught in schools, their higher objective was the opening of not only secondary schools but also grammar schools, where languages such as Finnish, Czech and Slovak would be the languages of tuition.

Whereas the national movement in Cisleithania proved very successful in this respect, especially after 1861, the situation was far more complicated in Transleithania, Prussia and Russia, where there were strong tendencies to assimilate the 'minorities' by means of school education. The Magyarisation of the education system in Hungary started after 1870, and the Russification of the schools in the Baltics in the 1880s – in a similar manner in which schools were Germanised after the unification of Germany. Consequently, the once-permitted grammar schools where the language of tuition was not Magyar were abolished in Hungary, and Magyar was increasingly enforced even in primary schools, at the expense of the local languages. Russification put an end, above all, to the first attempts at building Latvian and Estonian secondary schools, while the Finnish education system managed to retain some degree of independence. It should be remembered that Swedish was the language of higher education in Finland and German in the Baltics, and that, prior to Russification, the Finnish, Estonian and Latvian patriots had struggled against the resistance of the local – Swedish and German – elites and their determination to maintain their monopoly on education.[38]

Only in a few countries was there a university within the territory of an ethnic group. This was the case of the Magyar, Czech, Norwegian, Finnish and Flemish national movements. The Magyar and Norwegian movements succeeded in introducing the national language to their universities in the shortest space of time, followed by the Polish movement in Galicia and in 1882 also by the Czech movement. Universities were important for the language agenda of national movements as places where the norm of the language was institutionalised, in the form of a Chair who was responsible for teaching the national language.[39] This placed national movements with such an opportunity within their territory or its vicinity at an advantage – compared, for instance, with those in the Balkans or Russia.

Problems with complete language equality

In the context of state-nations, the notion that a literary language of a non-dominant ethnic group could be placed on a completely equal footing with the state language was a matter of wishful thinking and utopianism. Allowing two official languages into public life, administration, postal and railway communications, and so on, was contrary to the fundamental principles of running a centralised civic state. The situation was quite different in multi-ethnic empires, where the determining factor was the extent to which ethnicity-based federalisation or autonomy occurred. Such an arrangement was naturally adopted in the Union between Sweden and Norway and, for a short time, was also applied to the relationship between Swedish and Finnish, and Russian and German, in the Baltic provinces of Russia. Austrian-Hungarian dualism allowed Magyar to become the language of administration in Hungary – although this achievement had its darker side, in that it led to a suppression of non-Magyar languages. Polish acquired its status as an official language in Galicia in the second half of the nineteenth century.

The constitutional system of the Habsburg monarchy enabled not only the Magyar but also the Czech and Croatian national movements to try to enforce the use of the national language in the lower levels of state administration and the courts. In Bohemia and Moravia, attempts to achieve equal rights for Czech were firmly resisted by the local German elites, for whom they would result in the duty to learn the Czech language. Outside the Habsburg monarchy, Finnish demands for linguistic equality celebrated partial successes as early as the 1850–60s,[40] but even there the local Swedish-speaking elites were against a complete adoption of Finnish by the authorities, and refused to learn it. Until 1905 national movements everywhere else in the Russian Empire tried in vain to achieve at least small concessions with regard to the authorities' linguistic practices. When Latvian and Estonian patriots did achieve some minor concessions within the local administration, these were at the expense of German, not Russian.[41] Dutch began to be integrated at the lower levels of administration in the Flemish parts of Belgium in the 1870s.[42]

The issue of complete linguistic equality naturally became an object of political struggle. When linguistic demands achieved partial successes, they entered the realm of social demands and conflicts, as they sooner or later began to threaten the monopoly on power enjoyed by the bureaucratic elites of the ruling nation. The struggle for linguistic equality thus simultaneously became a struggle over posts within state administration. For the growing numbers of qualified intellectuals from ethnic groups whose mother tongue was not the state language (i.e. non-Russians, non-Germans, later non-Magyars, and also non-French-speaking Belgians), calls for the complete equality of their (by then fully codified) mother tongue stood for more than an emphasis of the symbols of national prestige. They were an expression of their social demands for equal chances of upward social mobility for all of the state's citizens. It is perhaps unnecessary to add that such a shift in attitudes was more likely to occur in places where the principle of civic equality had been successfully applied – i.e. primarily in the Austro-Hungarian Empire.

For the sake of completeness, it should be noted that the issue of language in the Ottoman Empire also derived from the principle of religious segregation of the non-Muslim population. Elementary education in the local vernacular posed no difficulties when it was conducted in private settings, one form of which was the self-governing millets. The cultural-religious dominance of Greek at that time often played a major role – upward social mobility tended to go hand-in-hand with religious conversion rather than linguistic assimilation, although Greek was in many cases the 'second' ruling language.

The whim of intellectuals or a social need?

Whether we consider the language agenda to be a significant chapter in the history of national struggle or a childish and long-outmoded pastime of 'nationalist' intellectuals, we cannot disregard its political and cultural relevance. It had long-term consequences for the mentalities and cultures of state-nations as well as nations that rose from non-dominant ethnic groups. Therefore, it is essential to turn our attention to the questions of why the language agenda was present in most national movements, and whether the fact that it played such a major role in most movements is the key factor. It is also important to examine what made language demands successful.

Could it be that there were elements within the language itself that caused political or social conflict? There are a number of examples in the past when speaking the same language was an instrument, or at least an expression, of group solidarity, which could usually only be put into effect in rare circumstances.[43]

With the rise of absolutism, language became a more important group bond, which reached beyond the relationships within the consolidating national state. Opposition to absolutist language policies, as we know it from Hungary, the southern Netherlands and the Baltic provinces of Russia, had an integrating effect, although it remained restricted to the aristocracy, who were – together with their language – defending their old privileges (in Hungary it was

Latin rather than the national language that was defended at first). As has been noted, in the majority of the absolutist monarchies of Western and Eastern Europe, linguistic centralism and homogenisation of the language of administration were not initially met with any substantial resistance connected to national agitation. Even the scholarly phase A of national movements was not necessarily aimed at the language policy of absolutism. Why was it, then, that groups of intellectuals in various parts of Europe decided independently of each other to commence fighting for the literary language of 'their' ethnic group? One reason was undoubtedly the profound crisis of the old regime and its system of values and interrelationships. Another reason was the rise of modernisation, which, as we have seen, was connected with the secularisation of thought and the rationalisation of state administration. All these transformations gave rise to the need for a new type of group solidarity, which in the specific circumstances of non-dominant ethnic groups may have led to the perception that the language homogenisation, as practised by the Austrian government in the interest of the German language and by the Russian government in the interest of the Russian language, was detrimental to members of the non-dominant ethnic group, and so denied them equal opportunities within society. Increasingly, therefore, it came into conflict with the evolving tendency to assert the principles of civic equality and equal opportunities for everyone. These notions were initially advocated by only a handful of intellectuals, whose linguistic demands could not rely on any power arguments. However, the language agenda gained support in spite of this, and we thus need to ask what the specific causes of this were.

Admittedly, this development was not inevitable. There were several cases in which the linguistic and cultural agenda was not at the forefront of the demands made by the national movement, and was secondary to the political programme. We may thus wish to modify the question to take account of the alternatives where, while language was the bearer and expression of national identity, phase B of the national movement was dominated by political demands. Since it is not evident that the linguistic and cultural agenda was a priority in phase B everywhere, we must ask why the participants in national movements found the new standard language appealing. If we adopt the notion that patriots offered the linguistic alternative of the national programme as a specific type of 'goods', then it was of crucial importance what types of 'consumer' and social groups were approached with this specific offer, and if there was any social 'demand' for the newly forming national community's own standard language.[44]

Did the social structure of the non-dominant ethnic group and the content of the national programme correspond in any way? One noteworthy correlation is that each national movement that in its phase B focused primarily on political goals acted on behalf of a non-dominant ethnic group with a complete social structure – the measure of 'completeness' being the levels of social development reached within the whole region. This was the case of the Polish, Greek, Norwegian and Irish national movements, and even the rise of the Serbian national movement occurred at a point when the social structure of the Serbian ethnie was 'complete', if judged by the standards within the underdeveloped inland Balkans.

However, discovering a correlation is not the same as discovering causality. It merely indicates an important connection and a relationship which needs to be verified. Let us return to those cases in which the linguistic agenda dominated. If we accept the thesis proposed by sociolinguists that a change in the attitude to the language – and therefore also the adoption of a new literary language – was 'a response to great social processes' and changes,[45] then our question can be worded more precisely: why did the leaders of ethnic groups that lacked a complete social structure tend in phase B to give preference to linguistic and cultural demands?

Older literature commonly answers this question by referring to the influence of Herder and to the 'eastern' type of nationalism, which is emphasised by Kohn and his followers.[46] But it must be remembered that Herder's philosophy of language was not an 'eastern' peculiarity; it can also be found among the Flemish and Catalans, and even within the Irish, Welsh and Norwegian national movements.[47] There was also, of course, the influence of Rousseau and the German Romantics, such as Schelling and Fichte.[48] Unfortunately, this interpretation is based on the unverifiable idea of a 'spirit of nationalism' which has 'left its mark in various parts of Europe'. Even if we accepted this notion at an abstract level, as a cultural transfer, we would not be able to explain the above-mentioned correlation between the social structure and the content of the national programme. There was, doubtless, such a thing as transfer of thought and values, but that alone does not account for why national movements with a complete social structure were less inclined to embrace information about Herder's philosophy of language. Nor will the application of Karl Deutsch's theory of communication be of help here. While the increasing intensity of social communication will have been an essential precondition for the success of national agitation, and for the growing importance of language, it offers no answers as to why the importance of language varied from one national movement to the next.

Continual references to the influence of Romanticism are equally unhelpful. The role of Romanticism and Romantics in national movements is indisputable. However, they were present in national movements that gave priority to the political agenda as well as those that did not. National movements were no doubt related to Romanticism, but this relationship stemmed from the common roots of these two phenomena – Romanticism was also a reaction to the great crisis of legitimacy and of old values, caused in turn by the crisis of late feudal society.[49] It holds true that the national language, and the literature written in this language, were an obvious connection, which offered new certainties, and above all a new identity.[50] Causality could, therefore, also be identified in the opposite direction: the Romantics may have regarded an orientation towards identifying with a modern civic nation as a possible way out of the crisis of identities and value systems of the old society, from which they distanced themselves.

A deeper understanding requires more than mere references to influences and transfers; it requires a search for more general foundations. Let us start with the fact that the spreading literacy led to an increase in the number of people who were able to 'imagine' a nation, in Benedict Anderson's sense of the word. For this segment of the population, literacy and education became – to use Gellner's term – an 'entrance ticket' to full citizenship and human dignity. The difficulty was that in multi-ethnic states this ticket was only valid for those whose mother tongue was identical to the state language, which was usually also the language of secondary education.[51] As communication intensified, bilingualism became a solution for others – i.e. the speakers of a different 'L*-language' (as the term is used by Joshua Fishman). Diglossia was ceasing to be viable in societies where people were exchanging information with a growing intensity, and was inevitably supplemented by bilingualism, linked to the adoption of the state language. An alternative response to this pivotal situation was a national movement that offered the speakers of an 'L*-language' the prospect of being able to participate in society by enabling them to use, next to the state language ('H-language') that was unfamiliar to them, the codified, intellectualised version of their own 'H*-language', which claimed to be the successor to their 'pre-industrial language'.[52]

The actual historical circumstances were not as harmonious as may be inferred from Fishman's model. 'H-languages' and 'L*-languages' were not only different but also unequal, as a result of which the freedom of choice on the part of speakers of 'L-languages' and 'H*-languages' was negligible. This was partly because bilingualism was an absolute necessity for those who wished to rise socially, and largely because social rising was impossible for the vast majority of those who lacked the opportunity or ability to speak the 'H-language'. The fact that they came from lower social classes and spoke a language (or its dialect) that had a lower status permanently kept them in a 'lower category' of human beings, with all the associated feelings of degradation. Language acquired a specific role in this situation in terms of their outlook on the world. While they could theoretically still adopt the 'H-language' and become assimilated, from a certain point in time they were confronted with a different option: to adopt a new standard national language very similar or identical with their 'L*-language'.[53]

It is valid to argue that language inferiority had existed since medieval times without causing discontent among the speakers of an 'L*-language'. There is a simple explanation for this: in feudal society, where inequality among people was dictated by birth, the unequal status of the people's language was part of the system, and considered to be natural. The gradual loosening of feudal ties and the disruption of the stereotypes of the 'old regime', together with growing access to education, led to the spread of basic Enlightenment notions of human worth and equality. It was increasingly unacceptable for individuals who adopted this new value system, even if only partially, to be regarded as less worthy purely on the basis of their not speaking the state language as well as its native speakers.

Why did they not adopt the state language? And why did all the places occupied by non-dominant ethnic groups not experience mass assimilation, as was the case in France? The answers are not clear-cut, and a number of factors must be considered. First, it is obvious that assimilation, connected to upward social mobility, was not simply a question of personal choice. It would not even be possible for everyone who decided to adopt the state language to become part of the middle or higher social classes. The number of educated individuals grew not only within the non-dominant ethnic group but also, and more markedly, among the elites of the state-nation. Consequently, the 'proto-elite' came into being – a group of people who belonged to the elites by education but whose origin kept them 'aside', preventing them from joining the ranks of the state elites. These were the people for whom the alternative of a new, linguistically defined community was the most attractive – and a group that many leaders of national movements stemmed from. In addition, this alternative promised the opportunity to rise socially and gain prestige without the need for assimilation.[54]

These observations lead us back to the initial question of whether the nature of the social structure and the importance of language for the national movement correlated in any meaningful, causal manner.

1. As modernisation progressed, access to education broadened, which presented even the members of the lower classes with the chance to rise socially. However, this opportunity was not equal, and was much less favourable for members of 'non-dominant ethnic groups', even those who had become bilingual. The greater the difficulties they encountered on their path to a higher social standing, the more they associated their social standing (and difficulties) with the language they spoke and considered to be their own.[55] This correlation between social situation and language was weaker in places where non-dominant ethnic group had a complete social structure. Difficulties with upward social mobility were therefore connected with social origin, and cannot be seen as stemming from linguistic differences.

2. Even if we assumed that everyone who chose to learn the state language could rise socially, this would not automatically lead to universal assimilation. It must be remembered that, for the speakers of an 'L*-language', complete bilingualism was not merely a question of attending school. Speaking the state language perfectly was also dependent on the individual's linguistic

skills, which varied. Linguistic talent cannot be directly linked to the value of IQ. Those, who could become familiar with the state language during their childhood were naturally in a different, advantageous position. This was true of mixed territories and, above all, families from the middle classes, which cared about their children's linguistic education. In addition, a perfect command of the state language also depended on the intellectual level at which the child's parents communicated. When linguistic talent was the same, the results of language teaching differed in relation to what social and intellectual background the child came from.[56] For example, Czech patriots issued a memorandum in 1832, in which they pointed out that children from the Czech lower classes who were attending German-speaking schools would not learn proper German, and nor would they have a command of standard Czech.[57]

3. Political culture also played an important role. In non-dominant ethnic groups whose social structure lacked higher classes and educated elites, the patriots involved in the initial stages of phase B came from the lower or lower-middle classes, and it was this part of society to which they tried to appeal. Artisans in Bohemia and peasants in Estonia and Lithuania alike were social strata that had received no previous political experience or political education prior to national agitation. This is the reason why their national communities needed to be defined in terms that these social groups could easily understand.[58] They would hardly have understood from the very beginning the abstract terms of the civic programme. For an ordinary person, 'constitution' was an unfamiliar neologism. To a peasant, 'freedom' referred to being free from feudal levies and oppression, rather than freedom of speech and the press.[59] What made much more sense to these classes was group integration based on linguistic categories, and the language agenda continued to be seen as the priority even after the members of the forming nations had embraced the notions of civic rights.

Language as an object of political struggle

The one question that remains is why language retained its important position in the programmes of many national movements even after it was no longer under threat, since national agitation had succeeded, the national community had achieved a complete social structure, and it was engaged in a political struggle. As a consequence of national agitation, language had gained a permanent place among national values. Its position was so firm, in fact, that no political party could afford to disregard the linguistic demands of its nation, as Social Democrats discovered in some countries when they had distanced themselves from overplaying the importance of linguistic demands at the expense of social ones. Language, together with national culture, became the symbol of national existence and acquired a role extending far beyond its communication function.

Another socio-psychological factor that encouraged the cult of language within national life was the general feeling that a newly forming nation, if defined in terms of language and culture, was under threat. Consequently, every mistreatment of its language and each imposition on its equal rights during phase B was perceived as damage to national existence and a sign of a threat to the nation. Educated as well as ordinary people now shared the view – or, rather, the illusion – that their nation would perish unless sufficient care and protection were given to its language. Simultaneously, the (almost) general spread of the new linguistic norm and the intensification of mutual contact among people both helped bring the communication function of the language to the fore. Language facilitated direct contact between the speakers of the language, who were partners of communication. Not only did this strengthen group identity and a sense of solidarity among the speakers of the same language; it also made them more perceptive of any seeming or real inequality between languages.[60]

When national movements in multi-ethnic states proved successful, the language of the given forming nation gained a certain position, giving rise to a new diglossia that guaranteed the hegemony of the state language over new rival languages. This new diglossia no longer concerned two unequal languages H and L*, but two written languages H and H*. Although these languages were linguistically equal and intellectualised, they were unequal in terms of prestige and status, which meant that the struggle for complete equality of language could not abate. The opposite was true, since in mass national movements inequality of language was perceived as social inequality.[61]

The struggle for the language continued to be pursued 'inwardly'. The nurturing of the codified standard language did not rest solely upon efforts to secure equal rights for it, but also upon preserving its purity.[62] This was true of state-nations as well as national movements; use of the correct form of the standard language characterised the nationally conscious members of all nations, not only activists in national movements.[63] The use of the standard language increased the prestige of intellectuals and, at the same time, served the function of national discipline. It was a practicable and easily monitored appeal to people to uphold a code that strengthened national unity and the nation's readiness for action, which in turn provided the power base for the national leaders. This function of literary language was not exclusive to national movements, but was also present in the relationship between the elites and 'the people' once nation-states had emerged.

The previous statement has a broader validity. Once a national movement had achieved a mass response, language assumed an indisputable place in public and political life. It became similarly important in national movements as it was to the established 'historical' state-nations. In state-nations and mass national movements alike, efforts to ideologise and politicise language were not made only by intellectuals. Provided that national agitation proved successful, the forming nations sooner or later achieved a complete social composition; intellectuals, who had occupied the leading positions, were joined by the enterprising middle classes – the petty and wealthy bourgeoisie. Like the elites of state-nations, these new leaders of the forming nations considered linguistic culture to be a source of social prestige – it differentiated them from the members of the lower classes who did not use the standard language. From this perspective, language helped strengthen national identity and, simultaneously, also the social identity of the new elites.[64]

An important difference must be noted. Even when a language had been successfully codified and made more equal in the circumstances of a new diglossia, it remained at a disadvantage for as long as the multi-ethnic empire in question continued to exist. The state language – German, Magyar or Russian – retained its prestige and, as a consequence, language was greatly 'ideologised' by members of the forming nations and by the ruling elites.[65] It is of little surprise that, once full independence had been achieved, politicians as well as ordinary members of the nations embraced the language that they felt symbolised and reflected their newly formed nation-state's worth.[66] This is how language retained the emotional potential that the first generation of patriots had given it long after any threat of assimilation had faded. This strong emotional bond connected members of a nation, without excluding the major communication function of language.[67]

An important fact that must not be overlooked is that, in the circumstances of a constitutional regime and civic society, language became a criterion of civic equality. This included the expectation that all languages (in the same manner as all nations) ought to be regarded as equally worthy. In addition to this, the existence of a codified and intellectualised language, which had transcended fragmented vernaculars, provided all the citizens – members of the nation – with an equal opportunity to express themselves, at least in theory. The opportunity to learn the standard form of their mother tongue and use it in public was perceived as one of civic rights.[68]

It may be appropriate at this point to list at least some arguments that will to an extent call into question the importance of language in national movements. Many of the circumstances that have been characterised as 'nationally mobilising' can also be found in situations that did not give rise to national movements. Most members of state-nations only spoke a local dialect – i.e. an L-language – which placed them at a social disadvantage. They had very little chance of rising socially, could not fully participate in public life, and were socially stigmatised by not speaking the standard language.[69] This raises the question of why, for instance, Provençal, Low German, Sicilian or Breton attempts at agitation for a national movement (albeit aimed 'only' at the national culture) proved unsuccessful, and why Jutlandic, Mecklenburgian or Saxon national movements did not occur at all.

It should be remembered that language became politicised and acquired a symbolic value even in places where there was no need to defend its rights or fend off threats of assimilation. This applied to Christian ethnies under Ottoman rule, where assimilation was not a threat partly due to the fact that the official state language – Ottoman – was not a living language. When assimilation-like processes did occur, they took the form of religious assimilation, which was not accompanied by linguistic assimilation in the case of the Bosnians and Albanians. Clashes of languages in the Balkans took the form of Slavonic patriots resisting the dominance of the Greek language.

Instead of generalising prematurely, let us limit ourselves to the statement that linguistic bonds and ethnic belonging were not the only decisive factors in modern nation-forming, and need to be placed in the context of other interconnections and relationships. We can also illustrate the usefulness of the terminology employed with greater accuracy. If we decided to use the term 'nationalism', we would have to describe the above-mentioned problems as conflicts between two 'nationalisms' – Provençal (Occitan) and French, for example. Using, instead, the term 'identity' would make the statement clearer, making the conflict, for instance, one between French state-national identity and Provençal regional identity. The regional and the state-national identities might theoretically be compatible. Research can examine the circumstances under which a regional identity, combined with a different ethnicity, gradually transformed (or had the potential to transform) into a national identity. The general understanding was that, while an individual cannot belong to two nations simultaneously, belonging to both a nation and a regional identity was compatible. That being said, we know that in some situations regional identity gave rise to the notion that the regional-national culture was distinctive and different from the state-national culture. The intensity with which state-national identity was forming at the time when conditions were becoming favourable for the national movement of the non-dominant ethnic group was, therefore, an important consideration. For example, the French revolution focused (in keeping with the tradition of absolute centralism) on state-national identity so strongly that any later attempts at alternative 'secessionist' national identities were rendered ineffective.

In conclusion, the weight of the role of language in national movements cannot be seen as the result of activities by capricious Romantic intellectuals. This relationship was determined by the transformations that had taken place within society and its thinking, and it had firm roots in society.

It could be verified empirically that the priority of the linguistic programme in phase B of national movements correlated with an incomplete social structure of 'non-dominant ethnic groups', in which national movements originated. This correlation can be expressed by two rules:

1. During phase B, linguistic and cultural demands dominated (alongside social demands) the programmes of national movements whose social structure was clearly incomplete – i.e. where the academic elites, aristocracy or bourgeoisie were absent. The political programmes of most national movements were developed later, usually at the beginning or during phase C.
2. Political (and social) demands predominated in the programmes of phase B in national movements whose social structure included the economic and intellectual elites. The linguistic programme was secondary, or became part of the national programme at a later stage.

In other words, the importance of linguistic demands in phase B of national movements was inversely proportional to the share of the ruling classes and intellectual elites in the social structure of the non-dominant ethnic group at the outset of this phase.

This correlation was not accidental; it represented a causal relationship. In some social circumstances the rising national movement had no other alternative than to emphasise linguistic demands. These demands must not be seen as a cohesive unit, but rather as a set of at least five groups of demands. For social and social-psychological reasons, language had an important extra-linguistic, extra-communicational function, and influenced the political programme.

Focusing on the linguistic programme and on the ethnically defined nation was the way in which the educated members of the peripheral ethnic groups responded to the upheavals accompanying the rise of modernisation. In the general crisis of legitimacy of the old and absolutist regimes, these patriots used linguistic differences to define their group's inferiority. The success of their agitation depended chiefly on the extra-linguistic circumstances – above all on social communication and mobility, in combination with nationally relevant conflicts of interest. This is not to imply that national agitation was always synonymous with the needs of the modernisation process.

CHAPTER 10

The Nation as a Cultural Construct

In the past decade there has been an increase in the number of scholars who perceive a nation as a 'cultural construct' or even an 'invented community'. Research into programmes, social bases and forms of organisation has been replaced by research into the role of national symbols, celebrations, myths, and women in national movements.[1] The question asked is now 'How?' rather than 'Why?' This means that causal connections are no longer sought in the world of 'outer' relationships, but instead in the 'inner' world of the key players, who are often seen as the 'creators' of the nations. The implicit assumption is that national programmes stemmed from the idea of the nation (nationalism), and hence derived forms of national life and sentiment. There is an explicit emphasis on the importance of irrational factors over rational interests, of emotions over reason.

In its essence this approach is neither methodologically innovative nor ground-breaking. Whether openly or without any direct references, it builds upon the tradition of a subjective definition of 'nation', based on Ernest Renan, Hans Kohn and others. A British board of experts, which for pragmatic reasons examined the issue of 'methods' of nationalism in 1939, concluded, among other things, that not only school education but also celebrations, parades, national anniversaries, cultural activities and radio broadcasting played a major role in helping shape nationalistic attitudes.[2]

It needs to be said that the view that a nation is truly formed only when it has reached the stage of an 'imagined community' (Benedict Anderson) or, phrased more elegantly, that the 'social construct of nation lies in self depiction' (Dieter Langewiesche) is not particularly revolutionary.[3] As Étienne Balibar has stated, only 'imaginary communities' are real under certain circumstances.[4] That said, the ability to imagine a nation was not an anthropological certainty; it depended on very specific circumstances that were the result of the spread of a certain degree of social communication and a particular type of education.[5] Anderson's frequently cited parallel between reading a novel and imagining a nation is justified in this context.

The Role of Emotions

In order for people to self-identify with a nation, they needed more than just skills of abstraction and imagination as any relationship to a nation contains emotional aspects. Interwar anthropology already defined nation as a 'community of emotional life', where the emotional connections with the nation rest upon everyday habits, ways of thinking and acting.[6] Many authors believe that the greater the mass of people which national identity or 'nationalism' involves, the more powerful and effective the range of emotional ties to the nation needs to be. This in turn leads to the need to research the type of nationalistic activities which strove for emotional mobilisation of individuals as members of a homogenised nation.[7]

The roots of emotional ties to one's nation have naturally become a subject of interest for psychologists. There is a general agreement that these ties came into existence within the context of socialisation and grew stronger when individuals were feeling insecure and under external threat at times of crises. Ties to the nation were not permanent: they grew stronger in turbulent times and times of external threat and weaker in times of peace.[8] Eugen Lemberg regarded not only feelings of group superiority over other groups but also feelings of inferiority, which easily led to xenophobia, as a specific source of emotional ties to a nation. He detected such feelings of inferiority among the Flemish authors who had already, in the fourteenth and fifteenth centuries, voiced their awareness of the French language and literature being more advanced and refined.[9]

The need for dignity, which had been damaged for various reasons, would have been another source of nationalism. The important factor was whether the person whose dignity had suffered was a member of a national community, a professional group or a family. With regard to a national community, it needs to be taken into account that dignity (and its loss) would have been felt differently by members of the elites than by members of the masses and that their responses would, therefore, also vary.[10]

Emotionalised collective values, which had irrational

foundations and compensated the feelings of being threatened, tended to 'free themselves of the outer, objective world and of the mutual inter-connectedness of the different roles within civic society'. Consequently, ideas and illusions could easily become more powerful than the actual experience and this in turn opened doors to mass psychoses, within the framework of a state nation or once a national community had been formed.[11]

Consideration needs to be given to the different conditions under which emotionalisation of national identity occurred in state nations as against national movements. The nurturing of positive emotions towards one's own nation and negative (or neutral) attitudes towards other nations formed part of the states' educational policies, implemented not only through schools and military service but also through public life, celebrations, parades, etc. In contrast to state nations, national movements seldom had these educational means at their disposal and only in exceptional cases had any influence over elements of school education (e.g. from the 1860s in the Habsburg monarchy).

A gradual personification of nation was a significant outcome of and, simultaneously, a precondition for further emotionalisation of the relationship with the nation. Personifying the idea of the nation allowed the abstract value of 'the love of the nation' to gain a verbalised form of a 'love relationship', i.e. in which patriotism and passionate love became intertwined.[12] Established state nations as well as nations which had only begun to fight for their recognition were equally likely to become the object of this type of relationship. The love of the nation was just as often motivated by an irrational admiration of the nation's size and strength as by self-pitying reflection on its weakness and noble helplessness. The other side of the same coin was the opportunity to foster and personify feelings of hostility towards other nations or their members.

We can only fully appreciate how potent the emotional charge of the image of a personified nation was when we realise that in the nineteenth century 'nation' was conceived of as an age-old community. This gave it an 'immortal' quality and a personalised national community, which had existed from time immemorial. Therefore, contained in its abstract 'body' were generations of ancient ancestors as well as contemporaries and their future descendants. Everyone who blended with the nation and felt like an integral part of that nation earned the opportunity and the right to help maintain its immortality.

There were other attitudes which were affected by the personification of the nation and whose political impact was marked. First and foremost, it was the parallel between civic equality and the equality among nations within the framework of civic society: if all citizens were equal, regardless of their wealth or social standing, then nations should also be equal, however small, weak or powerful. By being seen as an entity, 'nation' could implicitly (and sometimes even explicitly) serve as a reminder of unity: if together we form a single entity, it is not in the interest of our health to be racked by internal conflicts. Even more dangerous was – and still is – the notion of a personalised nation in places where some members of the nation (or those who are regarded as such) live within the territory of another nation state and are in danger of assimilation, i.e. blending with this other nation.

The threat of losing a part of one's nation to another identity was felt as a loss of a 'body part' and thus considered a threat to the nation as a whole. In this context, members of a state nation who lived as a minority in another state nation were seen as an integral part of their home nation's 'body' and any injustice which they suffered was perceived as an injustice done to all the members of the nation. It is this emotional charge which had the potential to push the issues of national minorities to the extreme.

The personification of a nation was, therefore, closely connected to the idea that a nation was a body, which turned the abstract term into something tangible. The fact that 'nation' materialised in this way led to its folklorisation, the fostering of 'national' music, costumes and dances, joint sports activities both in gyms and in public, parades and other similar pursuits, which will be addressed later. At this point it suffices to say that the aim of these joint activities was not merely to demonstrate the strength of the nation to the outside world. In addition, it facilitated internal discipline, compatible with the above-mentioned tendency towards asserting a monolithic national unity.[13]

Body symbolism made it possible to reinforce the emotional attitude to one's nation through the use of physical characteristics. In this vein, the association made with the German 'body' was 'moral warmth' (*sittliche Wärme*), while the English were a 'cold' nation. The body of one's own nation was commonly seen as healthy and, as such, needed to be protected from being infected, whereas other nations were easily degraded through the use of a metaphor about a body which was ill or had deteriorated.[14]

Natural Instincts

According to many authors, the irrational aspect of the emotional background of love of one's nation and national identity is paradoxically closely connected to natural and biological attributes. As early as the interwar years, psychologists concluded that the basis of identity was bio-psychological – primarily a biological programme, which was only secondarily related to the need for a stable social system and social interaction.[15] Eugen Lemberg went so far as to suggest that national egotism, which came to dominate 'integral nationalism' in the nineteenth century, was influenced by the ideas of natural selection and the survival of the fittest. What was true of individual animals and human beings also had to apply to different species and groups of people. The fittest nation was bound to win the fight over natural resources and living space. Lemberg concluded that, in the latter stages of the development of nationalism, Darwinist thought prevailed over Herder's.[16]

Scholarly work by Konrad Lorenz inspired some – mostly Anglo-Saxon – researchers to perceive nationalism as a form of primordial tie, stemming from the instinctive drive in all living creatures to defend the territory that supplies them with food. Louis L. Snyder referred to this drive as the 'territorial imperative', concluding that nationalism was quite 'natural' – i.e. essentially a natural force whose purpose was the protection and provision of living space for the group. At the same time, he cautioned that historians ought to consider biological research with caution, and employ the 'territorial imperative' only as a possible secondary factor in the context of the social anchoring of nationalism.[17]

This view is shared by some psychologists and psychiatrists, who believe that 'ethno-national' behaviour is determined by specific biological moments and is analogous with the instinctive behaviour of animals. Like animals, people group together in order to ward off the enemy. Identification with a group is driven by the individual's need for survival and procreation, which is how 'primordial ties' came into existence and gradually became a fact – an anthropological constant. Some authors have even advanced the claim that certain ethno-national attitudes are products of biochemical and physiological processes, which are independent of the cultural circumstances. In addition, there is the factor of conformity to group norms.[18] These views constitute a revival of the old idea of a nation, dating back to the end of the nineteenth century, which regards a nation as a consanguineous community. An important development is that researchers, unlike for instance ideologists of fascism, have rarely agreed with these attitudes.

According to some anthropologists, there is a territorial dimension to human aggression, as it is based on man's 'innate territorial nature' – the inherent instinct to defend his territory. Although this 'age-old' instinct may have become modified and tempered by the advance of civilisation, it is still present whenever a community controls and defends a territory it regards as its own. Patriotism has come to be seen as the civilised, foreseeable form of this attitude, which in certain circumstances motivates man to adhere to the territorial imperative. Conversely, xenophobia, which sometimes leads to aggressive nationalism, is unpredictable.[19]

The biological concept of nationalism thus holds that the sense of belonging is firmly rooted in the human psyche, and dates back to tribal societies, and that ethnies provide material for the constructing and reinforcing of identity. When in a group, people and animals utilise their altruistic as well as egoistic components of their genetic inheritance in response to different situations. As is the case with herds that become too large, there is a similar tendency for 'separatist movements' among people. This poses a problem for those in power, who have often succeeded in reinforcing the cohesiveness of the group by making use of images of an 'external threat' and a 'common enemy'. This corresponds to auto- and hetero-stereotypes.[20] These basic naturalistic concepts allow us to conclude that self-identification with 'ethno-nationalistic' movements – national movements founded upon the existence of an ethnic group – is chiefly connected with natural instincts. In contrast, militant self-identification with a state appears, in the light of these concepts, to have purely human qualities.

Symbols

Max Weber described symbols as the precondition for social inter-action. At the same time, however, by entering the public arena, symbols also represented a claim to power and control. Theodor Schieder regarded symbols as an inevitable concession to irration-ality in an otherwise rational world.[21] If we accept the view that nation-forming was partly, or even fully, dependent on people's ability to imagine the nation as a community, we must acknowledge that the role of symbols in this process would have been rather unique. In other words, communication and social interaction within a group that was so large that its members did not come into personal contact depended on the use of symbols. Karl W. Deutsch considered the mutual knowledge of customs, symbols and past events to be fundamental in enabling the members of a nation to communicate with a greater intensity with each other than with members of other national communities. Bernhard Giesen later spoke about cultural and other codes.[22] In this context, we are chiefly interested in symbols as a factor that helped spread national identity and encouraged people to believe in the nation. Nevertheless, sym-bols had a further function in state-nations and in forming national states – they represented the nation to the outside world, strength-ened the citizens' faith in the state, and legitimised political parties.

Experts disagree about the ways in which national symbols came into being. As is clear from his theory of ethno-nationalism, Anthony Smith believes that the symbolisation of ethnic categories played a central role in nation-forming. Opinions can already be found already in older literature (for example, Carlton Hayes and Albert Mathiez) that national symbols were created 'from below' (as a result of a spontaneous secularisation of religious cults) rather than 'from above' (through manipulated propaganda). It can be argued that national symbols 'from below' dominated in revolutions and in phase B of national movements. These symbols were not always uni-versally adopted, but when they were they eventually (after the successful revolution or national movement) acquired the nature of symbols implemented 'from above'. If symbols employed in the phase of national agitation were adopted spontaneously, they continued to live until the nation was fully formed. It is noteworthy that almost identical basic forms or types of national symbols were deployed in all forming nations and nation-states.[23] There was, undoubtedly, an intensive transfer of symbols and their purpose, facilitated by the asynchronous progression of European nation-forming.

It remains an open question which methods helped, in the nineteenth century, to transform the abstract ideas expressed by these symbols into concrete, analytically applicable forms of thinking and behaviour. References to a common language or a greater degree of education will not suffice in this context. Another open question is that of the relationship between the process of nation-forming and the application of national symbols. On the one hand, symbols clearly played an essential role in strengthening national identity. On the other hand, it is equally evident that in order for symbols to be effective, the people for whom these symbols were intended needed to have already formed an idea of a nation, and to share a certain degree of ethnic or national identity.[24] It is crucial to appreciate that the role national symbols had played in the stage of nation-forming and the role they played once the nation was fully formed and in the setting of 'integral nationalism' were very different. Non-historians in particular often inadmissibly engage in backward-projection, which fails to differentiate between the role of symbols in the context of contemporary nationalism and the role they played under very different political and social circumstances in the past.

Generally, it may hold true that a universal application of symbols turned them into stereotypes through which political power could be exercised in national life. This is supported by the observation that some simple symbols, such as flags, national costumes and colours, were adopted relatively easily, while more complex symbols, such as those that drew on history and mythology, became stereotypes only if their recipients had gained at least an elementary knowledge of facts from national history within the framework of general education. It appears that similar prerequisites needed to be fulfilled in the events of what some contemporary authors refer to as 'performative acts', through which national symbolism creates a new reality and turns into an experience.[25]

It is a great challenge to try to categorise and typologise national symbols and the other cultural phenomena used to strengthen national identity. However, at least for basic orientation, a working classification is needed. Symbols can be grouped as follows, based on the context and form in which they were used: 1. public activities (parades, celebrations, funerals, meetings); 2. verbal addresses (mottos, declarations, songs, anthems); 3. iconographic symbols (pictures, portraits, historical painting, flags, stamps, posters); 4. monuments; and 5. 'national' landscape and its parts.[26]

In the context of considering the role and meaning of symbols, it is important to address the place women occupied in the national discourse.[27] Their direct involvement in national movements grew in significance only once the mass phase had been achieved. Inevitably, they were not found among the scholars of phase A, and were very rarely present among the agitators and activists of phase B – either as poets and writers or as those who assisted the creation of artistic symbols of national movements, such as costumes, flags, celebration decorations, and so on. This does not mean, however, that they did not play their part in the process of nation-forming. Considerable value was attached to women in the process of the emancipation of state-nations, as well as in national movements as mothers and educators of the future generations of members of the nation. Women already had a firm position in patriarchal society, and as this was transformed into a civic society, they symbolised and guaranteed the continuity of national existence. One manifestation of this was in their becoming an important symbol – the bearers of national history.[28] The female element was also the most suitable instrument to strengthen emotional ties to the nation, and this is reflected in the artistic design of the nation's symbols.

Symbolisation of the female role was perhaps even more significant with regard to the existence of the nation in the circumstances of national movements. Most of these movements could not build on a national existence, and in the majority of cases the nation was defined by means of a common language and culture. A woman in the role of a mother emerged as the main guardian of the purity and survival of the language, and a guarantee that cultural customs would be preserved. The term 'mother tongue' speaks for itself. In her role as keeper of national continuity, the woman-mother was to be revered and protected.[29]

Women continued to be part of the national discourse in all these contexts, even when some women began to participate actively in public life during the mass phase of national movements. According to some authors, women's role in phase C was specific, in that they

brought peace and consensus-seeking tendencies into the movements. This is what set them apart from the distinctive attitudes of
men, who were radical and inclined towards violence.

Stereotypes

If we follow Wolfgang Kaschuba's example and ask how (and why)
abstract national ideas and values were transformed in the nineteenth century into 'real', analytically viable forms of thought and
behaviour, we will need to study the role of stereotypes.[30] Abstract
ideas and complex symbols could serve as the foundation for national
imagination only once they had become stereotypes. These tend to
be characterised as, for instance, 'uncritical generalisations, which
are not open to critical re-examination' (Hermann Bausinger),
'over-simplified, generalising judgements, which are based on an
emotional value system' (Uta Quasthoff) or 'firm convictions, daily
categorisation and standardisation of the world around us' which
relate to reality (Klaus Roth).[31]

Stereotypes – whether they are ideas about others (hetero-stereotypes) or about oneself (auto-stereotypes) – act as a systemic
instrument for the creation and reinforcement of the perceptions
that members of a group have of themselves. Stereotypes make it
possible to categorise individuals according to certain predetermined
criteria, which in turn further accentuates the differentiation between
'us' and 'them'. Classification stereotypes help individuals to orientate
themselves in the deluge of information. In the context of nation-
forming, they guide them towards 'national imagination' by teaching
them to reduce the complexity of reality and simplify the way in
which they evaluate their place in society. In so doing, they make it
easier for individuals to adopt the newly available identification with
their nation.[32]

The judgemental nature of national stereotypes inevitably entails
a dichotomy between mostly positive auto-stereotypes (notions
about one's own nation) and usually negative hetero-stereotypes
(notions about other nations). As Arnold Suppan rightly points out,
national stereotypes and their emergence cannot be examined in
isolation from their sociopolitical context at any given time. He pro-
poses that social circumstances, social relations and work contacts
should be included among the factors that influenced the emergence

of stereotypes; the weakening of all these relationships provided a breeding ground for negative stereotypes. The economic sphere gave rise to both positive and negative stereotypes, depending on the nationally relevant conflicts of interests. National stereotypes were naturally most closely related to the political–ideological sphere. Stereotypical negative views of the characteristics of the nation's enemy led to the formation of positive hetero-stereotypes about the 'enemies of the enemy'.[33] Besides the social, economic and political contexts, there was also the historical context – and, as has been discussed, 'collective memory' was a major source of positive as well as negative stereotypes.

When examining the role of stereotypes in nation-forming, we must take account not only of the various sources from which they originated, but also of the variations in their social relevance – i.e. their 'representativeness'. We must not see national stereotypes as something that was set and unchangeable, or as attitudes adopted automatically by all members of a national community from the very beginning. The social and cultural circumstances under which a given stereotype arose always need to be separated from its further fate – from the degree to which it was (not) adopted by the members of the national community.

Let us illustrate this difference through the example of the stereotypical German hero. If we reconstruct this stereotype according to how it evolved in the works of two German authors – the composer Richard Wagner and the writer Felix von Dahn – we arrive at a very compelling dichotomy between the Germanic and non-Germanic heroes. The Germanic hero had fair hair, blue eyes and a healthy complexion; the non-Germanic hero was black-haired and pallid. The former was a hopeful optimist; the latter a pessimist without any hope. When the Germanic hero was cruel, it was an act of impulsive cruelty, as opposed to the purposeful cruelty of the non-Germanic hero. The former was a leader and a liberator, the latter merely a leader.[34] Although we know that both authors' works were very popular, there is no doubt that this dichotomy had not originated as a 'universally German' stereotype. It began as the view of a relatively small circle of intellectuals, and it is very probable that the German intellectuals of the time would have had a very different image of the German hero if different authors' works had served as the source of inspiration. It was only with time that von Dahn and Wagner's views became national stereotypes. As was typical, the stereotype arose from the context of historical consciousness, rather than social or work relationships – hence the primarily warrior-like characteristics of the national hero.

National Monuments and Iconographic Symbols

The historical parallel between the assertion of civic society and the path to a modern nation is clearly reflected in the development of monuments in the eighteenth and nineteenth centuries. Until the eighteenth century, monuments were almost exclusively built for rulers and saints (or biblical figures), and symbolic figures from history were connected with antiquity. By the end of the century, monuments started to be erected to eminent contemporaries and specific heroes from the nation's history, regardless of their descent. The symbolism of monuments was no longer confined to the celebration of rulers, piety and abstract virtues – it had extended to celebrations of specific successes and achievements.[35]

The different timing with which this new concept of monuments was implemented is significant. In France, it occurred simultaneously with the rise of revolution and the Napoleonic wars. In contrast, central Europe during that time was characterised by mere modifications to the old concept. While the Panthéon and the Arc de Triomphe both conveyed distinctly national ideals, 'La Marseillaise', by François Rude, depicted ordinary soldiers in action from as early as 1836.[36] While French monuments to fallen soldiers were conceived as monuments to heroes who had fought for the nation, Prussian monuments speak of battles for the king and homeland – even soldiers who died fighting against the revolution in 1848 received gravestones as heroes who had given their lives in those causes.[37] By then Austria was also erecting monuments to army commanders that, until the mid nineteenth century, claimed that the commanders in question had died for their ruler (and very seldom also for their homeland). As changes occurred, the reference to the homeland on Prussian monuments could be converted into the idea of the nation. Austrian monuments, in contrast, had no explicit national potential.[38] Even the inscription above a mass grave of Austrian soldiers who died in Prague putting down the rebellion in June 1848 speaks only of 'good soldiers', rather than of the king and the homeland.

The concept of genuine national monuments was formed in two ways in the framework of forming nations. Firstly, it came 'from above', as a political decision by the ruling elites, as the Arc de Triomphe and the Walhalla memorial, which was conceived by King Ludwig I of Bavaria. The building of national monuments or memorials could be initiated from above if the national community possessed a complete social structure – i.e. in state-nations such as France or in nationally unifying movements like the German and Italian cases.[39] The alternative to this first option was for the initiative to come 'from below', which often remained a mere wish due to limited financial resources – such as the calls at the Hambach Festival of 1832 for the creation of a national monument that would be an expression of the 'German nation's grandeur'.[40] An initiative 'from below' that had more realistic foundations was to erect a monument to Arminius (Hermann) at the presumed site of the Germanic victory over the Romans in the Teutoburg Forest. The collection, which had begun in support of a celebration of a regional hero, was transformed into a nationally motivated one. The actual building of the vast, costly monument became an initiative 'from above' in the 1860s, and eventually became what was essentially an exercise in national megalomania.[41]

The idea of national monuments remained only a wishful dream for two reasons: first, their leaders could not count on securing the necessary funds for such a project; and second, the building of national monuments was dependent on the state elites' political approval. Therefore, when the patriot and enlightened autodidact, veteran commander Jan Jeník from Bratřice wrote a statement at the turn of the nineteenth century proposing that the statues of saints on Charles Bridge in Prague should be replaced with statues of famous Czechs, such as Jan Hus, it was meant in jest, and not even the author himself believed in the feasibility of such a plan. It should also be remembered that monument building had originally been primarily an urban matter, and thus remained for a long time outside the imagination of members of ethnic communities.

Only when a national movement moved into its mass phase could the dream of national monuments become reality. In the Czech lands, the first such monument was erected to Josef Jungmann, the founder of the Czech national programme. This was not an exception, since monuments as a general rule had not acquired their nationally demonstrative role until the rise of a mass national move-ment. All three major German national monuments – Hermann's monument, the Niederwald 'Germania' Monument and the monu-ment to Frederick Barbarossa (Kyffhäuser) – were only erected once Germany had been unified. The (much more modest) French coun-terpart of Hermann's Monument, the monument to the Gallic chieftain Vercingetorix, was not built until the rise of 'integral nationalism' during the reign and at the initiative of Emperor Napoleon III.

Italy also began to build national monuments after the nation was politically united, and they bore clear signs of the two-track approach to the struggle for national unity. While the democratic wing of the Italian public advocated monuments to Garibaldi, the conservative wing called for monuments to King Victor Emmanuel II. This was despite the fact that certain attributes of Garibaldi, such as his riding a horse or wearing a dress sword, were in German set-tings reserved to the aristocracy. The depiction of the meeting at Teano, where Garibaldi handed power over to the king, represented a symbolic compromise.[42] It was only within the framework of inte-gral nationalism that the megalomaniac project of the monument to Victor Emmanuel II in Rome became feasible.

The typology of national monuments evidently cannot be atem-poral, nor can it disregard the crucial difference between the two ways in which modern nations were formed. From this viewpoint, we need to assess the applicability of German typology, which dis-tinguished among 'nationally dynastic' (monarchic) monuments, 'nationally democratic' monuments, the remembrance church (i.e. Cologne cathedral), the monument to national education and cul-ture, and the monument to national unification. Apart from the fact that the criterion of comparison appears rather disparate, this typology cannot be applied to monuments that were built in the context of national movements.

In order to assume a critical attitude towards the role of monu-ments in the process of nation-forming, a number of other circumstances need to be considered. First and foremost, monu-ments (and national symbols in general) cannot be perceived as an unequivocal expression of national consensus, as disputes over the national relevance and significance of monuments were a common part of public life. The role of monuments thus needs to be analysed from an overall perspective rather than in isolated cases.[43] It must also be remembered that monuments were simultaneously works of art and, therefore, cannot be reduced to their political function alone.[44]

The most significant factor in assessing the national importance of monuments is the place they occupied within the communication network. In contrast to the printed word and images spread through of the press, monuments had a permanent location; and instead of coming to their objects – i.e. citizens – citizens had to travel to them. On one hand, this initially limited their audiences to those who lived locally and those who were sufficiently wealthy to be able to afford to visit them from further afield. On the other hand, their placing in open spaces meant that they could later be transformed into places of pilgrimage and specific national celebrations, during which participants were fully informed of the monument's national symbolism. In this context, the question of whether monuments of national significance were placed in metropolises or in open spaces was more of a formality.

Based on all of this, it is evident that national symbols expressed through monuments did not serve as a source of national agitation and were thus not a factor in the initial stages of modern nation-building. They did become a major force and *lieux de mémoire*, once nations were formed – they reinforced, modified and made more concrete the newly existing national awareness and national identity. The content and interpretation of each particular monument determined whether its symbolic legacy was more likely to lead to the reinforcement of aggressive nationalism, the military attributes of the nation, or merely of the sense of belonging together and respect for the cultural legacy of the ancestors.

Monuments were not the only form of iconographic symbolism. Illustrations of the national past, ranging from Historicism in painting to history being reduced to a symbolic figure, location or event, played a specific role in national agitation. Historicism is the iconographic counterpart of the construction of national histories and myths. Therefore, it was characterised by all that was stated earlier about the use of history in the process of raising national awareness. Images of historical scenes tended to accompany historical narratives from the very beginning of the national movement, and were an effective tool of national agitation. It also holds true in this context that, besides the agitation, images that were intended for ordinary people, the state (its wealthy elites) commissioned complex, large works – epics from ancient or recent times. Their originals ordinary members of the nation could see only rarely, by visiting a travelling exhibition. But this type of historicism was not invented within the framework of nation-states – it has its roots in the Italian Renaissance.

What proved more effective in relation to the masses was simplified iconographic symbolism, which made use of either existing or historical symbols of statehood (the eagle, the lion), national saints (St Louis in France, St Wenceslas in the Czech lands, St Olaf in Norway, St Stephen in Hungary, St Patrick in Ireland, and so on), or stylised and generalised figures from national mythology. They were not always only positive figures, representing one's own nation, but also figures that symbolised negative stereotypes about the 'enemy' – for example, John Bull representing England in the eyes of the Germans, German Michl representing the negative stereotype of Germans as seen by French or Czech eyes, and the French revolutionary, Marianne, perceived by the Germans as an 'easy' woman and a negative symbol of France.[45]

Despite the fact that women played an inferior role in the political life of nations and in national movements, and that national struggle was almost exclusively a male matter, the female figure usually occupied a prominent position among national symbols. Marianne symbolised to Frenchmen a united nation and a self-governing people. Her German counterpart, Germania, was also initially the symbol of the new German nation, which had risen from the will of the people. By 1848, another image of Germania had emerged – a woman armed with a sword and a shield – that was later adapted to suit the needs of the united German state. The symbol of the nation's freedom was thus transformed into a symbol of a loyal armed people.[46]

In a parallel fashion, the symbolic figures of Italia, Polonia, Mother Denmark, Hispania and Czechia were constructed, but none reached the popularity of Marianne and Germania. In contrast, the symbolic figure of Helvetia had come into existence earlier – written references to her date back to 1750, and her first depiction as a symbol of freedom (Helvetia libera) to 1780. This version was unacceptable to the conservative mountain cantons, which favoured the symbolic depiction of William Tell, and it was not until the Liberals' victory in 1848 that Helvetia became the symbol of constitutionality and appeared on stamps and coins, despite the disapproval of the mountain cantons and their preference for the Helvetic cross.[47]

The image of a woman as a symbol of the nation often entered a more general context, in which the nation was presented as the motherland who made legitimate demands on her sons – the members of the nation. This shift occurred easily in places with a tradition of a state-nation, where the notions of *pro patria mori* and *amor patriae* had occupied an important position within the moral code since the late Middle Ages. Association of one's nation with a woman-mother was also easier when the term 'nation' was a feminine noun in the local language, such as in German and French (in contrast to Czech, for example, where it is a masculine noun). In comparison, the anthropological construct seems much less convincing. It explains the connection between a nation and a woman by pointing out that the modern nation was a new organism, and as such could not be associated with a man, a representation of continuity and tradition. A woman, on the other hand, by virtue of motherhood alone, evoked the image of the birth of something new.[48]

All that has been said here about the role of woman as a national symbol is based on research into state-nations and Germany. We know relatively little about whether this construct also applies to nations formed through national movements. Partial findings indicate that, although similar symbolism can be found in these nations, its role does not appear to have been as significant as in the German and French cases. The causes of this difference are a matter of speculation, and so I hope it will suffice to point out at this stage that there was a parallel between the role of a woman as a symbol and the role of national monuments. Women as national symbols, in the same manner as national monuments, had a crucial function in the stage of a mass national movement – i.e. in the context of reinforcing rather than initiating national cohesion. This does not mean that women's involvement in the phase of national agitation was altogether absent.

National Celebrations

The main difference between celebrations and the other aforementioned forms of the cultural construct of a nation was that celebrations were not one-way activities. They essentially constituted an interaction between the organisers and the addressees of activities aiming to raise national awareness. Their interaction did not occur by means of printed texts or iconographic symbols; the actual presence of people meant that the fundamental (but not the only) means of communication was the spoken word. The public nature of national festivities – their placement within the public arena – was thus a natural trait and a precondition of their success. Only in the public arena was it possible to develop forms of communication that were strongly purposeful, in that they strove to influence and form collective consciousness.[49] 'The public' had a broad meaning: it was one of the key categories within efforts to modernise political life and create a modern political culture, and encompassed the notions of transparency, free exchange of opinions and consensus-seeking. The success of celebrations that strove for political emancipation and national agitation was unthinkable without public opinion.[50]

In the same way that public opinion could not exist without the freedom of the press, political and national celebrations could not exist without the freedom to assemble in an open space; political oppression prevented them from happening. This is not to imply that celebrations were absent in absolutist regimes, and of course they occurred in early modern societies. But they lacked the aspect of occurring in open political spaces. If we utilise the German categorisation that distinguishes between a spontaneous, joyful 'Fest' – *festivity* – and a planned, organised, goal-oriented 'Feier' – *celebration*[51] – we arrive at the realisation that, although both types of activities had already existed in premodern times, they usually occurred as essentially religious events and under strict church, state or manorial control. Some researchers thus believe that the distinction between Fest and Feier cannot be applied to the premodern era, as it was not until the French Revolution that Feier was transformed into an instrument of political mobilisation and separated from the apolitical, non-binding Fest.[52]

Whatever the truth about Fest and Feier, revolution was the

means through which celebrations were turned into an instrument of political emancipation and uniformity. Their organisers made conscious use of various forms of religious celebrations with which people were familiar, but gave them a new meaning that focused on earthly matters. These open-air celebrations evoked a sense of unity and togetherness in their participants, despite the fact that people returned to their everyday disputes and conflicts once the celebrations had come to an end. Besides fostering mass loyalty, celebrations were also an important means of 'inward' communication and an 'outward' demonstration of strength. Claims that they first occurred during the French Revolution have a major flaw: English meetings, which date back to before the Revolution, were already a manifestation of the formation of the political public. They bore neither the characteristics of celebrations nor elements of national zeal and, most importantly, they did not become the model for political celebrations in other countries across Europe. Unlike in England, and in a similar fashion to France, the organisers of national celebrations on the continent made use of traditional festivities and other forms of gathering that had originally had a religious content and encompassed contemporary as well as traditional components, including celebrations of feudal landlords.

A ritual formed part of national celebrations, ensuring and demonstrating that an individual accepted their affiliation to a national community. The ritual strengthened the individual's relationship with the nation and its past, reaffirming this relationship through repetition and creating the illusion of timelessness. Rituals worked on an emotional rather than a rational basis, and brought on the feeling of belonging together. Adherence to a ritual that was common to all and that took shape gradually reinforced the perception of a nation as a single body, and facilitated the process of socialisation within the nation.[53]

Besides the ritual, a number of other traits determined the specificity of national celebrations. They were the antithesis of the monotony of everyday life, and often marked a joyful escape from it. As some authors point out, they were – without verbalising it – simultaneously an instrument of the rule of the politically and economically powerful elites.[54] For the purposes of a historical interpretation, it is just as important to examine the contexts in which celebrations were held as the contents they thematised.

This viewpoint presents the opportunity to outline a typology of celebrations based on their different contexts:

1. Celebrations that consciously or unconsciously built upon older traditions of religious, dynastic or folk festivities
2. Reminders of significant events from national history
3. Anniversaries of important figures from national life or of their monuments
4. Funerals of national heroes
5. Political meetings expressing political demands
6. Sporting (and military) celebrations

Celebrations which built upon religious and dynastic festivities can be found primarily in the early phase of national movements. Polish pilgrimages to Virgin Mary of Czestochowa, who had saved Poland from the Swedes in the mid seventeenth century, acquired their 'national' overtones by the early modern period. However, they could not continue to take place after Czestochowa was annexed by Russia. An example of building on an old dynastic tradition was the attempts to turn Wawel in Cracow into a Polish equivalent of Panthéon, as the resting place not only of kings but also of major leaders of the national struggle, such as Tadeusz Kościuszko.[55] Church celebrations in Hungary gained a Magyar national aspect by the end of the eighteenth century. Characteristically, St Stephen's Day was added to the list of national holidays and celebrated also by the Calvinists. Similarly, dynastic holidays, such as the emperor's birthday or his visit to Hungary in 1817, were also perceived as national celebrations, which naturally culminated in the coronation of Franz Joseph as King of Hungary after the monarchy had divided in 1867.[56]

In contrast, dynastic holidays in the Czech setting occurred merely as official holidays, without a national overtone. Not only were they not transformed into national celebrations, but during Emperor Franz Joseph's visit to Prague in 1868, for example, Czech patriots even ostentatiously organised trips outside the metropolis. A connection with the dynastic tradition manifested itself in the cult of coronation jewels as a symbol of long-gone statehood. The celebration of the jewels in 1866 was an echo of their ceremonial 'return' from Vienna to Prague in 1790.[57] The first large national celebrations took place in 1848 at the foot of Říp Mountain, the mythical place of arrival and settlement of the first Czechs.

German national celebrations had also been initially held in the vein of religious tradition, especially due to Martin Luther, but gradually began to extend beyond religion as Luther came to be celebrated above all as a great German. Tellingly, the image of the German oak was slowly incorporated into the celebrations.[58] The first celebrations of German *Burschenschafts* in 1817 were deliberately placed and timed with regard to Luther's anniversary. Celebrations that marked the first anniversary of the Battle of Leipzig (the 'Battle of the Nations'), organised by a group of patriots around Ernst Moritz Arndt, were essentially folk merrymaking with a bonfire and singing, which built upon older folk traditions. The songs were religious as well as patriotic, and there was an altar and prayers for the dead. The analogy with the Old Testament was verbalised by mention of the Lord who revealed to Moses that the people of Israel would be freed. The battle was first interpreted as the victory of Good over Evil – and then, in this context, the longing for national unity was expressed.[59]

The first national celebrations organised by patriots in Estonia and Latvia, from the end of the 1860s, were an extension of folk festivities. They were a form of patriotic festival, celebrating singing and hosting village choirs that had previously sung at church services in individual parishes. At first the celebrations consisted mainly of religious songs, but increasingly also of patriotic songs and public announcements made in Estonian or Latvian. When interpreting these singing celebrations, it should be taken into consideration that other forms of public assembly and celebration were unthinkable in Tsarist Russia. Similar national singing celebrations also started being organised in the mid nineteenth century by patriots in Wales, where the political circumstances were very different. The tradition they built upon was that of medieval epic singers, the Celtic bards, whose tradition had been completely discontinued, and whose 'resurrection' was in fact a new beginning.

Celebrations commemorating anniversaries of major national events were a truly modern phenomenon, as was the spread of historical consciousness to the non-privileged classes of citizens. The symbolic beginning of this type of celebration, and a source of inspiration, was the celebration of the first anniversary of the fall of the Bastille, held in Paris, which still included strong elements of a folk festivity. Indeed, the process of transforming 14 July from an important anniversary to a national holiday was not straightforward in the post-Revolution period. During the reign of Louis Philippe, there was a tendency to celebrate 31 July (1830). Monarchists favoured Joan of Arc Day over revolutionary anniversaries. Napoleon III attempted to combine the anniversary of the plebiscite that had brought him to power with a religious holiday, the Assumption of Virgin Mary, on 15 August. It was not until 1880 that the Third Republic turned 14 July into a national holiday, which involved celebrations and demonstrations of military power.[60]

The absence of a national holiday in Germany was partially compensated by celebrations of the anniversaries of the Battle of Leipzig. While the speeches and rituals continued to be essentially the same, the political content of the celebrations was altered according to the situation. The same applies to the already-mentioned celebrations of Martin Luther, whose focus changed from celebrating the Reformation to becoming national celebrations. Significantly, the Society for German National Celebrations (Gesellschaft Deutscher Nationalfeste) was founded during the period of 'integral nationalism'.[61]

In established nation-states, national celebrations tended to become national holidays, and this shift, therefore, occurred outside the context of nation-forming. The exceptions to the rule were the nationalisation of St Patrick's Day in Ireland and the celebration of Constitution Day in Norway. The Norwegian case was specific in that the assembly of the representatives of the nation passed the constitution and declared independence in Eidsvoll, but this independence did not follow. The Constitution Day on 17 May thus began to be celebrated from the 1830s as an unofficial national holiday – a manifestation of national unity.

Major national anniversaries were also commonly celebrated within national movements as long as the construction of the national history led to the discovery of such anniversaries. Polish patriots, for instance, organised events to celebrate the anniversary of the May Constitution of 1791, Kościuszko's uprising of 1794, the Union of Lublin between Poland and Lithuania of 1569, and even the victory over the Teutonic Knights in the Battle of Grunwald in 1410 – although these could only be held in the Austrian-occupied territories of Cracow and Lwow. Similarly, Magyar national festivities

– apart from the main holiday, St Stephen's Day – were commemorations of the liberation of Buda from the Turks in 1686 and the revolution in 1848.

Important figures from mythological and recent history were a rich source of inspiration for national celebrations, their anniversaries and the unveiling of their monuments being the most frequently utilised occasions. The German celebrations of the unveiling of Herrmann's Monument (the Herrmannsdenkmal) in the Teutoburg Forest were paralleled by the French celebrations of the Gallic commander Vercingetorix. The 1859 celebrations of Schiller in Germany reached a mass scale, as did celebrations within the Magyar national movement of the poet Sándor Petőfi, accompanied by collections of money to fund the building of his monument, which was unveiled in 1882. At that time, monuments were also erected to other Magyar political leaders, such as Széchenyi, József Eötvös and Ferenc Deák. Polish history offered relatively rich material for celebrations and the national re-evaluation of Polish kings – in particular the kings of the Jagiellonian dynasty, John III Sobieski, the liberator of Vienna in 1683, and Stanisław Poniatowski, who had fought for the restoration of Poland. Czech history was less rich in nationally relevant rulers, of whom George of Poděbrady, the 'national king', and Charles IV, the 'Father of the Homeland', were the most celebrated. In the Czech settings, which were not particularly wealthy, monuments to Czech patriots were seldom built. One was erected in 1873 to Josef Jungmann, the next to Karel Havlíček, and one much later to František Palacký.

Although celebrations of Jan Hus were controversial for a long time, the anniversary of his death at the stake in 1415 became an occasion for national celebrations. There was a specific background to the mass building of monuments to Joseph II, which occurred in German-speaking towns from the 1860s: in the context of the times, the emperor was celebrated as a supporter of the German language and a pioneer of Germanisation.

Grand funeral celebrations were a common way of revering major national figures after their death, and can be found wherever the law permitted them. Funerals occasionally even turned into quiet demonstrations against oppression – for example, the funeral of the journalist Karel Havlíček in 1856 during Austrian neo-absolutism and of the Magyar national poet Mihály Vörösmarty in 1855.

Symbolic funeral celebrations took place across Hungary for István Széchenyi in 1860. In places where a connection could be made between the national struggle and the national dynasty, funerals of monarchs also became national celebrations, such as the burial of Victor Emmanuel II at the Roman Pantheon in 1878. The idiosyncratic form of the funeral cult is worth noting – i.e. the subsequent burials of remains, usually involving their transfer. For example, the remains of the national poet Ugo Foscolo were ceremonially transferred in this manner to Santa Croce Church in Florence in 1871. There was an additional funeral of the Magyar politician Lajos Batthyány in 1870, who had been executed after the revolution in 1848. The 'second funeral' of the Polish king Casimir III the Great, in 1869, became a Polish national celebration, as did the relocation of the remains of the poet Adam Mickiewicz from Poland to Wawel in Cracow.

In extreme political circumstances, national celebrations acquired the form of political meetings. There the anniversary or celebration of the significant figure did not serve as an excuse for or instrument of national agitation. Instead, people gathered to listen to their leaders' speeches, which offered explanations for national demands and aimed to win popular support for them. Typical among this type of national meeting were those held by the Repeal Association in the rising Irish national movement. Their parallels in central Europe were undoubtedly the Hambach Festival of 1832, spontaneous as well as organised mass meetings during the revolution of 1848–49, and the Czech movement protesting against the legalisation of Austro-Hungarian dualism in 1867. Political meetings were primarily about protest, expressing the demands of those who were not in power towards those who were. As such, they fell within the context of national movements. In the circumstances of nation-states, political demands were demands made by only a part of the society, and sometimes even became an instrument of the 'anti-national' opposition, as can be observed within the German and Austrian social democracies.

Celebrations of physical training that had a national content were not very widespread in Europe. Until the mid nineteenth century, the combining of this form of physical education with a national movement can be seen as specifically German. Despite being persecuted, the Turner movement was probably the largest national organisation until 1848. Following the unification of Germany, the movement was confronted with the task of forming a state within the framework of an established nation.[62] Utilising the Turners' experience, the German Empire implemented physical education at schools with the objective of disciplining the young and improving their paramilitary training.

It was only the impression of German superiority or threat that led to the Turner movement being copied. Its earliest imitation was perhaps the Czech movement Sokol, formed in the early 1860s with the aim of defending Czech national rights and fostering individuals' general development – both physical and intellectual. Sokol directed its attention to a democratic programme; its red shirts were a symbol of support for Garibaldi. The movement soon won wide support from the urban middle classes, and consequently within two decades it was able to organise large regular sporting celebrations, whose objective was to demonstrate the strength and unity of the Czech national movement. The pan-Slavic elements of the Sokol movement predominated in the second half of the nineteenth century, and similar types of organisation sprang up in other Slavic nations, including among the Poles, Croats, Ukrainians, Slovenes and Lusatian Sorbs. However, despite being modelled on the Czech example, these movements never became as widespread as in the Czech lands.[63]

France responded to the German threat after the defeat in 1870 by beginning to support physical fitness in connection with the strengthening of the national and republican spirit. Exercise was organised, and disciplined pupils by means of exercising them in unison. The notion of compulsory physical education, which prevailed and was adopted with the rise of the Third Republic, involved elements of defence as a preparation for the planned compulsory military service. Children were taught from an early age that the well-being and very existence of the nation depended on obligations being fulfilled and on individuals being subordinated to the whole. Voluntary 'school battalions' began to be formed from 1882, in which pupils wore uniforms and received paramilitary training. These battalions did not prove popular, and were abandoned by the end of the decade in favour of defence associations. The purpose of the movement was to integrate the population into the revolutionary ideals of freedom, equality and solidarity, complemented by discipline and respect for authority.[64]

Physical education and public exercises not only disciplined the participants, but also served as national educational spectacles. This was especially true of the German and French military celebrations, which combined a military performance with the state's self-representation.[65] Military celebrations were bound by a strong sense of ritual, which involved strict ceremonial rules, the entrance of the political representatives, rigid 'choreography', and of course the presence of an audience. The educational aim was to link the military spirit with national enthusiasm. After compulsory military service had been implemented in Prussia in 1814, the educational policy perceived 'the army' as 'the people in arms'. This was only a small step away from 'a nation in arms'. In France, where compulsory military service was later passed by law, the army was seen as 'the image of the nation' and as 'the nation in arms'. A rather distorted by-product of the cult of 'the nation in arms' was the cult of 'the fallen national heroes', who had died for the homeland and whom the nation had promised not to forget. In this sense, the impassioned, heroic symbolism in victorious Germany corresponded with that of defeated France.[66]

The final question is what role celebrations and their symbolism played in the process of modern nation-forming. General answers cannot be given without addressing the types of celebration. It is evident that neither sporting nor military celebrations were a widely present aspect of this process. Indeed, from a pan-European perspective, they were an exception to the rule. As regards the celebration of historical anniversaries and unveiling of national monuments, differentiation needs to be made between national movements and state-nations. In national movements, these types of celebration were not integral to the entire nation-forming process, but only started playing a major part in their mass phase C. In contrast, celebrations that we have categorised as meetings were more natural and commonplace in national movements, including their agitation phase B.

There has been an increase in the volume of research into national celebrations in the past two decades, which is especially valueable in the context of gaining a better understanding of individual national movements. However, for a number of reasons the findings of these studies need to be generalised with utmost care:

1. Consideration must be given to the fundamental difference between the social and cultural circumstances of state-nations (or nation-states) and national movements.
2. It is essential to respect the fact that most types of celebration looked to the past and the kind of historical information that was available to the leaders of individual nations for adaptation, who thus played a determining role.
3. National celebrations were by definition a public matter, and their implementation was dependent on the degree of political freedom in the given state.
4. Participation in celebrations required a certain level of wealth and political culture, neither of which was necessarily present in national movements from the very beginning.

The greatest objection to overplaying the importance of celebrations and symbols in national movements is based on the fact that attention is usually only paid to those celebrations that were employed to demonstrate national strength and unity, rather than as instruments of national agitation, and thus an offer of a new identity. Consequently, they are seen as an active agent that reinforced the existing national identity that had already been embraced by the masses. Under conditions of nation-states, celebrations sometimes modified national stereotypes and ideology in accordance to what the leaders of the movements, or those who were in control of the state power, considered to be the national interest.

National Territory and Its Borders

Not even radical supporters of the claim that a nation is determined primarily by the idea of nationalism call into question the fact that a nation is a territorial community, and that its members thus occupy a certain territory.[67] The relationship between the members of a nation and this territory was not a simple one between individuals and a neutral space, but an emotionalised relationship that conveyed value. Taking into account the spatial dimension of national existence leads to the need to answer the question of how the process of 'imagining' a nation, invoked by Benedict Anderson, took place. The ability to imagine 'belonging to a nation' was the principle way in which the national territory could be dealt with, organised and structured. The first attempts to project the existence of a forming (state-)national community into an area date back as far as the early modern period. In England, maps became a very popular subject of scholarly study in the second half of the sixteenth century, and particular in the seventeenth century. The emphasis was placed on the fact that England was not the outcome of the monarch's will but a territory occupied by members of the nation. The first descriptions of England from the end of the sixteenth century portray a nation whose bearers were the social elites – the gentry. England was not alone in politicising the image of the country. In the northern Netherlands, the search for specific aspects of national life was reflected in paintings whose authors consciously captured the life of the people and the distinctive landscape, often also expressing their republican national views.[68]

The country's location within Europe also had a symbolic meaning, which had already been thematised in the early modern period. The features highlighted were naturally those that could be interpreted as positive and prestigious. The country that idealised and ideologised its island location the most (and probably first) was England, later joined by Iceland, Ireland, Sardinia and Corsica. Another privileged location was a central one, described in metaphoric terms as 'the heart' of Europe, which was claimed chiefly by the Germans, as illustrated by Lamprecht's declaration that 'Germany had started becoming the heart of Europe both in geographic and historical terms' as early as the tenth century. Even Hölderlin refers to the German homeland as 'the holy heart of nations'.[69] Understandably, the Czechs also vehemently claimed the honourable location of the heart of Europe.

Not all nations could pride themselves on being located centrally, and being 'on the periphery' was often redeemed by an ideology of national mission – a vital role in the service of Europe or humanity. Such missions tended to be associated with historical mythologies about acting as a buffer against the foes of Europe – such as the Moors in Spain, the Mongolians in Russia, and the Turks in Hungary and Poland.

The cardinal points – i.e. the west–east axis – started to be used relatively late as a means of determining a prestigious location within Europe. The myth of the privileged western position spread in the nineteenth century, according to which the 'West' was associated with belonging to the civilised world, while the 'East' began to be seen as economically backward and politically reactionary. This dichotomisation was subsequently complemented by the myth of the capable and morally pure 'North', while the ideologisation of the 'South' of Europe gestured towards the myth of the Mediterranean keepers of the tradition of antiquity.

The projection of the nation into a space became a universal cultural need in the nineteenth century, first in state-nations and soon after that in the mass phase of national movements. The need to learn about one's homeland and to be able to describe it in scientific terms gave rise to geographic science, which started forming during the Enlightenment and became institutionalised a century later as a subject taught at state universities. In established state-nations, the development of geographic science was connected with its application in their respective colonies.[70]

There was much more to the process than merely the specialist affair of geographic science. The national territory was understood to mean 'home', and thus possessed qualitative characteristics, such as the national landscape. Nations were symbolised by certain types of landscape, with a particular structure of nationally relevant locations. According to Simon Schama, national identity was also dependent on the topography and image of a home.[71] Landscape was seen as a product of culture, and it was unimportant whether it was defined by a state boundary or only by the core of a nationally defined region, which was different from the other national regions in its vicinity. It is no accident that celebration and evocation of the landscape form a substantial part of the anthems of a number of European nations, such as those of the Czechs and Norwegians.

The cult of the landscape as the quintessence of national virtues characterised English (and later British) national identity. Since the early modern period, landscape scenes have reflected the worshipping of places that were reminders of famous battles, figures and myths. These places of remembrance (*lieux de mémoire*) were often only of local, rather than national significance. This alone signifies a certain degree of intellectualisation – an elitist view of the English countryside that encompassed ancient megaliths as well as aristocratic parks. There was also a historical dimension to the worshipping of the landscape: both the Romans and the Anglo-Saxons had found the land in which they were settling beautiful.

Foggy marshes and fenced-off pastures were another distinctive features of the English landscape. Irish landscape scenes combined natural uniqueness with memorable locations – chiefly those that served as reminders of events from the lives of clans and as proof of Irish distinctness.[72]

Although the German perspective retained its idealised view of the uniqueness of landscapes in individual countries for a long time, the national ideology soon became dominated by a romantic obsession with the forest. The Germanic forest was a symbolic expression of resistance to the expansive Roman urban civilisation, and thus a symbol of the superiority of the German spirit over urban materialism. From 1871 German imperial education focused on creating an image of a single, albeit multifaceted, landscape with villages amid greenery as the natural base of the nation and, simultaneously, of Berlin as the metropolis of all Germans.[73]

The focal point of the French landscape scene was the stable state entity, for which borders and political ties were more important than ethnicity. The outline of France was popularly presented as a hexagon, and the French landscape was seen as typically multifaceted, containing all types of landscape from fertile flat lands to giant mountains. It was also seen as characterised by climatic variety, incorporating Mediterranean, Atlantic and continental climates. Another important feature was the myth about the land having been cultivated continually for centuries, and the related cult of the small peasant and his work.[74]

It was relatively easy for nations that lived within smaller, more consistent territories to construct an idealised image of their landscape or a particular part of it. Indeed, the *pars pro toto* method was a necessary part of all constructs of national landscapes. The Magyars opted for the cult of an open flat land – *puszta* – in combination with three mountain ranges in the north of the country. Lithuanian (and similarly Latvian) landscape scenes depicted melancholy flat lands, deep pine forests and peasant settlements surrounded by fields and birch trees. The Finnish national landscape scenes depicted endless lakes, surrounded by forests. The Czech hilly landscape was a harmonious combination of meadows, fields, woods and bodies of water. The Norwegian scene combined rugged rocks covered with pine trees, lined with fjords on one side and mountain glaciers on the other. The Norwegian patriots emphasised the contrast between the 'vertical' nature of their land with the 'horizontal' nature of Denmark, to whose rule they were subjected.

Places of remembrance were an essential component of national landscape scenes, and architecture occupied a prime position in this context, as a 'materialised' form of connection with the past. A consensus was gradually reached about certain objects being reminiscent of the same thing – i.e. evoking in everyone the same association within collective memory. In state-nations, this consensus was facilitated by the fact they each had a single system of school education for the elites. In national movements, state control restricted the influence of school education, and therefore communication combined with national agitation played a decisive role: calendars, journals, pictures and in many places also preaching by the clergy. Educational tourism represented a specific element of the inculcation of respect for places of remembrance. Initially, it was of course confined to the educated elites, but in circumstances of extreme oppression, such as in Catalonia under the Franco regime, this type of tourism was almost the sole means of national activation.

There were a number of layers to 'places of remembrance'. Chronologically, the oldest layer comprised mythological sacred places, and in some cases also religious sites of pilgrimage. The next layer consisted of places reminiscent of the glorious aspects of the nation's history – victorious battles, key national figures' birthplaces and places of residences (castles and basic little cottages alike), national institutions and institutions that could be interpreted as national, and so on. The places most often employed for purposes of national agitation were those in which events had taken place that were later interpreted as the cause of national humiliation and suffering. Last but not least, a national value was assigned to outstanding or remarkable natural phenomena – mountains, rivers, rock formations, bodies of water, even mineral wealth.[75]

The construction of national landscape scenes and places of remembrance was undeniably difficult for multi-ethnic empires. The dynastic 'state' monuments represented such efforts in the Habsburg monarchy, but their appeal to non-dominant ethnic groups was limited. With the exception of marginal efforts, the monarchy essentially abandoned attempts at constructing 'national', pan-Austrian landscape scenes or universally applicable places of remembrance. By contrast, the tsarist administration endeavoured to facilitate learning about the whole of Russia in order to reinforce the sense of belonging together at least among the educated part of the population. The state financed geographic expeditions – to Siberia in particular, and also to the Caucasus region and central Asia – and supported the popularisation of their findings. But these efforts did not appear to be very effective in strengthening national identity, and were complicated by Russia's transitional position between Europe and Asia.[76]

The sea was a singular component of national landscape scenes, whose role varied greatly in relation to the geographic situation of any given country in Europe. There were the 'seafaring' nations, for whom the sea was integral to the image of the national landscape, and seafaring was naturally a nationally integrating activity. Seafaring nations that were successful at colonial expansion – the Spanish, English, French, Portuguese, Italian and Dutch, for example – date back to the early modern period. They were later joined by other seafaring nations, this time commercial entrepreneurs such as the Greeks, Norwegians and Germans. For all these, the sea and seafaring were a defining aspect of national confidence. Sometimes, the proximity to the sea had little national importance – neither the Finnish, Irish, Bulgarians, Estonians, Croatians, Slovenians nor the Ukrainians became sea traders. Among the Baltic nations, only the Latvians had plans (albeit utopian) to reinforce their position as a nation by using the sea to become 'the Dutchmen of Russia'.

In some cases the sea acquired a political and symbolic meaning. An obvious example was that of the Polish national movement, in which the notion was maintained of restoring Poland to its size before the division, when Polish territory had 'connected the seas' (the Baltic and Black seas). Despite being unrealistic, this concept was so deeply rooted that, even within a unified Poland, the Polish public continued to be encouraged to believe in the idea of 'maritimity'.[77]

Nation-forming in Europe also extended to nations that had no access to a sea. The vast majority of these were nations that arose from non-dominant ethnic groups, as Switzerland was the only landlocked state in Europe in the eighteenth century. While the absence of a coastline did not prevent the forming of the Czech, Slovak, Lithuanian, Magyar and Serbian nations, it affected their social structure and very likely influenced their national stereotypes and their elites' views of Europe.

The natural need to define national borders and demarcate national territories collided with the complex structure of relationships that were far from harmonious. It has already been stated that the process of nation-forming took place in historically determined circumstances, including the ambiguous nature of national borders. Borders were defined politically as well as ethnically, and these two definitions seldom corresponded. It is also essential at this point to consider the typological differentiation between state-nations, whose borders were the result of centuries' worth of foreign policies, and national movements, which were in the process of defining their borders.

In the process of nation-forming, state borders from the early modern period began to be nationalised and seen as a 'natural' demarcation of a given nation as against other nations. The inhabitants found within the framework of state-national borders were intended to be homogenised into a modern nation, which implied that the political borders were also going to become cultural borders. Nevertheless, any border is always a two-sided issue, and can divide as well as unite nations. A political border tended not to be questioned when it corresponded with an ethnic or natural border.[78]

The phenomenon of a natural border had fascinated politicians since medieval times, as it evoked the idea of the state territory being safer. The process of nationalising borders added the concept of an enclosed national 'body', also in the territorial sense of the word. Both of these factors were combined, for instance, in Danton's demand of 1793 that France demarcate its national territory definitively by the mountains (the Pyrenees and the Alps) and the Rhine, and thereby make the country defensible.[79] Plans to implement natural borders were easily ideologised and given a symbolic context, as illustrated in the notorious first stanza of the German anthem, although the rivers (the Meuse, the Memel, the Adige and the Belt) symbolise claims to the ethnic, rather than strategic, border of Germany.

The ethnic and cultural borders were especially important in defining the territory of nations without a state – i.e. in the circumstances of national movements. Endeavours to establish a national territory in this context were confronted with at least two issues. Firstly, it was unclear, particularly in the phase of national agitation, who were all the people who embraced the newly forming nation, and it was relatively difficult to arrive at any 'objective' statistics regarding nationality. Secondly, a historical factor entered the national discourse in several national movements: the Magyar, Czech, Croatian, Basque and Welsh nations claimed the borders of a political entity that had existed in the past, and with which it was legitimate to self-identify. When this 'historical right' was successfully applied and the national movement culminated in the establishment of a nation-state, the historically defined national border did not correspond with the ethnic one.

A specific case of a conflict between the ethnic and historical definition of the national territory can be seen in the German example, where the 'national' historical formation was considered to be the medieval Holy Roman Empire. If 'the German future lay in the German Middle Ages', as Hagen Schulze wrote, this implied a megalomaniac historical self-reflection, which both supported and required correspondingly megalomaniac plans for the national future.[80]

Combining two or more identities (national, ethnic, state, and so on) was not always as viable as it proved in the case of minorities in France. Even there, a cartographic image of France started to be purposefully spread from 1871; maps of France were displayed in all schools, so that they would become firmly engraved in pupils' minds.[81] By the twentieth century, it was common for schools to equip classroom walls with maps.

Like state-nations, the newly formed national states also strove to anchor the image of 'our territory' in the 'mental map' of their citizens. Wherever the boundary was disputed or questioned, its importance as a symbol and a base of national identity grew.[82] When the actual national boundary did not correlate with the idea of the size of the national body, it gave rise to the notion that the 'body' has been maimed and that the whole nation was thus suffering. This corresponded with the production of national maps, some of which showed the current boundaries (for example, Spain) while others were altered to encompass national claims, *irredenta* (for example, Italy, France and Denmark). Maps of colonial dominions often belonged among the images of the 'national' territory.[83] The borders of nation-states were naturalised, projected into the past as 'age-old', and promoted to the level of symbols in a way that would make it possible not only to homogenise but also to 'territorially socialise' the members of national communities.[84] We know that these efforts were not always successful: the issue of ethnic or national minorities became an inevitable consequence of a successful nation-state forming everywhere in Europe.

By way of conclusion, it should be emphasised that all the aforementioned manifestations of borders becoming naturalised and ideologised were not the causes but the effects of successful modern nation-forming, as were the conflicts that resulted. Therefore, a similar objection applies here to the one made earlier in relation to the role of cultural activities, celebrations and monuments. Research into borders can bring valuable findings about *the ways* in which nations integrated internally and the *mechanisms* through which they could be controlled and manipulated. But it will not suffice when we wish to *explain and interpret* the nation-forming processes in Europe.

Conclusions and Hypotheses

Readers will no doubt have noticed that the term 'nationalism' has been used in only a handful of contexts. The notions mentioned and considered in this book are national consciousness, people's self-identification with a group designated as a nation, the forming of this group, and its historical roots. This is by intent rather than by accident, since I regard the term 'nationalism' to be an insufficient tool of scientific historical analysis – in particular when it is employed excessively and in the all-encompassing and even personalised sense commonly encountered especially in the Anglo-Saxon linguistic context. If we considered 'nationalism' to be an atemporal phenomenon, unconstrained by time or space, it would enable us to arrive at a rather banal conclusion that people (certain classes or groups) were 'nationalist' already in the Middle Ages, as they associated their awareness of belonging, their language and value systems, with the community that they sometimes referred to as a nation. But the social structure (and mentality) of these communities were very different to those of the communities that formed as 'modern nations' during the nineteenth and twentieth centuries.

As was stated in the opening chapter, it is of no use getting involved in a dispute over whether a nation should be seen as a product of nationalism or the other way around. The question as to why modern nations emerged in Europe cannot be fully explained merely by pointing out that they were a cultural construct – the outcome of a cultural transfer in the form of the effects of nationalism or similar. This only pushes the question into a different terminological context, which in turn demands a clarification of why the phenomenon of nationalism (assuming we know what it is) achieved success quickly in some cases, slowly in other cases, and sometimes not at all. An awareness of belonging to a nation was not spread by a virus, nor was it a pandemic with a biological cause, but rather the result of decisions made by people in specific historical circumstances. The fact that different people made the same choices in the past cannot be explained solely by the transfer of ideas. To presume that the type of media-induced manipulation commonly encountered nowadays was present in the circumstances of the nineteenth century is an unacceptably ahistorical approach.

The basis of my work is the opinion that a modern nation – i.e. a large social group – is not an age-old phenomenon, and that the precondition for its existence was an increasing number of individuals who saw themselves as its members and self-identified with it. Identification with a nation was thus a result of more or less spontaneous decisions, which were 'arbitrary' in the sense that they depended on a whole range of circumstances, influences and events, specific to each individual. However, given that the same decision was made – sometimes sooner and sometimes later – by hundreds, thousands, and even tens of thousands of people, we must assume that it was an outcome not of coincidence but of decision-making influenced by recurrent circumstances or similar experiences among large numbers of people. Four decades ago, this view provided a base for my research, and further research has showed that it can serve, albeit in modified form, as a starting point in both developing and verifying crucial hypotheses.

This book aims to demonstrate that decision-making related to national identity and an awareness of belonging to a nation cannot be explained satisfactorily until we abandon the mono-causal interpretation – whether its claims lie in 'objective truths' or emotionally orientated 'constructs'. Nation-forming would have been inconceivable without the propagation of the idea of national identity and the positive value of belonging to a nation. It would have been equally unlikely for national agitation to succeed if it had not been for earlier, historically rooted cultural (ethnic) ties, common historical experiences, and certain political institutions or institutionalised social and cultural relationships. However, abandoning the mono-causal interpretation alone will not be sufficient.

A principal finding that I have built upon is the fact that two types of European nation-building processes must be differentiated. On one hand, nations were formed under the conditions of what I refer to as a 'state-nation', which had originated from an early modern state with only one dominant national culture. Here, an awareness of existing as a distinct 'nation' had been present among the members of the ruling classes since at least the Middle Ages. On the other hand, there were the circumstances of national movements, which had risen from the national mobilisation of the non-dominant, non-state ethnic group. This usually (but not always) culminated in the forming of a 'small nation' and, as the case may be, also its nation-state. Most institutions, many terms and contexts played different roles in the two sets of circumstances, and we know that there were a few transitional cases.

Another major finding is that, in the framework of small-nation building, phases A and B of national movements rarely contained manifestations that were typical of most state-nations – i.e. feelings of superiority over other nations and attempts to dominate them or subject their interests to the interests of one's own nation. That being said, these attitudes were latently present in the newly forming self-identification with a nation. However, it was not until the nation had been fully established and contained its own ruling classes that opinions emerged among its members that I consider to be nationalism in the true sense of the word: a truly dangerous intolerance, justified by 'typical' national arguments, aggression, and an uncritical overestimation of one's own nation. Nationalism in this sense of the word occurred in state-nations as well as nation-states that rose from successful national movements. This, however, belongs to a developmental stage that lies outside the temporal scope of this book, whose objective has been to focus on the nation-forming process and its causes.

If, in conclusion, we ask why the intention to 'construct' nations in Europe in most cases led to the formation of modern nations – i.e. if we ask what the causes and preconditions of a successful culmination of the nation-forming processes were – we need to break up the question into smaller parts. First of all, we must distinguish between two situational contexts: whether the starting point was a state-nation or a national movement. In addition to this, two time-frames need to be differentiated with regard to causal explanations. Firstly, we need to ask why attempts to 'create' – i.e. establish – a nation occurred in the first place, and, secondly, we need to investigate in what situations and due to what circumstances these efforts proved successful. This approach was used in individual chapters, and the summary of its findings is as follows.

What gave rise to the intention and subsequent efforts to spread national consciousness? Most historians agree that the decision to self-identify with a nation and assign it a key value stemmed from a situation in which the old society, which had been based on coercion, privileges and inequality, began to disintegrate, when the existing patriarchal, feudal or Estates relationships and the old value systems had begun to falter, and when religious legitimacy, upon which the old social system had been founded, had started to be questioned.

The solution was straightforward in state-nations: elevate ties to a state to the status of a binding national norm. Endeavours to achieve civic equality assumed the form of integrating the members of the forming civic society into an organic community, which was perceived as embodying value and given the label 'nation'. The term 'nation' had already been used in earlier times, and while at that time it referred to a political (and usually simultaneously also linguistic) community, its new purpose was to transform the monarch's subjects into equal citizens – members of a nation. This is the way in which evolution towards a nation occurred in England from the seventeenth century onwards – and in France a century later, albeit with considerable Revolutionary civic rhetoric. Most authors have traditionally regarded the French model of a 'single indivisible nation' as typical and exemplary for western Europe. However, this stereotypically repeated notion needs to be contrasted across the whole of Europe. As we saw, the so-called French model was more of an exception than the rule, when compared with more than twenty nation-forming processes across the entire continent.

The majority of modern European nations were formed under the conditions of national movements, where the search for a new identity was much less straightforward and had many more alternatives than in state-nations. The question that always needs to be considered is: what were the alternatives to the path that led from an ethnic community to a national movement, and then to a fully formed, distinctive nation? In almost all cases, the other option was to merge and identify ('assimilate') with the ruling nation, but this was viable only where the national movement had arisen within a clearly defined, well-established state-nation – i.e. only in west European, multi-ethnic empires such as Great Britain and Spain. One reason why this option of merging with the ruling nation was less realistic in the three eastern multi-ethnic empires was that their ruling state elites still lacked a firmly defined national identity in the modern sense of the word.

Assimilation was a highly unlikely option when the ethnic group was large, and the national movement was able to build upon strong memories of a state and was led by the aristocracy (for example, the Magyars and the Polish). It is important not to perceive alternatives solely in the context of assimilation: an alternative development to forming a single nation was a disintegration of the national movement into several streams, with a view to establishing independent entities. This option proved unsuccessful in Transylvania in relation to the Magyar nation and in Moravia in relation to the Czech nation, and is still an unresolved issue for Carpathian Rusyns in relation to the Ukrainian nation. On the other hand, it succeeded in the case of the Macedonians in relation to Bulgarians.

In the circumstances of non-state ethnic groups, the solutions to the crisis of old identities, and thus a new group identity, were sought by focusing, on one hand, on the relics of past political entities and institutionalised remnants of a common fate, and, on the other, on the ethnically, culturally and primarily linguistically (sometimes also religiously) defined community. But this focus was not dictated by the will of intellectuals or their love of power; it originated from the experience of a linguistic and cultural disadvantage and, in some cases, even inferiority among the members of one's ethnic group, in comparison with those who comprised the ruling elites.

The actual success of the resulting national identity was not determined by the philosophical concept or legacy of thought upon which the protagonists of the nation-forming process in a given state-nation or national movement built, whether these took the form of rational Enlightenment, Romantic rebellion or Christian religious zeal. Despite this, it is essential to pay attention to the thought structure of the national consciousness and national ideology, rather than content oneself with the superficial label 'nationalism' – which is, strictly speaking, empty.

One of the founding concepts for modern European nations was undoubtedly the Judeo-Christian religious tradition, which was familiar with terms and values such as 'chosen nation' and 'promised land', and the notion of an ethnically defined enemy (as presented in the Old Testament). These aspects of the religious tradition were not necessarily in conflict with the legacies of the Enlightenment: rationality, tolerance, secularisation, the ideal of civic equality and enlightened patriotism. Already at this point, the context of enlightened patriotism was influenced by the specifically European ethos of work for a common good (probably of Christian origin) – i.e. the commitment to benefit 'humanity' through one's own work. Humanity had the specific form of a given community, whether organised within a region, a state or – as a new phenomenon – a national community. The notion of working for people made the shift from the context of regional patriotism to acquire the meaning of working for the nation and its members. Simultaneously, an older, Baroque version of patriotism was still influential in many parts of Europe at the turn of the nineteenth century, which was anchored in religion and became part of some national programmes. This type of patriotism already advocated love for the homeland, defined as both a state and a land-region. From the point of view of the motivation towards patriotism, the situation of state-nations was simpler than that of national movements, as they were able to build upon 'state interests' sanctified by tradition.

The principles of enlightened patriotism obliged the educated to take care of the people living in their region (or state) and study their life and culture. Scholars 'discovered' national customs, either constructed the national language based on the spoken vernaculars or modernised its older literary form, and studied the climate and also the history of 'their' people, which included pietism as well as Johann Herder's idea that, by working for the nation, one benefits humanity as a whole. In the scholarly phase A, the culture of the existing state-nation was defined as much as the features of the nation-to-be, where nation-building took place under the conditions of an ethnic community. At this stage, definitions were sought without a bias that would cross the line of a scholar's zeal for the topic in question. However, this interest did give rise to clear notions about what characterises *us* and who *they* are – which was of crucial importance in particular in the circumstances of an ethnic community.

It was a natural extension of the scholarly activities that a proportion of the educated elites sooner or later arrived at the conclusion that the members of an ethnic community (citizens of a state) need to be encouraged to embrace the ideas of a new national community and a new national identity. In believing this, they embarked upon the agitation phase B of national movements. In contrast to state-nations, ethnic communities did not automatically comprise the educated elites. The first, most basic precondition of success was to broaden access to school education, which would make social ascent possible for at least some young members of the ethnic group. This factor alone was responsible for the marked difference between the social anchoring of the leaders of national movements and of the members of the elites in state-nations. A secondary difference lay in the composition of the educated audience, and thus also in the shape of the forming national culture: whereas state-nations continued to display the dichotomy between high and folk culture, in national movements these two kinds of culture were initially (and often for a long time) intertwined.

The idea of a nation – each vision or 'construct' of a modern nation – could be effective only if it reached those for whom it was intended. For national consciousness to spread successfully, the required level of social communication was one that would allow regular contact between patriotic agitators and the recipients of their nationally mobilising efforts. This intensification of social communication was facilitated by a number of changes that occurred at the outset of the modernisation of society. One such change was increasing horizontal mobility – regular mobility and mutual communication between people that reached beyond the village, manor or town, and included visits to marketplaces, seasonal work, migration, and military service. Other changes included improvements to transport networks and postal connections, and intensification and rationalisation of the state and regional administration. Other important factors in communication were the spread of literacy and education, at the level of both elementary and secondary (usually municipal) schools.

Once again, all these preconditions of communication played a different role in situations where they served as an instrument of the state's nationally mobilising politics, on one hand, and in situations where the agitation activities of national movements entered communication 'from below', on the other. For example, school education was in its essence a state-organised national education, and the degree of magnanimity, national tolerance or indifference of the state apparatus of the multi-ethnic empires determined the extent to which schools could offer a national identity to the members of a non-dominant ethnic group. Even the selection of the language of tuition could be crucial from the point of view of national mobilisation.

Literacy was not an automatic or universal catalyst for national consciousness, either. It acquired this function only if the new national identity on offer could be presented in periodical and non-periodical publications. What mattered, therefore, was whether the political system was so liberal as to tolerate national agitation in the press. However, freedom of speech alone was not enough: there had to be sufficient financial means to make it possible to publish periodicals in the language of the ethnic group in question.

The significance of national public celebrations for agitation, regardless of their occasion or form, lay in the fact that they could appeal to illiterate as well as literate audiences, and their social impact was thus much broader. Despite this, it would be far from the truth to see them as ubiquitous. For the ruling elites of state-nations, national celebrations and the propagation of national symbols gradually became part of their exercising of authority. But this was not the case until the 'ones at the top' first realised that, in order to pursue their power interests (both domestic and foreign), they needed to mobilise the masses behind the national idea. This usually followed after the principles of constitutionalism and people's participation in political decision-making had begun to gain ground. This form of national agitation was much less accessible to the leaders of national movements. Due to their limited financial resources, and often also to state control, they could make use only of some forms of public celebration, such as funerals, newly defined national religious and folk festivities, singing festivals, and so on.

Social communication was a consequence of modernisation changes that not even the most enthusiastic among the protagonists of the national idea could foresee. Nor could they artificially bring about the secularisation of thought or the crisis of legitimacy of old social dependencies, values and identities. As we have seen, these modernisation changes need to be examined in the broadest possible scope, from the evolution of market relations and new forms of trade and production business, to the political revolution, rationalisation of state administration, and bureaucratisation.

A major difficulty in explaining national mobilisation by

'modernisation' is that nation-building did not occur evenly, and that the asynchronous nature of modern nation-building did not correlate with the speed of modernisation. In other words, although modern nations were sometimes built in developed parts of Europe first and in less developed parts later, this was not always the case. Let us remember that the beginning and the process of nation-forming were more or less synchronous in developed Germany and relatively underdeveloped Greece, in the proto-industrial Czech lands, and in agrarian Hungary. The national movement in developed Catalonia emerged approximately at the same time as the one in very underdeveloped Lithuania. Therefore, successful modern nation-forming was not in itself a sign of being developed or underdeveloped. Furthermore, the intensity of social communication does not fully explain the nation-forming processes, either.

In view of this, we need to take into consideration a further two important circumstances, described in this book as 'nationally relevant conflicts' and 'external factors'. If national identity was to be received positively, national arguments (in whatever form) needed to 'resonate' with what given individuals – or, rather, social groups – considered to be their own interests. The appeal of the newly offered identification with a nation increased when socially or economically defined rivals and competitors could also be labelled national enemies. There was no universal concept of a national enemy; it depended on the type of the nation-building process. In state-nations, the image of an external enemy most often had a nationally mobilising function, and its mobilisation efficiency was high in situations of war or under foreign occupation (or having memories of such an occupation). This is how 'the French threat', for instance, facilitated national mobilisation in Germany, and how 'the German threat' facilitated national mobilisation in Denmark. Classic examples include the situation of 'the homeland being under threat' during the French Revolution, and a new wave of national integration during the times of reaction against the German threat after 1871. If a war can be seen as an important nationally mobilising factor, then it was particularly relevant in state-nations.

In national movements – with the exception of those that emerged within the territory of the Ottoman Empire – the 'national enemy' was determined chiefly according to relationships between different strata of society. Conflicts between peasants and their 'foreign' nobility, between the countryside and the town, between artisans and the emerging industry, between the established educated elites and the new academic intelligentsia that was struggling to apply itself, between the centre and the provinces – all had the potential to have a mobilising effect.

In state-nations, these social divisions often complicated a spontaneous and complete integration of all classes into a national community. It was no coincidence that the idea of proletarian internationalism in the workers' movement proved successful in state-nations, whereas the workers in most national movements self-identified with their own nation in its struggle against the rule of 'foreign' capital. Latvian Bolsheviks and Catalan anarchists are the exceptions that prove this rule.

A whole range of relatively disparate relationships and circumstances can be listed in the category of external factors, which undoubtedly include international conflicts and great-power interests. In fact, the very spreading of the idea of a nation, as part of cultural transfer, has often been perceived as an 'external factor'. The opportunity to find moral and possibly even financial support in the construct of a broader togetherness played an important role, whether this togetherness is characterised as pan-Slavism, pan-Germanism, Scandinavianism or Finno-Ugrism. An external factor that was specific to national movements was external support and the interest of 'friendly' foreign powers in the weakening of a given multi-ethnic empire, or in acquiring strategic positions within the territory of the emerging small nations. While this type of support was rather rare during phase B, the external factor became decisive when the nation-building process culminated in statehood-seeking efforts. This is because national movements seldom resulted in the formation of their respective states effortlessly against the will of great powers, as was the case in Norway and Ireland. The vast majority of European nation-states were formed on the basis of a decision made by the great powers.

The complexity of the small-nation building and the causality of the path towards the success of phase B can be illustrated by the following model:

Figure 3

Model of Interactions between Social Reality and the Activity of National Movements

SOCIAL REALITY	NATIONAL ACTIVITY
Findings of scholarly research of phase A	Their application to the needs of the national movement
The past and its relics	Search for national history
Ethnic and linguistic situation	Linguistic and cultural demands
Social and economic modernisation	Social emancipation
Modernisation of the political system	National political programme
New conflicts of interest	Nationally relevant conflicts of interest
Modernisation of education	Struggle for national schools
Possibility of social ascent	The building of academic elites
Social communication	Cultural construct of a nation

Modern nations were not simply 'products of nationalism', nor a result of unlucky chance. They were a consequence of a combination of efforts at national mobilisation and objective circumstances – i.e. circumstances independent of the wishes of 'nationalists', which included ethnic relationships, relics from the past, and modernisation processes. National awareness, and consequently also patriotism, was an expression (an external manifestation) of the progressing national imagination – i.e. the spread and adoption of self-identification with a new type of a community: a nation. While it is true that this community was inconceivable without its members becoming nationally conscious, this does not mean that we can elevate the idea of a nation to a *primus movens* of the entire process. National identities could be constructed, but not put into practice independently of the historical, political, social and cultural contexts and circumstances. The failure of Czechoslovakism, Scandinavianism and Yugoslavism are examples that prove this point, as are the disintegrating constructs of the Belgian, Spanish and British nations.

Notes

Preface to the English Edition

1 Miroslav Hroch, *Social Preconditions of National Revival in Europe* (Cambridge, 1985).

2 Miroslav Hroch, *In the National Interest: Demands and Goals of European National Movements of the Nineteenth Century* (Prague, 2000).

3 See especially Anthony Smith, *Nationalism and Modernism: A Critical Survey of Recent Theories of Nations and Nationalism* (London/New York, 1998).

4 See *Nationalities Papers* 38: 6 (November 2010), 'Special Issue: Twenty-Five Years of A-B-C: Miroslav Hroch's Impact on Nationalism Studies'.

5 Miroslav Hroch, *Die Vorkämpfer der nationalen Bewegung bei den kleinen Völkern Europas* (*Acta Universitatis Carolinae* XXIV) (Prague, 1968).

Part I

1 This need has been addressed in numerous publications, such as Anthony Smith, *Nationalism and Modernism: A Critical Survey of Recent Theories of Nations and Nationalism* (London/New York, 1998); Athena Leoussi, ed., *Encyclopedia of Nationalism* (New Brunswick/London, 2001); and, in the last decade, in works by John Hutchinson, Paul Lawrence and Umut Özkirimli.

1. Definitional Disputes

1 The Finnish historian Aira Kemiläinen was the first author to draw attention to the fundamental difference in interpretations of these terms in the opening chapters of her *Nationalism: Problems Concerning the Word, the Concept and Classification* (Jyväskylä, 1964) – a book that remained outside the attention of the western sciences. More recently,

see for example "'Nation": A Survey of the Term in European Languages', in Athena Leoussi, ed., *Encyclopedia of Nationalism*, pp. 203–8.

2   See the treatise *Gentis felicitas*, published in 1659.

3   Perhaps the first such tendency can be found in Bernard Joseph, *Nationality: Its Nature and Problems* (London, 1929), pp. 24–5, and later also in Carlton Hayes, *Nationalism: A Religion* (New York, 1960).

4   For typical examples of literature from the end of the nineteenth century that attempted to define a nation in terms of a set of objective 'attributes', see Friedrich Julius Neumann, *Volk und Nation* (Leipzig, 1888); Friedrich Meinecke, *Weltbürgertum und Nationalstaat* (Munich/ Berlin, 1907); Otto Bauer, *Die Nationalitätenfrage und Sozialdemokratie* (Vienna, 1907), pp. 84ff, 135. Bauer's concept served as an inspiration to the young Bolshevik emigrant Joseph Stalin, who made us of its simplified account in forming his definition of a nation based on binding characteristics, which from the 1930s constituted the official Soviet 'Marxist-Leninist' view of the nation. See Ephrain Nimni, *Marxism and Nationalism: Theoretical Origins of Political Crisis* (London/Boulder, 1991), Chapter 7.

5   Ernest Renan, 'Qu'est-ce qu'une nation?' in *Oeuvres Completes I* (Paris, 1947). Gustav von Rümelin, *Kanzlerreden* (Tübingen, 1907). For the role of 'statisticians', compare Siegfried Weichlein, "'Qu'est-ce qu'une nation?'" Stationen der deutschen statistischen Debatte um Nation und Nationalität in der Reichsgründungszueit', in: Wolther von Kreseritzky and Klaus-Peter Sick, eds, *Demokratie in Deutschland. Chancen und Gefährdungen im 19. und 20. Jahrhundert* (Munich, 1999), pp. 71.

6   Max Weber, *Wirtschaft und Gesellschaft II* (Tübingen, 1976), pp. 675ff. On the other hand, Weber explained the difference between the living standards of the Germans and the Polish by pointing to racial predispositions. See Jean-Rodrigue Paré, 'Les "écrits de jeunesse" de Max Weber: l'histoire agraire, le nationalisme et les paysants', in *Revue Canadienne de science politique*, September 1995, p. 440; Michael Banton, 'Max Weber on "Ethnic Communities": A Critique', in *Nations and Nationalism* 13 (2007), pp. 23ff. See also Pierre Birnbaum, ed., *Sociologie des nationalismes* (Paris, 1997), pp. 13–14.

7   As is the opinion of, for example, Paul James, or recently also Umut Özkirimli, *Contemporary Debates on Nationalism: A Critical Engagement* (Basingstoke, 2005), p. 30.

8   The Nazi concept was influenced, for instance, by Max Boehm, *Das*

eigenständige Volk (Göttingen, 1932). A large number of authors, such as Kurt Stavenhagen, in *Das Wesen der Nation* (Berlin, 1934), advocated markedly subjectivist, nationalism-laden views. A theoretical concept that was differentiated and balanced was presented in Heinz Ziegler, *Die moderne Nation. Ein Beitrag zur politischen Soziologie* (Tübingen, 1932), but was, unfortunately, forgotten by later research.

9   Carlton Hayes, *The Historical Evolution of Modern Nationalism* (New York, 1931).

10   Hayes, *Nationalism: A Religion*, p. 2.

11   Frederick Hertz, *Nationality in History and Politics: A Study of the Psychology and Sociology of National Sentiment and Character* (London, 1945); E. H. Carr, *Nationalism and After* (London, 1945); Elie Kedourie, *Nationalism* (London, 1960).

12   His founding work, *The Idea of Nationalism: A Study of Its Origins and Background*, was first published in 1944, then reprinted many times. His publication *Nationalism: Its Meaning and History* (Princeton, 1955) contained some modifications.

13   Louis Leo Snyder, *The Meaning of Nationalism* (New Brunswick, NJ, 1954), pp. 118ff. The ideological and political aspects of the 'German' ethnic definition of a nation had been pointed out a whole fifteen years before Kohn, in Ziegler, *Die moderne Nation*, pp. 37–8.

14   Aira Kemiläinen, *Nationalismus*, pp. 111ff.

15   See Michael Billig, *Banal Nationalism* (London/New Delhi, 1997), pp. 46–7, 55–6; George Schopflin, *Nations, Identity, Power: The New Politics of Europe* (London, 2000), pp. 4–5; Jarosław Kilias, *Wspólnota abstrakcyjna. Zarys socjologii naroda* (Warsaw, 2004), pp. 60–1; Anne-Marie Thiesse, 'National Identities: A Transnational Paradigm', in Alain Dieckhoff and Christophe Jaffelot, eds, *Revisiting Nationalism: Theories and Processes* (London, 2005), pp. 123–4. A rather specific case is that of Liah Greenfeld, who based her concept of *Nationalism: Five Roads to Modernity* (Cambridge, MA, 1992) on Hans Kohn's dichotomy without quoting Kohn even once.

16   Boyd Shafer, *Nationalism: Myth and Reality* (New York, 1955); Boyd Shafer, 'If Only We Knew More about Nationalism', *Canadian Review of Studies in Nationalism* 7 (1980), pp. 197ff.

17   Pitirim Sorokin, *Society, Culture, and Personalities: Their Structure and Dynamics – A System of General Sociology* (New York, 1947).

18   Anthony Smith, *National Identity* (London, 1991), p. 14.

19   Miroslav Hroch, *Die Vorkämpfer der nationalen Bewegung bei den*

kleinen Völkern Europas (Prague, 1968). I modified and clarified this interpretation later: 'From National Movement to the Fully-Fledged Nation', *New Left Review* I/198 (1993), pp. 3ff.

20 Karl W. Deutsch, *Nationalism and Social Communication* (Cambridge, MA, 1953); Miroslav Hroch, 'Three Encounters with Karl W. Deutsch', *Czech Sociological Review* 48 (2012), pp. 1,115ff.

21 Carl J. Friedrich, 'Nation-Building', in Karl Deutsch and William Foltz, eds, *Nation-Building* (New York, 1966).

22 Stein Rokkan, ed., *Comparative Research across Cultures and Nations* (Paris/The Hague, 1968); Stein Rokkan, Kirsti Sælen and Joan Warmbrunn, 'Nation-Building: A Review of Recent Comparative Research and a Selected Bibliography of Analytical Studies', *Current Sociology* 19: 3 (1973); Charles Tilly, ed., *The Formation of National States in Western Europe* (Princeton, NJ, 1975); Louis Leo Snyder, *Varieties of Nationalism: A Comparative Study* (Hinsdale, IL, 1976); John Breuilly, *Nationalism and the State* (Manchester, 1982). For a more recent emphasis on the link between the nation and the state (and simultaneously also ethnicity), made by a non-Western author, see Bronislav Geremek, *The Common Roots of Europe* (Cambridge, 1996), pp. 165ff.

23 Ernest Gellner, *Nations and Nationalism* (Oxford, 1983), pp. 12–13. Note the shift in opinion in his posthumous publication *Nationalism* (London, 1997).

24 Michael Keating, *Nations against the State: The New Politics of Nationalism in Quebec, Catalonia and Scotland*, 2nd edn (London, 2001), p. 15.

25 Walker Connor, *Ethnonationalism: The Quest for Understanding* (Princeton, NJ, 1994); Daniele Conversi, ed., *Ethnonationalism in the Contemporary World: Walker Connor and the Study of Nationalism* (London, 2004).

26 Kilias, *Wspólnota abstrakcyjna*.

27 Eugen Lemberg, *Nationalismus, vol. I* (Hamburg, 1964), pp. 28ff. For more information on Lemberg, see Miroslav Hroch, 'Eugen Lemberg's "Nationalismustheorie"', *Bohemia* 45 (2005), pp. 1ff.

28 According to Paul James, *Nation Formation: Towards a Theory of Abstract Community* (London, 1996), p. 63.

29 Kedourie, *Nationalism*, p. 9.

30 From the rich literature on Gellner, see in particular John Hall, ed.,

The State of the Nation: Ernest Gellner and the Theory of Nationalism (Cambridge, 1998).

31 Benedict Anderson, *Imagined Communities: Reflections on the Origin and Spread of Nationalism* (London, 1983). With characteristic irony, Anderson himself refers to the 'other life' of his term in the Afterword to the second edition of his book.

32 James, *Nation Formation*, pp. 5ff.

33 For probably the most noticeable critic of 'essentialism' as regards the understanding of a nation, see Rogers Brubaker, *Nationalism Reframed: Nationhood and the National Question in New Europe* (Cambridge, 1996), pp. 13ff. In addition to this, Brubaker has recently also argued against 'groupism' – i.e. research methods that regard groups as constituent parts of human society. See Rogers Brubaker, *Ethnicity without Groups* (Cambridge, MA, 2004), and the critique of this concept in *Nations and Nationalism* 12 (2006), pp. 699ff.

34 In particular, see Rudolf Speth, *Nation und Revolution. Politische Mythen im 19. Jahrhundert* (Opladen, 2000), p. 153; Leopoldo Mármora, *Nation und internationalismus* (Bremen, 1983), pp. 119–20; Anthony Birch, *Nationalism and National Integration* (London, 1989), pp. 6–7; Bernd Estel, 'Grundaspekte der Nation', in Bernd Estel and Tilman Mayer, eds, *Das Prinzip Nation in modernen Gesellschaften* (Opladen, 1994), pp. 13ff.

35 Tom Nairn, *The Break-Up of Britain: Crisis and Neo-Nationalism* (London, 1977), esp. Chapter 9.

36 Étienne Balibar and Immanuel Wallerstein, *Race, Nation, Class: Ambiguous Identities* (London/New York, 1991), pp. 47ff. For comments on Isaiah Berlin's differentiation between aggressive and cooperative nationalism, see Nathan Gardels, 'Two Concepts of Nationalism: An Interview with Isaiah Berlin', *New York Review of Books*, 20 November 1991. Anthony Smith refers to the positive type of nationalism by employing John Hutchinson's adjective 'cultural'. Smith, *Nationalism and Modernism*, pp. 176–7.

37 Louis Leo Snyder, *The New Nationalism* (Ithaca, NY, 1968), pp. 13ff.

38 Josep R. Llobera, *The God of Modernity: The Development of Nationalism in Western Europe* (Oxford, 1994).

39 Daniel Bar-Tal, 'Patriotism as Fundamental Belief of Group Members', *Politics and the Individual* 3 (1993), p. 48. For a critique of the hypocrisy of counterposing patriotism and nationalism, see Billig, *Banal*

Nationalism, pp. 5, 43; and also David McCrone in his Foreword to *The Sociology of Nationalism* (London/New York, 1998). It is worth noting that Bar-Tal's definition of patriotism is quite reminiscent of Lemberg's definition of nationalism.

40 Theodor Schieder, *Nationalismus und Nationalstaat: Studien zum nationalen Problem im modernen Europa* (Göttingen 1991), p. 347.

41 Greenfeld, *Nationalism.*

42 This political rather than scientific typology does not exclude the authors high appreciation of nationalism as a basic factor of human spirit. See Liah Greenfeld, 'Nationalism and the Mind', *Nations and Nationalism* 11 (2005), p. 333.

43 This matter appears to be considered within the fields of social and political psychology. See, for example, Amélie Mummendey, Andreas Klink and Rupert Brown, 'Nationalism and Patriotism: National Identification and Outgroup Rejection', *British Journal of Social Psychology* 40 (2001), pp. 159ff.

44 This view is advocated in Germany, for instance, by Otto Dann, *Nation und Nationalismus in Deutschland 1770–1990* (Munich, 1993), pp. 12ff. It is also commonly found in Polish, and not only in Catholic literature.

45 Michael Keating, *State and Regional Nationalism: Territorial Politics and the European State* (New York, 1988).

46 Patriotism is used as the positive counterpart of nationalism more frequently in the British and American contexts than in the German one. Earle Hunter had already characterised (American) patriotism in 1932 as an 'emotional relationship of individuals with their homeland, the consequence of which is that individuals will subject their personal wishes to the good and interests of their homeland'. Earle Leslie Hunter, *A Sociological Analysis of Certain Types of Patriotism* (New York, 1932), pp. 27–8. Patriotism is also seen as the opposite of the negatively perceived nationalism by the contributors to Raphael Samuel, ed., *Patriotism: The Making and Unmaking of British National Unity*, 3 vols (London/New York, 1989). See Peter Sugar, 'The Roots of Eastern European Nationalism', in *1er Congrès international des études balkaniques et sud-est européennes* (Sofia, 1966), p. 163; Leonard Doob, *Patriotism and Nationalism: Their Psychological Foundations* (New Haven, CT, 1964). See also Maurizio Viroli, *For Love of Country: An Essay on Patriotism and Nationalism* (Oxford, 1995). On the rare occasion when the term has been used in French, it has been with

reference to the interwar period: see Piere-André Taguieff, 'Le nationalisme des nationalistes', in Gil Delannoi, ed., *Théories du nationalisme* (Paris, 1991), pp. 52ff. More recently, it has also been utilised as an umbrella term for a positive relationship with one's nation and region: see Sandrine Kott and Stéphane Michonneau, *Dictionnaire des nations et des nationalismes* (Paris, 2006), pp. 305ff.

47 Povl Bagge, 'Nationalisme, antinationalisme og nationalfølelse i Danmark omkring 1900', in *Festskrift til Astrid Friis* (Copenhagen, 1963), pp. 1ff. For more terms, see also Robert LeVine and Donald Campbell, *Ethnocentrism: Theories of Conflict, Ethnic Attitudes, and Group Behavior* (New York, 1972); Sugar, 'Roots of Eastern European Nationalism', p. 163. Doob, *Patriotism and Nationalism*; Jeff McMahan and Robert McKim, *The Morality of Nationalism* (Oxford, 1997).

48 For an early use of the term 'national consciousness', see, for example, Florian Znaniecki, *Modern Nationalities: A Sociological Study* (Urbana, IL, 1952). More recently, it has re-emerged, for instance, in Michael Seymour, 'Redefining the Nation', in Nenad Miscevic, ed., *Nationalism and Ethnic Conflict* (Chicago, IL, 2000), p. 41; and in Joep Leerssen, *National Thought in Europe: A Cultural History* (Amsterdam, 2006). In relation to specific circumstances, Leerssen also uses the terms 'national identity' and 'nationalism'.

49 Kott and Michonneau, *Dictionnaire des nations et des nationalismes*, pp. 305ff.

50 This term had already been employed in René Johannet, *Le principe des nationalités* (Paris, 1918). For a later example, see Alain Renault, 'Logique de la nation', in Delannoi, *Théories du nationalisme*, pp. 34ff.

51 For the most recent use in German literature, see Rudolf von Thadden, Steffen Kaudelka and Thomas Serrier, eds, *Europa der Zugehörigkeiten* (Göttingen, 2007). For 'national belonging', see recently Montserrat Guibernau, *Belonging: Solidarity and Division in Modern Societies* (London, 2013).

52 Thomas Hylland Eriksen, *Ethnicity and Nationalism* (London, 1993), pp. 152–3.

53 John Armstrong, *Nations before Nationalism* (Chapel Hill, NC, 1982), p. 288.

54 Raymond Grew, 'The Construction of National Identity', in Peter Boerner, ed., *Concepts of National Identity* (Baden-Baden, 1986), pp. 31ff; Sven Tägil, ed., *Regions in Upheaval: Ethnic Conflict and Political Mobilization* (Lund, 1984), p. 22.

55   Smith, *National Identity*; William Bloom, *Personal Identity, National Identity and International Relations* (Cambridge, 1990). Alain Dieckhoff and Natividad Gutierréz, *Modern Roots: Studies of National Identity* (Aldershot, 2001); Oliver Zimmer, 'Boundary Mechanisms and Symbolic Resources: Towards a Process-Oriented approach to national identity', *Nations and Nationalism* 9: 2 (2003), pp. 173ff. In German literature, see Bernhard Giesen, ed., *Nationale und kulturelle Identität. Studien zur Entwicklung des kollektiven Bewusstseins in der Neuzeit* (Frankfurt am Main, 1991); and, among more recent texts, Montserrat Guibernau, *The Identity of Nations* (Malden, 2008).

56   Smith, *National Identity*, Chapter 1.

57   Bloom, *Personal Identity*, pp. 52ff.

58   Fernand Braudel, *L'identité de la France* (Paris, 2000).

59   Tägil, *Regions in Upheaval*, pp. 241–2.

60   Lauri Honko, 'Traditions in the Construction of Cultural Identity', in Michael Branch, ed., *National History and Identity* (Helsinki, 1999), pp. 17ff; Ray Abrahams, 'Nation and Identity: A View from Social Anthropology', in ibid., pp. 34ff; Heinz-Gerhard Haupt, Michael Müller and Stuart Woolf, eds, *Regional and National Identities in Europe in the XIXth and XXth Centuries* (The Hague, London, Boston 1998).

61   Albert F. Reiterer, *Soziale Identität. Ethnizität und sozialer Wandel. Zur Entwicklung einer anthropologischen Struktur* (Frankfurt, 1993); Charles Taylor, *Die Quellen des Selbst. Die Entstehung der neuzeitlichen Identität* (Frankfurt am Main, 1994); Thomas Meyer, *Identitätswahn. Die Politisierung des kulturellen Unterschieds* (Berlin, 1997).

62   Lutz Niethammer, *Kollektive Identität. Heimliche Quellen einer unheimlichen Konjunktur* (Reinbek, 2001); Andrew Heywood, *Political Ideologies: An Introduction* (Basingstoke, 1992), p. 159; Brubaker, *Nationalism Reframed*, pp. 10ff. Nationhood is also recommended by Margaret Canovan, *Nationhood and Political Theory* (Cheltenham, 1996) – compare Gellner, *Nations and Nationalism*, pp. 298–9.

63   Anthony Smith had already criticised the concept of 'diffusionism' severely in the 1970s, in Anthony Smith, 'The Diffusion of Nationalism: Some Historical and Sociological Perspectives', *British Journal of Sociology* 29 (1978), pp. 238–9.

64   Anthony Smith, *Nationalism and Modernism*, pp. 133ff.

65   Ibid., pp. 223ff.

66   James, *Nation Formation*, Chapter 8.

67   This overlaps to an extent with the six main 'institutional dimensions'

recommended for future research by Anthony Smith: 1. state and citizenship, 2. territory, 3. language, 4. religion, 5. history, and 6. rites and
ceremonies. See Smith, *Nationalism and Modernism*, pp. 226–7.

68 The exceptions include Michael Mann, who distinguishes between
developmental types on the path to the national state. See Michael
Mann, *The Sources of Power, vol. 1: The Rise of Classes and Nation-
States, 1760–1914* (Cambridge, 1993), pp. 218ff.

69 I use the term 'small nations' not as a reflection of the size of these
nations but according to the circumstances in which modern nations
formed. Therefore, while the large Ukrainian nation, for instance, is
part of this category, the much smaller Danish and Dutch nations are
not. For this reason, the term I use as the opposite to 'small nations' is
'state-nations'. It is difficult to understand this important difference, if
you use the term 'nation' as identical with state. We have to accept that
there existed (and still exist) nations without state in Europe.
Nevertheless, even though these nations achieved in most cases the
stage of nation-state, they kept for some decades important specificities
in mentality, social behaviour and stereotypes. Maybe the term 'small
nation' could be better explained to English readership as "nations,
originally without state.

70 It is a positive development that 'nations without state' have been the
focus of research in the last decade. See in particular the above-mentioned works by Michael Keating and Montserrat Guibernau.

2. Typological Characterisation

1 The term 'state-nation', while not very common, appears to be the most
suitable equivalent of the German *Staatsnation*, and will be used in this
book to refer to state formations with their own national culture, which
preceded the modern nation and nation-state.

2 Schieder, *Nationalismus und Nationalstaat*, pp. 110–11.

3 Breuilly, *Nationalism and the State*, pp. 95–6.

4 Michael Mann, *The Sources of Power, vol. 2: The Rise of Classes and
Nation States, 1760–1914* (Cambridge, 1993), pp. 218–19.

5 Charles Tilly, *States and Nationalism in Europe since 1600* (New York,
1991), p. 133–4. Tilly's 'state-led nation' might be an alternative to the
term 'state-nation', that I am using in this book. It is another acceptable
equivalent of the German *Staatsnation*.

6 Dieter Langewiesche, 'Staatsbildung und Nationsbildung in

Deutschland – ein Sonderweg?', in Ulrike von Hirschhausen and Jörn Leonhard, eds, *Nationalismen in Europa. West- und Osteuropa im Vergleich* (Göttingen, 2001), pp. 61–2.

7   Smith, *National Identity*, pp. 20–1.

3. The Legacy of the Past

1   František Graus, *Lebendige Vergangenheit* (Cologne/Vienna, 1975), pp. 17–18.

2   Jan Assmann, *Kulturelles Gedächtniss* (Munich, 1992), p. 78.

3   For detailed information on this topic, see Anthony Smith, *The Ethnic Origins of Nations* (Oxford/Cambridge, 1986), especially Chapters 8 and 9.

4   Hagen Schulze gives many examples in his *State, Nations and Nationalism: From the Middle Ages to the Present* (London, 1996), pp. 97ff.

5   Jenö Szücs, *Nation und Geschichte* (Cologne/Vienna, 1981), pp. 28ff. This topic is covered in detail by the German medievalists in the series 'Nationes' – compare, for example, Helmut Beumann and Werner Schröder, eds, *Aspekte der Nationenbildung im Mittelalter* (Sigmaringen, 1978). For historical consciousness in medieval central Europe, compare the pioneering compilation, Roman Heck, ed., *Dawna swiadomość historyczna w Polsce, Czechach i Slowacji* (Ossolineum, 1978).

6   Anthony Smith, 'The "Golden Age" and National Renewal', in George Schöpflin and Geoffrey Hosking, eds, *Myths and Nationhood* (London, 1997).

4. Ethnic Roots

1   Among the extensive literature on the topic of medieval nations, see in particular John Armstrong, *Nations before Nationalism* (Chapel Hill, NC, 1982); Beumann and Schröder, *Aspekte der Nationsbildung*; Smith, *Ethnic Origins of Nations*.

2   William Bloom, *Personal Identity, National Identity and International Relations* (Cambridge, 1990), pp. 143–4.

3   Benedict Anderson, *Imagined Communities: Reflections on the Origin and Spread of Nationalism* (London, 1983), pp. 43ff.

4   Einar Haugen, *The Scandinavian Languages: An Introduction to Their History* (London 1976), pp. 361ff.

5   Renée Balibar and Dominique Laporte, *Le Francais national: Politique et pratiques de la langue nationale sous la Révolution Francaise* (Paris, 1974); Michel de Certeau, Dominique Julia and Jacques Revel, eds, *Une politique de la langue. La Révolution Francaise et les patois: l'enquete de Grégoire* (Paris, 1975); Jean-Yves Lartichaux, 'Linguistic Politics during the French Revolution', *Diogenes*, June 1997, pp. 65–84.

6   Joshua Fishman, *Language and Nationalism: Two Integrative Essays* (Rowley, MA, 1972), pp. 53ff.

7   Pierre Bourdieu, *Ce que parler veut dire. L'économie des échanges linguistiques* (Paris, 1982), p. 31.

8   Scholarly works on absolutism omit this subject – even the more comparative ones, such as Perry Anderson, *Lineages of the Absolutist State* (London, 1974).

9   Fishman, *Language and Nationalism*, p. 41.

10   Charles Ferguson, 'Diglossia', *Word* 15 (1959), pp. 325ff.

11   Joshua Fishman, 'Bilingualism with and without Diglossia, Diglossia with and without Bilingualism', *Journal of Social Issues* 23 (1967), pp. 29ff.; Joshua Fishman, *Language in Sociocultural Change* (Stanford, CA, 1972), pp. 135ff.

12   John Edwards, *Language, Society and Identity* (Oxford, 1985), pp. 143–4.

13   William Foltz, 'Ethnicity, Status and Conflict', in Wendell Bell and Walter Freeman, eds, *Ethnicity and Nation-Building* (Beverly Hills/ London, 1974), pp. 103–4.

14   There is also a terminological reservation. Smith's definition of an ethnic community comes very close to my understanding of a nation, the only difference being that it lacks the principle of civic equality. Therefore, I make use of this term with the awareness that I could equally be using the synonyms 'nationality' or 'ethno-nationalism'. The advantage of Smith's terminology lies in making it possible to counterpose 'category' and 'community'.

15   Smith, *Ethnic Origins of Nations*, pp. 22–3. Some authors believe, however, that all ethnic groups are characterised by an awareness of being different and belonging together. Compare Thomas Hylland Eriksen, *Ethnicity and Nationalism* (London, 1993), p. 12; and John Comaroff and Jean Comaroff, *Ethnography and the Historical Imagination* (Boulder, CO, 1992), p. 54.

16   Smith, *Ethnic Origins of Nations*, pp. 42–3.

5. Modernisation

1   Hans Ulrich Wehler, *Modernisierungstheorie und Geschichte* (Göttingen, 1975), pp. 14–15; Hans-Jürgen Puhle, 'Nation States, Nations, and Nationalism in Western and Southern Europe', in Justo Beramendi, Ramón Máiz and Xosé Núñez, eds, *Nationalism in Europe: Past and Present II* (Santiago de Compostela, 1994), pp. 23–4.

2   See Jeffrey Alexander, 'Core Solidarity, Ethnic Outgroup and Social Differentiation: A Multidimensional Model of Inclusion in Modern Societies', in Jacques Dofny and Akinsola Akiwowo, eds, *National and Ethnic Movements* (London, 1980), pp. 10–11.

3   Anthony Giddens, *The Nation-State and Violence*, Cambridge 1985, pp. 35–6.

4   See Étienne Balibar and Immanuel Wallerstein, *Race, Nation, Class: Ambiguous Identities* (London/New York, 1991), pp. 135–6; ; David McCrone, *The Sociology of Nationalism* (London/New York, 1998), pp. 92–3.

5   In addition to the above-mentioned views of Karl Deutsch, see Shmuel Noah Eisenstadt, 'Die Konstruktion nationaler Identitäten in vergleichender Perspektive', in Bernhard Giesen, ed., *Nationale und kulturelle Identität* (Frankfurt am Main, 1991), pp. 21–2; Rudolf von Thadden, 'Aufbau nationaler Identität. Deutschland und Frankreich im Vergleich', in ibid., pp. 493–4.

6   Bernhard Giesen, *Die Intellektuellen und die Nation* (Frankfurt, 1993).

7   Heinrich Thimme, *Kirche und nationale Frage in Livland während der ersten Hälfte des 19. Jahrhunderts* (Königsberg, 1938), pp. 30–1.

8   Gerd Roellecke, 'Herrschaft und Nation', *Rechtsphilosophische Hefte* III (1994), p. 19.

9   Ernest Gellner, Nations and Nationalisms (Oxford, 1983), Chapter 3; Karl Deutsch and William Foltz, eds, *Nation-Building* (New York, 1966), p. 38.

10 For an analysis of the difference between List's and Marx's prognoses, see Roman Szporluk, *Communism and Nationalism* (Oxford, 1988). See also the critical commentary by Gale Stokes, 'Class and Nation: Competing Explanatory Systems', *East European Politics and Societies* 4 (1990), pp. 98–9.

11 Martin Greschat, *Das Zeitalter der Industriellen Revolution* (Stuttgart, 1980), p. 45.

12 Paul Bairoch, 'International Industrialization Levels from 1750 to 1980', *Journal of European Economic History* 11 (1982), pp. 29–30.

13 Michael Mann, *The Sources of Power, vol. 3* (Cambridge, 1993), pp. 113–14; McCrone, *Sociology of Nationalism* (London/New York, 1998), pp. 92–3.

14 See Sheilagh Ogilvie and Markus Cerman, eds, *European Proto-Industrialization* (Cambridge, 1996).

15 Giddens, *Nation State and Violence*, p. 216.

16 Further to the issue of unevenness, see Miroslav Hroch and Luďa Klusáková, eds, *Criteria and Indicators of Backwardness: Essays on Uneven Development in European History* (Prague, 1996), pp. 126–7.

17 For the latest evidence of the importance of the postal services and railways for the strengthening of German national identity, see Siegfried Weichlein, *Nation und Region. Integrationsprozesse im Bismarckreich* (Düsseldorf, 2004), Part I.

18 A classic work on this subject is Eugen Weber, *Peasants into Frenchmen: The Modernization of Rural France 1870–1914* (Stanford, 1976). But other authors have also noted the slow process of national integration in the French countryside – for example, Marie-Madeleine Martin, *The Making of France* (London, 1959).

19 Miroslav Hroch, *Social Preconditions of National Revival in Europe* (Cambridge, 1985), pp. 158–9.

20 Martin Bürgener, *Pripet-Polessie* (Gotha, 1939), pp. 107–8; Jerzy Tomszewski, *Z dziejów Polesia* (Warsaw, 1963). For a more contemporary work on the issue of *tutejší*, see Hans Christian Trepte, 'Die Hiessigen (Tutejsi/Tzutejšyja) – regionales Bewusstsein im polnisch-weissrussischen Grenzreum' in Philipp Ther and Holm Sundhaussen, eds, *Regionale Bewegungen und Regionalismen in europäischen Zwischenräumen seit der Mitte des 19. Jehunderts* (Marburg, 2003), pp. 1,345–6. For more on the industrialisation of Wales, see Karl Deutsch, *Nationalism and Social Communication* (Cambridge, MA, 1953), p. 111; Ness Edwards, *The Industrial Revolution in South Wales* (London, 1924); Gwyn Williams, *The Welsh in Their History* (London/Canberra, 1982).

21 Wolfgang Schmale and Nan Dodde, *Revolution des Wissens?* (Bochum, 1991), pp. 19–20.

22 Michal Römer, *Litwa. Studyum w odrodzeniu narodu litewskiego* (Lviv, 1908), pp. 228–9.

23 Gale Stokes, 'Cognitive Style and Nationalism', *Canadian Review of Studies in Nationalism* 9 (1982), pp. 2–3.

24 For an overview of school and system reforms, see Schmale and Dodde, *Revolution des Wissens?* See also Ulrich Herrmann, ed., *Volk, Nation,*

Vaterland. Studien zum Achtzehnten Jahrhundert, vol. 18 (Hamburg, 1996).

25 This view was put forward by Hans-Jürgen Puhle, 'Nation-States in Western and Southen Europe', in Beramendi et al., *Nationalism in Europe*, pp. 23–4.

26 This table is a combination of my older model and a modification introduced by Hans-Jürgen Puhle, 'Nation-States, Nations and Nationalisms', p. 31.

27 This has often been argued by advocates of a fundamental conflict between 'ethos' and 'demos' – i.e. between the progressive civic and reactive nationalistic understandings of the term 'nation'. This ahistorical approach will be addressed elsewhere in the book.

6. The Players

1 František Šmahel, 'The Hussite Movement: An Anomaly of European History', in Mikulas Teich, ed., *Bohemia in History* (New York, 1998), pp. 79–97. A noteworthy comparison between the Hussite movement and the movement of Flemish towns was attempted in the 1930s in Eugen Lemberg, *Wege und Wandlungen des Nationalbewustseins. Studien zur Geschichte der Volkswerdung in den Niederlanden und in Böhmen* (Münster, 1934).

2 Alfred Cobban, *The Social Interpretation of the French Revolution* (Cambridge, 1964). For a comprehensive overview on this issue, see the first chapter of François Furet, *Penser la Révolution Française* (Paris, 1978).

3 For the latest summary of this issue, see Robert Tombs, 'The Political Trajectory of Nationalism in Ninteenth-Century France', in Ulrike von Hirschhausen and Jörn Leonhard, eds, *Nationalismen in Europa. West- und Osteuropa im Vergleich* (Göttingen, 2001), pp. 133–4.

4 According to Liah Greenfeld, the foundations of English 'nationalism' were laid by this time. See Liah Greenfeld, *Nationalism: Five Roads to Modernity* (Cambridge, MA, 1992), Chapter 1.

5 See Raphael Samuel, ed., *Patriotism: The Making and Unmaking of British National Identity* (London/New York 1989); Linda Colley, *Britons: Forging the Nation, 1707–1837* (New Haven, CT, 1992). On the topic of the relationship between the aristocracy and the bourgeoisie, see for example Jamie Camplin, *The Rise of the Plutocrats: Wealth and Power in Edwardian England* (London 1978).

6   Roar Skovmand, Vagn Dybdahl, Erik Rasmussen and Olaf Klose, *Geschichte Dänemarks 1830–1939* (Neumünster, 1973), especially pp. 64–5, 206–7. For the latest information on this issue, see Uffe Östergaard, 'Nation-Building and Nationalism in the Oldenburg Empire', in Stefan Berger and Alexei Miller, *Nation-Building in the Core of Empires: A Comparative Perspective* (Budapest, 2008).

7   This was the general conclusion I drew on the basis of a comparative analysis of the social composition of the leaders of national movements. See Miroslav Hroch, *Social Preconditions of National Revival in Europe* (Cambridge, 1985), pp. 129–30.

8   This term is used here to refer to those people whose qualifications enabled them to earn their living through intellectual means, regardless of whether they had attended university or only secondary school. The use of 'white collar' as an alternative term seems only partially suitable for defining such people.

9   There are a number of other works besides the above-mentioned analysis and its findings, which were often inspired by this approach. See for example Gerhard Brunn, 'Die Organisationen der katalanischen Bewegung 1859-1923', in Gerhard Brunn and Hans Henning, *Nationale Bewegung und soziale Organisation I* (Munich, 1978), especially pp. 447–8; and Jutta de Jong, *Der nationale Kern des makedonischen Problems* (Frankfurt am Main/Bern, 1982)

10 Extensive research on the gender aspect in national context is concerned above all, unfortunately, with the twentieth centrury, i.e. the time of fully formed nations and nation-states. See for example Nira Yuval-Davis, *Gender and Nation* (London, 1997); Nira Yuval-Davis 'Gender Relations and the Nation', in Athena Leoussi, ed., *Encyclopedia of Nationalism* (New Brunswick/London, 2001), pp. 297–314. More historically oriented: Ida Blom and Katherine Hall, eds., *Gendered Nations: Nationalism and Gender Order in the Long Nineteenth Century* (Oxford/New York, 2000). On the historical discourse about women see Jitka Malecková, 'Where Are Women in National History?', in Stefan Berger and Chris Lorenz, eds, *The Contested Nation: Religion, Class and Gender in National History* (London, 2008), pp. 171–99.

11 This aspect is stressed already in Anthony Smith, *Theories of Nationalism,* London 1971, pp. 134ff..

12 The percentages are approximate, and represent mean values generated from figures that naturally fluctuated during phase B of national

movements. The calculations are based on Miroslav Hroch, 'Das Bürgertum in den nationalen Bewegungen des 19 Jahrhunderts', in Jürgen Kocka, ed., *Bürgertum im 19 Jahrhundert. Deutschland im europäischen Vergleich, Vol. 3* (Munich, 1988), pp. 346–5, which contains information on the sources used.

7. Nationally Relevant Conflicts of Interest

1   Gale Stokes, 'Cognition and the Function of Nationalism', *Journal of Interdisciplinary History* IV (1974), p. 539.
2   Wolfgang Kaschuba, 'Die Nation als Körper', in Étienne François, Hannes Siegrist and Jakob Vogel, eds, *Nation und Emotion* (Göttingen, 1995), p. 298.
3   Michael Mann, *The Sources of Social Power, vol. II: The Rise of Classes and Nation States 1760–1914* (Cambridge, 1993), Chapter 3.
4   See for example Peter Imbusch, *Macht und Herrschaft* (Opladen, 1998), pp. 9–10.
5   Max Weber, 'Soziologische Grundbegriffe', in his *Wirtschaft und Gesellschaft I* (Tübingen, 1976). Available in translation as *Economy and Society* (New York, 1968).
6   Michael Banton, 'Max Weber on "Ethnic Communities": A Critique', in *Nations and Nationalism* 13 (2007), p. 33.
7   Heinrich Popitz, *Phänomene der Macht* (Tübingen, 1986).
8   Imbusch, *Macht und Herrschaft*, p. 12.
9   Amitai Etzioni, 'Power as a Societal Force', in Marvin Olsen and Martin Marger, eds, *Power in Modern Societies* (Boulder, CO, 1993), pp. 34ff.
10 Popitz, *Phänomene der Macht*, pp. 38–9.
11 Marvin Olsen, 'Forms and Levels of Power Executions', Olsen and Marger, *Power in Modern Society*, pp. 34.
12 Peter Bacharach, Morton Baratz, *Power and Poverty: Theory and Practice* (New York, 1970), p. 44. See also Steven Lukes, *Power: A Radical View* (London, 1974), p. 19.
13 Karl Deutsch, *The Nerves of Government* (New York 1963), especially Chapter 7.
14 Lukes, *Power*, pp. 7ff.
15 Niklas Luhmann, *Macht* (Stuttgart, 1975).
16 Lukes, *Power*, pp. 17ff.
17 Norberto Bobbio, 'Gramsci and the Concept of Civil Society', in John

Keane, ed., *Civil Society and the State: New European Perspectives* (London 1888), p. 92

18 Étienne Balibar and Immanuel Wallerstein, *Race, Nation, Class: Ambiguous Identities* (London/New York, 1991), p. 82.

19 William Bloom, *Personal Identity, National Identity and International Relations* (Cambridge, 1990); Colley, *Britons.*

20 Dieter Langewiesche, *Nation*, pp. 192ff., and 'Staatsbildung und Nationsbildung in Deutschland – ein Sonderweg?' in Ulrike von Hirschhausen and Jörn Leonhard, eds, *Nationalismen in Europa. West- und Osteuropa im Vergleich* (Göttingen, 2001), pp. 57ff.

21 Thomas Hylland Eriksen, *Ethnicity and Nationalism: Anthropological Perspectives* (London, 1993), p. 68.

22 John Breuilly, *Nationalism and the State* (Manchester, 1982), p. 2.

23 Stein Rokkan, 'Dimensions of State Formation', in Charles Tilly, ed., *The Formation of National States in Western Europe* (Princeton, 1975), p. 564.

24 Michael Hechter, *Internal Colonialism: The Celtic Fringe in British National Development, 1536–1966* (London, 1975).

25 For debate on this matter, see Tom Nairn, Eric Hobsbawm and Régis Debray, *Nationalismus und Marxismus* (Berlin, 1978).

26 Balibar and Wallerstein, *Race, Nation, Class*, pp. 89–90.

27 Andrew Orridge, 'Uneven Development and Nationalism', *Political Studies* 29 (1982), pp. 181ff.

28 Michael Hechter, 'Nationalism as Group Solidarity', *Ethnic and Racial Studies* 10 (1987), pp. 418–19.

29 Alexander Motyl, 'How Empires Rise and Fall: Nations, Nationalism and Imperial Elites', in Justo Beramendi, Ramón Máiz and Xosé Núñez, eds, *Nationalism in Europe: Past and Present II* (Santiago de Compostela, 1994), pp. 383–4.

30 Hroch, *Social Preconditions*, Chapter 18.

31 Miroslav Hroch, 'Can Nation-Forming Processes Be Used as a Criterion of Uneven Development?' in Miroslav Hroch and Luda Klusáková, eds, *Criteria and Indicators of Backwardness: Essays on Uneven Development in European History* (Prague, 1996), pp. 129–41.

32 Ibid., pp. 134ff.

8. National Myths and the Search for a Common Destiny

1   Ivan Rudnytsky, 'Observations on the Problem of "Historical" and "Non-Historical" Nations', *Harvard Ukrainian Studies* 5 (1981), pp. 358–9.

2   Peter Sugar viewed this approach critically in 1996, in 'The Roots of Eastern European Nationalism' *1er Congrès international des études balkaniques et sud-est européennes* (Sofia, 1966), pp. 162–3.

3   See for example the work of Carlton Hayes and Charles Tilly, also Hagen Schulze's book, which is popular in Germany, and a similar selection can be found in a more contemporary publication by Hans-Ulrich Wehler, *Nationalismus. Geschichte, Formen, Folgen* (Munich, 2001).

4   Breuilly, *Nationalism and the State*, Chapters 3–5.

5   Stein Rokkan, Kirsti Sælen and Joan Warmbrunn, 'Nation-Building: A Review of Recent Comparative Research and a Selected Bibliography of Analytical Studies', *Current Sociology* 19: 3 (1973); Jeffrey Alexander, 'Core Solidarity, Ethnic Outgroup and Social Differentiation: A Multidimensional Model of Inclusion in Modern Societies', in Jacques Dofny and Akinsola Akiwowo, eds, *National and Ethnic Movements* (London, 1980), pp. 5–6.

6   Frederik Barth, *Ethnic Groups and Boundaries* (Bergen, 1969); Josep Llobera, *The God of Modernity: The Development of Nationalism in Western Europe* (Oxford, 1994).

7   According to Jenö Szücs, *Nation und Geschichte* (Cologne/Vienna, 1981), p. 223.

8   He explicitly deals with the 'small nations', for example in Anthony Smith, *The Ethnic Origins of Nations* (Oxford/Cambridge, 1986), pp. 217–18.

9   Adrian Hastings, *The Construction of Nationhood: Ethnicity, Religion and Nationalism* (Cambridge, 1997).

10 Reference is often made to Eric Hobsbawm and Terence Ranger, eds, *The Invention of Tradition* (Cambridge, 1983), but individual authors' opinions in this collection on the concept of 'invented traditions' differ.

11 A work of groundbreaking importance was a collection by Pierre Nora, *Les lieux de mémoire III. 1–3 La Nation* (Paris, 1986). However, his ideas gradually became so fashionable – like 'invented traditions' – that the manner in which they have been understood and applied has often bordered on misinterpretation.

12 Otto Dann, ed., *Nationalismus in vorindustrieller Zeit* (Munich, 1986); Jenö Szücs, Adrian Hastings, František Graus and others have also written valuable contributions on this topic.

13 Ulrich Bielefeld, 'Die lange Dauer der Nation', in Ulrich Bielefeld and Gisela Engel, eds, *Bilder der Nation* (Hamburg, 1998), pp. 402–3.

14 Szücs, *Nation und Geschichte*, pp. 104–5; Joep Leerssen, *National Thought in Europe: A Cultural History* (Amsterdam, 2006), pp. 71–2.

15 The relationship between the past and the present needs to be expanded to include this factor, not confined to myths and legends alone as is suggested by Anthony Smith (*Ethnic Origins of Nations*, Chapters 8 and 9).

16 This has repeatedly been the topic of international discussions and scientific conferences since the twentieth century. See especially Erik Lönnroth, Karl Molin and Ragnar Björk, eds, *Conceptions of National History* (Berlin/New York 1994); Chris Lorenz, *Konstruktion der Vergangenheit. Eine Einführung in die Geschichtstheorie* (Cologne, 1997); Stefan Berger, Mark Donovan and Kevin Passmore, eds, *Writing National Histories: Western Europe since 1800* (London, 1999); Michael Branch, ed., *National History and Identity: Approaches to the Writing of History in the North-East Baltic Region* (Helsinki, 1999); Christoph Conrad and Sebastian Conrad, eds, *Die Nation schreiben. Geschichtswissenschaft im internationalen Vergleich* (Göttingen 2002).

17 Stefan Berger, *The Search for Normality: National Identity and Historical Consciousness in Germany since 1800* (New York/Oxford, 1997).

18 As a follow-up to older discussions (see note 17, above), 'Writing National Histories', a large international project undertaken with the backing of the European Science Foundation and led by Stefan Berger, was devoted to this subject. Its outcomes were published in a number of collections: Stefan Berger, ed., *Narrating the Nation: The Representation of National History in Different Genres* (Oxford, 2007); Stefan Berger, ed., *Writing the Nation: A Global Perspective* (Oxford, 2007); Antonis Liakos, ed., *The European Canon* (Leipzig, 2007); Stefan Berger and Chris Lorenz, eds, *Nationalizing the Past: Historians as Nation-Builders in Modern Europe* (London, 2010). The main bulk of the text of the present volume was compiled prior to 2005 and does not take account of the outcomes of this project. However, since most of them correspond with my earlier hypotheses, I did not feel the need to rework the original version. It has been left essentially unaltered, as evidence that similar conclusions will be drawn at different research sites if similar methods are employed.

19 The latest major treatise on the issue of myths is presented by George Schöpflin, in Geoffrey Hosking and George Schöpflin, *Myths and Nationhood* (London, 1997), pp. 20–1. Among the numerous works published recently, mainly as comparative studies of national myths, see for example Eva Behring, Ludwig Richter and Wolfgang Schwarz, eds, *Geschichtliche Mythen in den Literaturen und Kulturen Ostmittel- und Südosteuropas* (Stuttgart, 1999); Jacques Revel and Giovanni Levi, eds, *Political Uses of the Past: The Recent Mediterranean Experience* (London, 2001); Jacques Le Rider, Moritz Csáky and Monika Sommer, eds, *Transnationale Gedächtnisorte in Zentraleuropa* (Innsbruck/ Vienna/Munich, 2002); Heidemarie Uhl, *Zivilisationsbruch und Gedächjtniskultur* (Innsbruck/Vienna/Munich, 2003); Heidi Hein-Kircher and Hans Henning Hahn, eds, *Politische Mythen im 19. und 20. Jahrhundert in Mittel- und Osteuropa* (Marburg, 2006).

20 Eberhard Jüngel, 'Die Wahrheit des Mythos und die Notwendigkeit der Entmythologisierung', in idem (ed.) *Das Wort, das Geschichte macht* (Tartu, 1996), pp. 73ff. ; Rudolf Speth, *Nation und Revolution. Politische Mythen im 19. Jahrhundert* (Opladen, 2000), p. 153; Rüdiger Voigt, ed., *Politik der Symbole. Symbole der Politik* (Opladen, 1989), p. 11; Christopher Flood, *Political Myth: A Theoretical Introduction* (New York, 1996).

21 George Schöpflin, in Introduction to *Myths*, pp. 22ff.

22 Joanna Overing, 'The Role of Myth: An Anthropological Perspective', in Hosking and Schöpflin, *Myths of Nationhood*, p. 18; Kurt Hübner, *Das Nationale. Verdrängtes. Unvermeidliches. Erstrebenswertes* (Graz/Vienna/Cologne, 1991), pp. 288–9. See also the Introduction by Pierre Nora in (see note 11) *Les lieux de mémoire II. 1–3 La Nation.*

23 Eric Hobsbawm, 'Inventing Traditions', in Eric Hobsbawm and Terence Ranger, *The Invention of Tradition* (Cambridge, 1983).

24 Anthony Smith, 'The Nation: Invented, Imagined, Reconstructed?' in Marjorie Ringrose and Adam Lerner, eds, *Reimagining the Nation* (London, 1993), p. 14. See also Paul James, *Nation Formation: Towards a Theory of Abstract Community* (London, 1996), pp. 115–16.

25 Herfried Münkler and Hans Grünberger, 'Origo at Vetustas. Herkunft und Alter als Topoi nationaler Identität', in Münkler, Grünberger, Konrad Maier, eds, *Nationenbildung. Die Nationalisierung Europas im Diskurs humanistischer Intellektueller:Italien und Deutschland* (Berlin, 1998), pp. 235–55; Berger, *Search for Normality*, pp. 24–5.

26 Suzanne Citron, *Le Mythe national. L'Histoire de France en question* (Paris, 1989); Eugen Weber, 'Gauls versus Franks', in Robert Tombs, ed., *Nationhood and Nationalism in France: From Boulangism to the Great War 1889–1918* (London, 1991), pp. 14–15.

27 Eduard Maur, 'Palackého koncepce českých agrárních dějin a její osudy', in *František Palacký 1798–1998* (Prague, 1999), pp. 139ff.

28 The European themes somewhat fade into the background in the thought-provoking chapter by Anthony Smith, 'The "Golden Age" and National Renewal', in Hosking and Schöpflin, *Myths and Nationhood*, pp. 36–7.

29 See the contribution by Andrew Wilson, and that by Agita Misāne and Aija Priedīte, in ibid., p. 165, pp. 185–6.

30 Szücs, *Nation und Geschichte*, pp. 33–4.

31 David McCrone, *The Sociology of Nationalism* (London/New York, 1998), pp. 57–8.

32 An achievement that is both commendable and revealing with regard to research into national and nationalistic motivations within the field of archaeology is a collection by Margarita Díaz-Andreu and Timothy Champion, *Nationalism and Archaeology in Europe* (London, 1996). Among the few collections of this kind, this one offers a truly European horizon, encompassing Irish, Spanish and German, as well as Lithuanian and Russian archaeology. This subject area was also covered in a special issue of *Nations and Nationalism* 7: 4 (2001), in which the most important contribution was perhaps that by Anthony Smith: 'Authenticity, Antiquity and Archaeology'.

33 A collection published on the occasion of the Berlin exhibition 'Mythen der Nationen' provides a rich source of information on national mythology. See Monika Flacke, *Mythen der Nationen: Ein europäisches Panorama* (Munich/Berlin, 1998). It should be taken into account that, in the selection of 'typical' national myths, authors were influenced not only by their knowledge of which myths dominated the nineteenth century but also by their ideas about what was relevant at the time (and perhaps even today).

34 Among the most recent works on the significance of wars in national myths, see Nikolaus Buschmann and Dieter Langewiesche, eds, *Der Krieg in den Gründungsmythen europäischer Nationen und der USA* (Frankfurt/New York, 2003).

35 For more on this pressing topic, see Holm Sundhaussen, 'Kriegserinnerung als Gesamtkunstwerk und Tatmotiv: Sechshundertzehn Jahre

Kosovo-Krieg (1389–1999)', in Dietrich Beyrau, ed., *Der Krieg in reliösen und nationalen Deutungen der Neuzeit* (Tübingen, 2001), pp. 11–12.

9. Fighting for a National Langauge and Culture

1   See the distinctively critical preface to Rogers Brubaker, *Ethnicity without Groups* (Cambridge, MA, 2004). See also Eric Hobsbawm, *Nations and Nationalism since 1780: Programme, Myth, Reality*, pp. 54–5; Juan Linz, 'From Primordialism to Nationalism', in Edward Tiryakian and Ronald Rogowski, eds, *New Nationalism of the Developed West* (London/Sydney, 1985), pp. 204–5. The terms 'ethnic', 'ethnicity' and 'ethnic group' are a subject of debate and even doubt – see Richard Jenkins, *Rethinking Ethnicity*, 2nd edn (London, 2008).

2   Greenfeld, *Nationalism*, Chapter 4.

3   Eugen Lemberg, *Nationalismus, vol. II*, pp. 34ff.. Anthony Smith, *Ethnic Origins of Nations*, especially Chapter 7.

4   Anthony D. Smith, *Nationalism and Modernism: A Critical Survey of Recent Theories of Nations and Nationalism* (London/New York, 1998), pp. 224–5.

5   Eriksen, *Ethnicity and Nationalism*, especially pp. 100–1.

6   Walker Connor, 'Nation-Building or Nation-Destroying?' *World Politics* 24 (1972), later Chapter 2 of his *Ethno-Nationalism: The Quest for Understanding* (Princeton, 1994). For positive reflections on these views, see Daniele Conversi, ed., *Ethnonationalism in the Contemporary World: Walker Connor and the Study of Nationalism* (London, 2004). For critical views, see Roland Breton, *Les ethnies* (Paris, 1981); Robert LeVine and Donald Campbell, *Ethnocentrism: Theories of Conflict, Ethnic Attitudes, and Group Behavior* (New York, 1972).

7   Pierre Fougeyrollas, *La Nation. Essor et déclin des sociétés modernes* (Paris, 1987).

8   They were published at the beginning of the 1990s by New York University Press and Dartmouth.

9   Karl Deutsch's theory of social communication has already been criticised for underestimating the role that subjective perception plays in the linguistic processes of assimilation and dissimilation. See Siegried Weichlein, 'Soziale Kommuniation: Karl Deutsch und die Folgen', in Pavel Kolář, Miloš Řezník, eds, *Historische Nationsforschung im geteilten Europa 1945–1989* (Cologne, 2012), pp. 36–7.

10   John Edwards, *Language, Society and Identity* (Oxford, 1985), espe-
     cially pp. 133–4.

11   Walter Freeman, 'Functions of Ethnic Conflict and Their Contributions
     to National Growth', in Wendell Bell, Walter Freeman, eds, *Ethnicity
     and Nation-Building* (London, 1974), pp. 177–8.

12   Eriksen, *Ethnicity and Nationalism*, pp. 56–7. Ladislav Holy and Milan
     Stuchlik, *Actions Norms and Representations: Foundations of
     Anthropological Inquiry* (Cambridge, 1983); Joshua Fishman, *Language
     and Nationalism: Two Integrative Essays* (Rowley, MA, 1972); Anthony
     Smith, *Nationalism and Modernism*, pp. 223–4. Smith's concept was
     criticised by Umut Özkimirli, 'The Nation as an Artichoke? A Critique
     of Ethnosymbolist Interpretations of Nationalism', in *Nations and
     Nationalism* 8 (2003), pp. 333–4.

13   Such as by institutions called 'Matica' (originally a Serbian word,
     meaning the queen bee), which were founded in almost all Slavic
     national movements.

14   Niccolò Machiavelli wrote a defence of the Italian language: *Discorso
     o Dialogo intorno alla nostra lingua*. See the modern edition by Bartolo
     Tommaso Sozzi (Turin, 1976) for examples of defence and celebration
     of the language by Pietro Bembo, Baldassar Castiglione, Leonardo
     Salviati and others. A defence of the French language (*Defence et
     Illustration de Langue francoyse*) was published in 1549 by bishop Jean
     du Bellay. More examples are listed in Eugen Lemberg, *Nationalismus,
     vol. I* (Hamburg, 1964), p. 122.

15   Karl Heinrich Rexroth, 'Volkssprache und werdendes Volksbewustsein im
     ostfränkischen Reich', in Helmut Beumann and Werner Schröder, eds,
     Aspekte der Nationenbildung im Mittelalter, (Sigmaringen, 1978), pp. 296–7.

16   Hendrik Elias, *Geschiedenis van de Vlaamse Gedachte I* (Antwerp,
     1963), pp. 119ff.

17   Daniele Conversi, 'Language or Race? The Choice of Core Values in
     the Development of Catalan and Basque Nationalisms', *Ethnic and
     Racial Studies* 13 (1990), pp. 53–4.

18   *Čechoslav*, 11 September 1824.

19   Conversi, 'Language or Race?', p. 60.

20   John Henry Wuorinen, *Nationalism in Modern Finland* (New York,
     1931), p. 65.

21   Česlao Sipovic, 'The Language Problem in the Catholic Church in
     Byelorussia from 1832 to the First World War', *Journal of Byelorussian
     Studies* III (l973), pp. 23ff.

22   Ernest Gellner, *Culture, Identity and Politics* (Cambridge, 1987), p. 24; Pierre Bourdieu, *Ce que parler veut dire. L'économie des échanges linguistiques* (Paris, 1982), p. 29.

23   Fischman, *Language and Nationalism*, p. 61.

24   Barth, *Ethnic Groups and Boundaries*, pp. 8ff.; Bud Khleif, 'Insiders, Outsiders and Renegades: Towards a Classification of Ethnolinguistic Labels', in Howard Giles and Bernard Saint-Jacques, eds, *Language and Ethnic Relations* (Pergamon, 1979), pp. 159–60.

25   Zdeněk Starý, *Ve jménu funkce a intervence*, AUC Philogica, Monographia CXXIII (1994),Chapters 3 and 4.

26   George Thomas, *Linguistic Purism* (London/ New York, 1991), pp. 116–17; Fishman, *Language and Nationalism*, pp. 66–7; Starý, *Ve jménu funkce a intervence*, pp. 59ff, 119–20.

27   For more details on this issue, see Edwards, *Language, Society and Identity*, pp. 16ff.

28   Achille Burgun, *Le développement linguistique en Norvege depuis 1814* (Ann Arobor, MI, 1921); Einar Haugen, *Language Planning: The Case of Modern Norwegian* (Cambridge, MA, 1966).

29   Joshua Fishman and Ofelia Garcia, eds, *Handbook of Language and Ethnic Identity, Vol. 1* (Oxford, 2010), pp. 276ff.

30   Grigorij Venediktov, *Iz istorii sovremennogo bolgarskogo jazyka* (Sofia, 1981), pp. 48ff; Paul Magocsi, 'The Language Question as a Factor in the National Movement in Eastern Galicia', in Andrei Markovits and Frank Sysyn, eds, *Nationbuilding and the Politics of Nationalism: Essays on Austrian Galicia* (Cambridge, MA, 1982), p. 232.

31   Venediktov, *Iz istorii sovremennogo bolgarskogo jazyka*, pp. 76, 141; Vladislas Kaupas, *Die Presse Litauens, unter Berücksichtigung des nationalen Gedankens und der öffentlichen Meinung I* (Klaipeda, 1934), pp. 141–2; Michał Römer, *Litwa, Studium o odrodzeniu narodu litewskiego* (Lviv, 1908), pp. 122–3; Jerzy Ochmanski, *Historia Litwy* (Wroclaw/ Warsaw/Krakow, 1990), p. 235; Carole Rogel, *The Slovenes and Jugoslavism 1890-1914* (New York 1977), Aina Blinkena, 'The Role of the Neo-Latvians in Forming the Latvian Literary Language', in Aleksander Loit, ed., *National Movements in the Baltic Countries during the 19th Century* (Stockholm, 1985), pp. 337ff.

32   Marjana Gross, *Die Anfänge des modernen Kroatiens. Gesellschaft, Politik und Kultur in Zivil-Kroatien und Slavonien in den ersten dreißig Jahren nach 1848* (Vienna/Cologne/Weimar, 1993), pp. 64ff; Robert Auty, 'The Linguistic Revival Among the Slavs of the Austrian Empire

1780–1850: the Role of Individuals in the Codification of New Literary Languages', *Modern Language Review* LIII (1958), pp. 399–400; R. Magocsi, 'Language Question', p. 237; Nicholas Platonovich Vakar, *Belorussia, The Making of a Nation: A Case Study and a Bibliographical Guide to Belorussia* (Cambridge, MA, 1956), p. 78.

33 František Daneš, 'Values and Attitudes in Language Standardization', in Jan Chloupek and Jiri Nekvapil, eds, *Reader in Czech Sociolinguistics* (Amsterdam, 1987), pp. 206ff.

34 This view is shared by Eric Hobsbawm and also by the Austrian authors of the collection 'Die Konstruktion des Nationalen', published as a booklet by the journal *Österreichische Zeitschrift für Geschichtswissenschaften* (1994). Shmuel Noah Eisenstadt, 'Die Konstruktion nationaler Identitäten in vergleichender Perspektive', in Bernhard Giesen, ed., *Nationale und kulturelle Identität* (Frankfurt am Main, 1991), pp. 1ff.

35 George Shevelov, *The Ukrainian Language in the First Half of the Twentieth Century (1900–1941): Its State and Status* (Cambridge, MA, 1989), pp. 98ff.

36 Georges Davy, *Élements de sociologie* (Paris, 1950), p. 233.

37 Bourdieu, *Ce que parler veut dire*, p. 32.

38 On the first grammar schools and the issue of upward social mobility, see Lolo Krusius-Ahrenberg, *Der Durchbruch des Nationalismus und Liberalismus im politischen Leben Finnlands 1856–1863* (Helsinki, 1934), pp. 98, 164. For more information on the Estonian project of the Alexander School, see Helmut Speer, *Das Bauernschulwesen im Gouvernement Estland vom Ende des achtzehenten Jahrhunderts bis zur Russifizierung* (Tartu, 1936), pp. 433ff; and Hans Kruus, *Grundriss der Geschichte des estnischen Volkes* (Tartu, 1932), p. 131. On the grammar school in Suwalki, see Wilhelm Gaigalat, *Litauen, das besetzte Gebiet, sein Volk und dessen geistige Strömungen* (Frankfurt am Main, 1917), p. 58.

39 The Chair in the Finnish language at the University of Helsinki was established in 1851.

40 Krusius-Ahrenberg, *Der Durchbruch des Nationalismus*, pp. 163–4; Magnus Gottfrid Schybergson, *Politische Geschichte Finnlands 1809–1919* (Gotha/Stuttgart, 1925), pp. 626–7.

41 'Zur Nationalitätenfrage', in *Baltische Monatsschrift* (1863), pp. 568ff, and (1864), p. 570.

42 Lode Wils, 'L'emploi des langues en matieres judiciaires et administratives dans le Royaume de Belgique', *Revue du Nord* LXXIII (1991), pp. 64ff.

43 Bloom, *Personal Identity*, p. 143.

44 Bourdieu, *Ce que parler veut dire*, Chapter 1.

45 Marilyn Martin-Jones, 'Language, Power and Linguistic Minorities: The Need for an Alternative Approach to Bilingualism, Language Maintenance and Shift', in Ralph Grillo, ed., *Social Anthropology and the Politics of Language* (London/New York, 1989), p. 118.

46 See for example Holm Sundhaussen, *Der Einfluss der Herderschen Ideen auf die Nationsbildung bei den Völkern der Habsburgermonarchie* (Munich, 1973). For a critique of Kohn's concept, see Aira Kemiläinen, *Nationalism: Problems Concerning the Word, the Concept and the Classification* (Jyväskylä, 1964). For the latest application of Kohn's dichotomy, with a strong political subtext, see Greenfeld, *Nationalism*.

47 Fishman, *Language and Nationalism*, p. 48.

48 Anne Cohler, *Rousseau and Nationalism* (New York/London, 1970).

49 Eric Hobsbawm, *The Age of Revolution* (London, 1973), pp. 312ff. For more on the relationship between Romanticism and national movements, see also Miroslav Hroch, 'National Romanticism', in Balázs Trencsényi and Michal Kopeček, eds, *Discourses of Collective Identity in Central and Southeast Europe, II. National Romanticism: The Formation of National Movements* (Budapest, 2007), pp. 4ff.

50 Stokes, 'Cognition and the Function of Nationalism', pp. 533ff.

51 Hermann Weilenman, 'The Interlocking of Nation and Personality Structure', in Karl Deutsch and William Foltz, eds, *Nation-Building* (New York, 1966), pp. 37ff.

52 Joshua Fishman, *Language in Sociocultural Change* (Stanford, CA, 1972), p. 148

53 Martin-Jones, 'Language, Power and Linguistic Minorities', pp. 109ff.

54 Stokes, 'Cognition and the Function of Nationalism', p. 536.

55 Glyn Williams, 'Language Group Allegiance and Ethnic Interaction', in Giles and Saint-Jacques, *Language and Ethnic Relations*, p. 58.

56 See George Mead, *Mind, Self and Society* (Chicago 1934), pp. 135ff; Einar Haugen, 'Bilinguals Have More Fun', *Journal of English Linguistics* 19 (1986), pp. 106–7; Jesper Hermann, 'Bilingualism versus Identity', *Multilingual Matters* 43 (1988), pp. 227ff.

57 The memorandum was compiled on the initiative of František Palacký, and subsequently published in 1872.

58 Weilenman, 'Interlocking of Nation and Personality Structure', p. 37.

59 Alphonse Dupront, 'Sémantique historique et analyse de contenu: culture et civilisation', in Maurice Cranston and Peter Mair, eds, *Langage*

et politique (Brussels, 1982), p. 87. Based on an analysis of *Cahiers de doléances*, Dupront proves that peasants associated the word 'culture' with only one word – 'agriculture'.

60   Georg Bossong, 'Sprache und regionale Identität', in Georg Bossong, Michael Erbe, Peter Frankenberg, Charles Grivel and Waldemar Lilli, eds, *Westeuropäische Regionen und ihre Identität. Mannheimer Historische Forschungen Bd. 4* (Mannheim, 1994), p. 48.

61   Hobsbawm, *Nations and Nationalism*, pp. 116ff.

62   Fishman, *Language and Nationalism*, p. 54.

63   Bourdieu, *Ce que parler veut dire*, pp. 64ff.

64   Dieter Cherubin, 'Zur bürgerlichen Sprache des 19. Jahrhunderts', *Wirkendes Wort* 33 (1983), pp. 406–7. The quote is based on Angelika Linke, 'Zum Sprachgebrauch des Bürgertums im 19. Jahrhundert. Überlegungen zur kultursemiotischen Funktion des Sprachverhaltens', in Rainer Wimmer, ed., *Das 19. Jahrhundert. Sprachgeschichtliche Wurzeln des heutigen Deutsch* (Berlin/New York, 1991), pp. 250ff.

65   Fishman, *Language and Nationalism*, p. 61; Williams, 'Language Group Allegiance', pp. 62ff.

66   Jeffrey Ross, 'Language and the Mobilization of Ethnic Identity', in Giles and Saint-Jacques, *Language and Ethnic Relations*, p. 10.

67   Otto Jespersen, *Mankind, Nation and Individual – from a Linguistic Point of View* (Oslo, 1925), p. 5; John Armstrong, *Nations before Nationalism* (Chapel Hill, NC, 1982), p. 242

68   Gellner, *Culture, Identity and Politics*, p. 17.

69   Edwards, *Language, Society and Identity*, pp. 93ff.

10. The Nation as Cultural Construct

1   A detailed overview of earlier research is offered in Heinz-Gerhard Haupt and Charlotte Tacke, 'Die Kultur des Nationalen. Sozial- und kulturgeschichtliche Ansätze bei der Erforschung des europäischen Nationalismus im 19. und 20. Jahrhundert', in Wolfgang Hartwig, Heinz-Gerhard Haupt, eds.,*Kulturgeschichte heute* (Göttingen, 1996), pp. 255ff.

2   The report was titled 'Nationalism: A Report by a Study Group of Members of the Royal Institute of International Affairs', and was not published until 1963.

3   Langewiesche, 'Staatsbildung und Nationsbildung in Deutschland, p. 60.

4   Balibar and Wallerstein, *Race, Nation, Class*, p. 93.

5 Stokes, 'Cognition and the Function of Nationalism', pp. 525–6.

6 Boyd Shafer, *Nationalism: Myth and Reality* (New York, 1955), p. 51.

7 A classic work on this topic is Georg Mosse, *Die Nationalisierung der Massen. Politische Symbolik und Massenbewegungen von den Napoleonischen Kriegen bis zum Driftem Reich* (Frankfurt am Main, 1975). For later works, see the contributions in François et al., *Nation und Emotion.*

8 For an overview of ideas about the roots of national identity, see Bloom, *Personal Identity*, Chapter 1. See also the collection published by the Committee on International Relations, Group for the Advancement of Psychiatry, under the title *Us and Them: The Psychology of Ethnonationalism* (New York, 1987); Daniel Katz, 'Nationalism and International Conflict Resolution', in Herbert Kelmen, eds, *International Behaviour: A Social-Psychological Analysis* (New York, 1965), pp. 356ff. (Katz's book *The Psychology of Nationalism* had been published in 1949). Eugene Anderson used the poet Heinrich von Kleist as an example to prove the correlation in his *Nationalism and the Cultural Crisis in Prussia, 1806–1815* (New York, 1939), pp. 135–6.

9 Lemberg, *Nationalismus, vol. I*, pp. 27ff, and *Wege und Wandlungen des Nationalbewusstseins. Studien zur Geschichte der Volkwerdung in den Niederlanden und in Böhmen* (Münster, 1934), pp. 56ff.

10 Walter Feinberg, 'Nationalism in a Comparative Mode', in Robert McKim and Jeff McMahan, eds, *The Morality of Nationalism* (Oxford, 1997), pp. 66ff.

11 Bedrich Loewenstein, 'Eine alte Geschichte? Massenpsychologie und Nationalismusforschung', in Eva Schmidt-Hartmann, ed., *Formen des nationalen Bewusstseins* (München, 1994), pp. 100ff. This contains references to further literature on the psychology of nationalism.

12 These specific factors had already been pointed out in George Mosse, *Nationalism and Sexuality: Respectability and Abnormal Sexuality in Modern Europe* (Madison, WI, 1985). In this context, some lines by the Czech poet Jan Neruda in his *Zpěvy páteční* are worth noting:

> I am running towards you, my darling nation,
> like a young maiden, the human warbler,
> rushing to meet her lover in a passionate song.

13 Kaschuba, 'Die Nation als Körper', pp. 293–4. Henning Eichberg, a Danish historian, had pointed at the roots of this relationship: 'Leistung, Spannung, Geschwindigkeit. Sport und Tanz im gesellschaftlichen

Wandel des 18/19. Jahrhunderts' (Stuttgart, 1987).

14 Ute Gerhard and Jürgen Link, 'Zum Anteil der Kollektivsymbolik an den nationalen Stereotypen', in Jürgen Link and Wulf Wülfing, eds, *Nationale Mythen und Symbole in der zweiten Hälfte des 19. Jahrhunderts* (Stuttgart, 1991), pp. 28–9.

15 Bloom, *Personal Identity*, pp. 33–4.

16 Lemberg, *Nationalismus I.*, p. 196.

17 Louis Snyder, 'Nationalism and the Territorial Imperative', *Canadian Review of Studies in Nationalism* 3 (1975), pp. 1–21. Boyd Shafer is even more cautious in this respect, and recommends that the issue of territorial imperative be treated merely as open: *Faces of Nationalism* (New York, 1972).

18 *Us and Them*, p. 33; William Hamilton, 'The Genetical Evolution of Social Behaviour', *Journal of Theoretical Biology* 7 (1964), pp. 1ff.

19 Robert Arderey, *The Territorial Imperative: A Personal Inquiry into the Animal Origins of Property and Nations* (New York, 1966).

20 Dirk Wendt, 'Feindbild-seine biologischen und psychologischen Ursachen', in Voigt, *Politik der Symbole*, pp. 73–4; Anne Katrin Flohr, *Fremdenfeindlichkeit. Biosoziale Grundlagen vom Ethnozentrismus* (Opladen, 1994), p. 251.

21 Max Weber, *Gesammelte Aufsätze zur Wirtschaftslehre* (Tübingen, 1973), p. 332; Franz J. Bauer, *Gehalt und Gestalt der Monumentalsymbolik. Zur Ikonologie des Nationalstaates in Deutschland und Italien 1860–1914* (Munich, 1992l), pp. 7ff.

22 Karl Deutsch, *Nationalism and Social Communication* (Cambridge, MA, 1953), p. 97. For a systematic study of this subject, see Bernhard Giesen, *Die Intellektuellen und die Nation* (Frankfurt, 1993).

23 Elisabeth Fehrenbach, 'Über die Bedeutung der politischen Symbole im Nationalstaat', *Historische Zeitschrift* 213 (1971), pp. 301ff; Thomas Nipperdey, 'Nationalidee und Nationaldenkmal im 19. Jahrhundert', *Historische Zeitschrift* 206 (1968), p. 531. For more on the topic of symbolism, see Lothar Gall, *Die Germania als Symbol* (Göttingen, 1992), and also the already mentionned collection by Link and Wülfing, *Nationale Mythen*. A clear, well-arranged study of the German case is offered by Hans Hattenauer, *Geschichte der deutschen Nationalsymbole* (Munich, 1990).

24 Kaschuba, 'Die Nation als Körper', p. 291

25 Fehrenbach, *Über die Bedeutung*, p. 297. For information on performativity, see Karel Šíma, 'Národní slavnosti šedesátých let 19.století jako

performativní akt konstruování národní identity', *ČČH* 104 (2006), pp. 84ff.

26 W. Smith, 'National Symbols' in Leoussi, *Encyclopedia of Nationalism*, vol. 1, pp. 522–3. Smith differentiates – more with regard to the present – between four important spheres in which national symbols are applied: 1. active symbolism expressed at public celebrations, fairs, anniversaries, funerals, and so on; 2. verbal symbolism expressed in addresses, announcements, anthems, songs and mottos; 3. specific symbolism found in national appreciations of landscape, rivers, mountains, buildings, and so on; and 4. graphic symbolism expressed in paintings, posters, decorations etc.

27 Most of the abundant literature that has, in the past two decades, concerned itself with the innovative, genre aspect of nation-forming has unfortunately focused on the relationship between women and 'nationalism'. It thereby places itself in a situation where it mainly analyses the present situation – or rather, remains in the context of the present times. See the 'classic' works such as Nira Yuval-Davis, *Gender and Nation* (London, 1997), or Nira Yuval-Davis, 'Gender Relations and the Nation', in 'Encyclopedia of Nationalism, vol. I', pp. 297ff..

28 Jitka Malečková, 'Where Are Women in National History?', in Stefan Berger, Chris Lorenz, eds, *The Contested Nation*, pp. 171–99.

29 See the contributions by Ida Blom, Geoff Ely and Silke Wenk in the collection edited by Ida Blom, Karen Hagemann, Catherine Hall, *Gendered Nations: Nationalism and Gender Order in the Long Nineteenth Century* (Oxford/New York, 2000).

30 Kaschuba, 'Die Nation als Körper', p. 291.

31 Uta Quasthoff, *Soziales Vorurteil und Kommunikation* (Frankfurt, 1973), p. 28; Klaus Roth, 'Bilder in den Köpfen', in Valeria Heuberger, Arnold Suppan and Elisabeth Vyslonzil, eds, *Das Bild vom Anderen* (Frankfurt, 1998), p. 23; Hermann Bausinger in *Jahrbuch für Deutch als Fremdsprache* 14 (1988), p. 160.

32 Roth, 'Bilder in den Köpfen', pp. 33ff.

33 Arnold Suppan, 'Identitäten und Stereotypen in multiethnischen europäischen Regionen', in Valeria Heuberger et al., eds., *Das Bild vom Anderen*, pp. 16f.

34 Michael Titzmann, 'Die Konzeption der "Germanen" in der deutschen Literatur des 19. Valerie Jahrhunderts', in Link and Wülfing, *Nationale Mythen*, p. 136.

35 Maurice Agulhon, 'La "statuomanie" et l'histoire', *Ethnologie francaise* 8 (1978), pp. 147ff; Adam Lerner, 'The Nineteenth-Century Monument' in Ringrose and Lerner, *Reimagining the Nation*, p. 179

36 Lerner, 'Nineteenth-Century Monument', p. 191; Hartmut Boockmann, 'Denkmäler. Eine Utopie des 19. Jahrhunderts', *Geschichte in Wissenschaft und Unterricht* 28 (1977), p. 165.

37 Michael Jeismann and Rolf Westheider, 'Wofür steht der Bürger?', in Reinhart Koselleck and Michael Jeismann, eds, *Der politische Totenkult. Kriegerdenkmäler in der Moderne* (Munich,1994), pp. 26–7; Manfred Hettling, 'Bürger oder Soldaten; Kriegerdenkmäler 1848–1854', in ibid, pp. 147ff.

38 Betka Matschke-von Wicht, 'Zum Problem des Kriegerdenkmals in Österreich in der 1. Hälfte des 19. Jahrhunderts', in Koselleck and Jeismann, p. 51ff.

39 Thomas Nipperdey, 'Nationalidee und Nationaldenkmal', p. 531.

40 Mosse, *Die Nationalisierung der Massen*, pp. 67–8.

41 Charlotte Tacke, *Denkmal im sozialen Raum. Nationale Symbole in Deutschland und Frankreich im 19. Jahrhundert* (Göttingen, 1995).

42 Bauer, *Gehalt und Gestalt in der Monumentalsymbolik*, p. 35.

43 Haupt and Tacke, *Die Kultur des Nationalen*, p. 272.

44 Nipperdey, 'Nationalidee und Nationaldenkmal', pp. 575–6; Hartmut Boockmann, 'Denkmäler', p. 163; Bauer, *Gehalt und Gestalt*, p. 19.

45 Gilbert Gadoffre, 'French National Images and the Problem of Stereotypes', *International Social Science Bulletin* 3 (1951), p. 583; McCrone, *Sociology of Nationalism*, pp. 46ff.

46 Lothar Gall, *Germania – eine deutsche Marianne?* (Bonn, 1993), pp. 14ff; Gerhard Brunn, 'Germania und die Wentstehung des deutschen Nationalstaates', in Voigt, *Symbole der Politik*, pp. 105ff.

47 Georg Kreis, *Helvetia im Wandel der Zeiten. Die Geschichte einer Repräsentationsfigur* (Zürich, 1991), pp. 35ff.

48 Thomas Sandkühler, Hans-Günter Schmidt, '"Geiasdtige Mütterlichkeit" als nationaler Mythos im Deutschen Kaiserreich', in Link and Wülfing, *Nationale Mythen*, especially pp. 241ff.

49 Bauer, *Gehalt und Gestalt*, pp. 5–6.

50 Dieter Düding, ed., *Öffentliche Festkultur. Politische Feste in Deutschland von der Aufklärung bis zum ersten Weltkrieg* (Reinbek, 1988), pp. 10ff; Manfred Hettling and Paul Nolte, eds, *Bürgerliche Feste. Symbolische Formen politischen Handelns im 19. Jahrhundert* (Göttingen, 1995).

51 Michael Maurer, 'Feste und Feiern als historischer forschungsgegen-stand', *Historische Zeitschrift* 253 (1991), pp. 103–4.

52 Winfried Gebhardt, *Fest, Feier, Alltag. Über die gesellschaftliche Wirklichkeit des Menschen und ihre Deutung* (Frankfurt, 1987), pp. 155ff.

53 Voigt, *Politik der Symbole*, pp. 12ff.

54 Maurer, *Feste und Feiern*, pp. 102–3.

55 Stanislaw Grodzinski, 'Nationalfeiertage und öffentliche Gedenktage Polens im 19. und 20. Jahrhundert', in Emil Brix, Hannes Stekl, eds, *Der Kampf um das Gedächtnis. Öffentliche Gedenktage in Mitteleuropa* (Vienna,1997), pp. 207–8.

56 Katalin Sinkö, 'Zur Entstehung der staatlichen und nationalen Feiertage in Ungarn', in ibid., pp. 253–4.

57 Jiří Pokorný and Jiří Rak, 'Öffentliche Festtage bei den Tschechen', in ibid., pp. 172–3.

58 Johannes Burkhardt, 'Reformations und Lutherfeiern. Die Verbürgerlichung des reformatorischen Jubiläumskultur', in Düding, *Öffentliche Festkultur*, pp. 212–13.

59 Stefan-Ludwig Hoffmann, 'Mythos und Geschichte. Leipziger Gedenkfeiern der Völkerschlacht im 19. und frühen 20. Jahrhundert', in François et al., *Nation und Emotion*, pp. 111ff; Dieter Düding, 'Das deutsche Nationalfest', in Düding, *Öffentliche Festkultur*, pp. 69ff.

60 Alain Corbin, 'La fête de la souveraineté', in Alain Corbin, Noëlle Gérôme, Danielle Tartakowsky, eds, *Les usages politiques des fetes aux XIXe-XXe siecle* (Paris, 1994), pp. 25ff.

61 Mosse, *Nationalisierung der Massen*, p. 112.

62 Among the plentiful literature on the Turner movement, see Stefan Illig, *Zwischen Körpertüchtigung und nationaler Bewegung: Turnvereine in Bayern 1848–1890* (Cologne, 1998).

63 Claire E. Nolte, *The Sokol in the Czech Lands to 1914: Training for the Nation* (New York, 2002). For a wider context, see Diethelm Blecking, ed., *Die slawische Sokolbewegung. Beiträge zur Geschichte von Sport und Nationalismus in Osteuropa* (Dortmund, 1991).

64 Pierre Arnaud and André Gounot, 'Mobilisierung der Körper und republikanische Selbstinszenierung in Frankreich 1789–1889', in François et al., *Nation und Emotion*, pp. 300ff.

65 Jakob Vogel, *Nationen im Gleichschritt. Der Kult der 'Nation in Waffen' in Deutschland und Frankreich 1870–1914* (Göttingen, 1997), pp. 15ff.

66 Annette Maas, 'Der Kult des toten Kriegers in Frankreich und

Deutschland 1870–1914', in François et al., *Nation und Emotion*, pp. 215ff.

67 This definition is often disputed by employing the argument that the Jews did not live within a compact territory. If we consider a modern nation to be a community of equal citizens, who communicate more intensively 'inwardly', within the group, than 'outwardly', the Jews constitute an ethnic community (as the term was used by Anthony Smith); and, in my view, the modern Jewish national movement did not occur until Zionism arose. See Miroslav Hroch, 'Zionism as a European National Movement', *Jewish Studies* 38 (1998), pp. 73–81.

68 Bernhard Klein, '"The Whole Empire of Great Britain". Zur Konstruktion des nationalen Raumes in Kartographie und Geographie', in Bielefeld and Engel, *Bilder der Nation*, pp. 40ff; Richard Helgerson, *Genremalerei, Landkarten und nationale Unsicherheit in Holland des 17. Jahrhunderts*, in ibid., pp. 123ff.

69 Gerhard and Link, 'Zum Anteil der Kollektivsymbolik an den Nationalstereotypen', pp. 19ff.

70 David Hooson, ed., *Geography and National Identity* (Oxford/Cambridge, 1994), pp. 5ff.

71 Simon Schama, *Landscape and Memory* (London, 1996), p. 15.

72 David Lowenthal, 'European and English Landscapes as National Symbols' in Hooson, *Geography and National Identity*, pp. 17ff.

73 Schama, *Landscape and Memory*, pp. 117–18; Gerhard Sandner, 'In Search of Identity: German Nationalism and Geography, 1871–1910', in Hooson, *Geography and National Identity*, pp. 71ff.

74 Armand Fremont, 'La Terre', in Pierre Nora, *Les lieux de memoire III* (Paris, 1992), pp. 18ff; Lowenthal, 'European and English Landscapes', p. 19.

75 Pierre Nora, 'Naissance du monument historique', in Nora, *Les lieux de mémoire II.* (Paris 1986), pp. 424ff.

76 Mark Bassin, 'Russian Geographers and the "National Mission" in the Far East', in Hooson, *Geography and National Identity*, pp. 112ff; Mark Bassin, 'Sibirien auf der kognitiven Landkarte Russlands im 19.Jahrhndert', *Geschichte und Gesellschaft* 28 (2002), pp. 378ff.

77 Stefan Troebst, '"Intermarium" und "Vermählung mit dem Meer". Kognitive Karten und Geschichtspolitik in Ostmitteleuropa', *Geschichte und Gesellschaft* 28 (2002), pp. 445ff.

78 Thomas Wilson and Hastings Donnan, *Border Identities: Nation and State in International Frontiers* (Cambridge, 1998), pp. 10ff.

79 Peter Sahlins, *Boundaries: The Making of Spain and France in the Pyrenees* (Berkeley, CA, 1989), pp. 187ff.

80 Hagen Schulze, *Gibt es überhaupt eine deutsche Geschichte?* (Berlin, 1989), p. 48.

81 Wilson and Donnan, *Border Identities*, p. 16; Eugen Weber, *Peasants into Frenchmen: The Modernization of Rural France 1870–1914* (Stanford, 1976), p. 334.

82 Eriksen, *Ethnicity and Nationalism*, p. 68. For more information on the theoretical aspects of research into border conflicts, see Sven Tägil, ed., *Studying Boundary Conflicts: A Theoretical Framework* (Stockholm, 1977).

83 McCrone, *Sociology of Nationalism*, p. 56.

84 Oren Yiftachel, 'The Homeland and Nationalism', in *Encyclopedia of Nationalism*, vol. 1, pp. 359ff.

Geographical Index

Index of Concepts